Mathematics Education in the Middle Grades

Teaching to Meet the Needs of Middle Grades Learners and to Maintain High Expectations

Proceedings of a National Convocation and Action Conferences

Center for Science, Mathematics, and Engineering Education

National Research Council

NATIONAL ACADEMY PRESS
Washington, DC

NOTICE: The project that is the subject of this report was approved by the Governing Board of the National Research Council, whose members are drawn from the councils of the National Academy of Sciences, the National Academy of Engineering, and the Institute of Medicine. The members of the committee responsible for the convocation and report were chosen for their special competences and with regard for appropriate balance.

The Center for Science, Mathematics, and Engineering Education (CSMEE) was established in 1995 to provide coordination of all the National Research Council's education activities and reform efforts for students at all levels, specifically those in kindergarten through twelfth grade, undergraduate institutions, school-to-work programs, and continuing education. The Center reports directly to the Governing Board of the National Research Council.

The Convocation and Action Conferences about which these proceedings report were funded by a grant from the U.S. Department of Education with additional funding from the American Educational Research Association. Any opinions, findings, or recommendations expressed in this report are those of members of the steering committee or participants in the Convocation and Action Conferences and do not necessarily reflect the views of the U.S. Department of Education.

Library of Congress Cataloging-in-Publication Data

Mathematics education in the middle grades : teaching to meet the needs of middle grades learners and to maintain high expectations : proceedings of a national convocation and action conferences / Center for Science, Mathematics, and Engineering Education, National Research Council.
        p. cm.
Includes bibliographical references.
  ISBN 0-309-06797-9 (pbk.)
  1. Mathematics—Study and teaching (Middle school)—United States—Congresses. I. Center for Science, Mathematics, and Engineering Education.
  QA13 .M156 1999
  510'.72—dc21

99-050765

Additional copies of this report are available from National Academy Press, 2101 Constitution Avenue, N.W., Lock Box 285, Washington, DC 20055. Call (800) 624-6242 or (202) 334-3313 (in the Washington metropolitan area).

This report is also available online at http://www.nap.edu.

Printed in the United States of America

THE NATIONAL ACADEMIES

National Academy of Sciences
National Academy of Engineering
Institute of Medicine
National Research Council

The *National Academy of Sciences* is a private, nonprofit, self-perpetuating society of distinguished scholars engaged in scientific and engineering research, dedicated to the furtherance of science and technology and to their use for the general welfare. Upon the authority of the charter granted to it by the Congress in 1863, the Academy has a mandate that requires it to advise the federal government on scientific and technical matters. Dr. Bruce M. Alberts is president of the National Academy of Sciences.

The *National Academy of Engineering* was established in 1964, under the charter of the National Academy of Sciences, as a parallel organization of outstanding engineers. It is autonomous in its administration and in the selection of its members, sharing with the National Academy of Sciences the responsibility for advising the federal government. The National Academy of Engineering also sponsors engineering programs aimed at meeting national needs, encourages education and research, and recognizes the superior achievements of engineers. Dr. William A. Wulf is president of the National Academy of Engineering.

The *Institute of Medicine* was established in 1970 by the National Academy of Sciences to secure the services of eminent members of appropriate professions in the examination of policy matters pertaining to the health of the public. The Institute acts under the responsibility given to the National Academy of Sciences by its congressional charter to be an adviser to the federal government and, upon its own initiative, to identify issues of medical care, research, and education. Dr. Kenneth I. Shine is president of the Institute of Medicine.

The *National Research Council* was organized by the National Academy of Sciences in 1916 to associate the broad community of science and technology with the Academy's purposes of furthering knowledge and advising the federal government. Functioning in accordance with general policies determined by the Academy, the Council has become the principal operating agency of both the National Academy of Sciences and the National Academy of Engineering in providing services to the government, the public, and the scientific and engineering communities. The Council is administered jointly by both Academies and the Institute of Medicine. Dr. Bruce M. Alberts and Dr. William A. Wulf are chairman and vice chairman, respectively, of the National Research Council.

NATIONAL CONVOCATION ON MATHEMATICS EDUCATION IN THE MIDDLE GRADES
Program Steering Committee

Edward Silver, *Chair*, Professor and Senior Scientist, Learning Research Development Center, University of Pittsburgh, Pittsburgh, PA

Representatives, Mathematical Sciences Education Board

Hyman Bass (NAS)*, Professor of Mathematics, Columbia University, New York, NY

Benjamin Blackhawk, Mathematics Teacher, St. Paul Academy and Summit School, Crystal, MN

Susan S. Wood, Professor of Mathematics, J. Sargeant Reynolds Community College, Richmond, VA

Representatives, American Educational Research Association

Robert Linn, Distinguished Professor of Education, University of Colorado, Boulder, CO

Sandra Wilcox, Associate Professor of Teacher Education, Michigan State University, East Lansing, MI

Representatives, National Council of Teachers of Mathematics

Catherine Brown, Associate Professor of Curriculum and Instruction, Indiana University, Bloomington, IN

Karen Longhart, Mathematics Teacher, Flathead High School, Kalispell, MT

Representatives, National Middle School Association

Sam Chattin, Science Teacher, William H. English Middle School, Scottsberg, IN

Katherine Rasch, Dean and Professor of Education, Maryville University, Chesterfield, MO

Member-At-Large

Shirley Sagawa, Executive Director, Learning First Alliance, Washington, DC

National Research Council Staff

Gail Burrill, Project Director

Rodger Bybee, Executive Director, CSMEE

Kristance Coates, Project Assistant

Joan Ferrini-Mundy, Associate Executive Director, CSMEE

Bradford Findell, Program Officer

DeVonne Robertson, Program Assistant

Kirsten Sampson Snyder, Administrative Officer

Doug Sprunger, Senior Project Assistant

Tina Winters, Senior Project Assistant

---

*NAS: Member of the National Academy of Sciences

Acknowledgments

The National Academy of Sciences gratefully acknowledges the U.S. Department of Education for its generous financial support of the Convocation and Action Conferences and these proceedings, the American Educational Research Association for its additional financial support and co-sponsorship of the Convocation and Action Conferences, and the National Middle School Association and National Council of Teachers of Mathematics for their co-sponsorship of the Convocation and Action Conferences. Any opinions, findings, and conclusions or recommendations expressed in this material are those of the authors and do not necessarily reflect those of the funders.

We would like to acknowledge the staff at the National Research Council's (NRC) Center for Science, Mathematics, and Engineering Education (CSMEE) for their efforts in putting the Convocation and Action Conferences together. In particular, Tina Winters was instrumental in overseeing logistical arrangements for the meetings, and in organizing these proceedings for review and publication. She was supported in her efforts by Kirsten Sampson Snyder and Doug Sprunger. Others who provided on-site support were Kristance Coates and DeVonne Robertson.

We are grateful to the members of the Program Steering Committee for their oversight in planning of the programs for the Convocation and Action Conferences. We would also like to thank Anthony Jackson for his contributions to the program planning and his assistance with resources for the Convocation. Additional thanks go to Deborah Loewenberg Ball, Hyman Bass, and Sandra Wilcox for their instrumental roles in the organization of the Action Conference on the Professional Development of Teachers of Mathematics in the Middle Grades, the Action Conference on the Nature and Teaching of Algebra in the Middle Grades, and the Action Conference on Research in the Teaching and Learning of Mathematics in the Middle Grades, respectively. We also wish to acknowledge the speakers and discussion group facilitators for their contributions and leadership that gave substance to the discussion.

It should be noted that these proceedings have been reviewed by individuals chosen for their diverse perspectives and technical expertise, in accordance with procedures approved by the NRC's Report Review Committee. The purpose of this independent review is to provide candid and critical comments that will assist the NRC in making the published report as sound as possible and to ensure that the report meets institutional standards for objectivity, evidence, and responsiveness to the study charge. The content of the review comments and draft manuscript remains confidential to protect the integrity of the deliberative process.

We wish to thank the following individuals for their participation in the review of this report:

Gilberto Cuevas, University of Miami
Nina Koltnow, Sidwell Friends School
Sidney L. Rachlin, East Carolina University
Marlyn Spivak, Jack London Middle School

While these individuals have provided many constructive comments and suggestions, responsibility for the final content of this report rests solely with the authoring committee and the NRC.

GAIL BURRILL
Project Director, Mathematics Education in the Middle Grades

Learning mathematics in the middle grades is a critical component in the education of our nation's youth. The mathematics foundation laid during these years provides students with the skills and knowledge to study higher level mathematics during high school, provides the necessary mathematical base for success in other disciplines such as science, and lays the groundwork for mathematically literate citizens. A variety of evidence suggests that the mathematics education landscape is shifting and evolving rapidly. Below average mathematics achievement scores for grade eight U. S. students as reported in the Third International Mathematics and Science Study (TIMSS) (U.S. Department of Education, 1996) stimulated national concern leading to a variety of activities and proposals focusing attention on mathematics education. Data from the National Assessment of Educational Progress (NAEP) (National Center for Education Statistics, 1997) indicates that while the nation has demonstrated progress over time, the achievement levels for all students are not yet satisfactory. Research about mathematics education has begun to have implications for classroom practice. States are setting high standards for student achievement and aligning their assessments with those standards. The National Council of Teachers of Mathematics (NCTM) is preparing *Principles and Standards for School Mathematics*, an updated version of its previous standards documents: *Curriculum and Evaluation Standards for School Mathematics*, (NCTM, 1989); *Professional Standards for Teaching Mathematics*, (NCTM, 1991); and *Assessment Standards for School Mathematics*, (NCTM, 1995).

As educators focus on improving mathematics education, they face a variety of issues. The problems of middle grades mathematics education are substantial and differ from those at the elementary and secondary levels. There are issues about:

- **Content.** What mathematics content is appropriate? How can the characterization of the U.S. mathematics curriculum as a "mile wide, inch deep" be addressed? How can the mathematics curriculum be strengthened yet respect the development issues so central to middle grades students? What is the nature of algebra at the middle grades and how does it influence the curriculum?

- **How middle grades students learn mathematics.** What is the balance between conceptual understanding and practice? What is the role of manipulatives in helping students learn? How do students build understanding of a concept over time?

- **Teaching mathematics at the middle grades.** To what extent do teacher background and preparation specifically for the teaching of mathematics have an impact on what students learn? How can the issue of specialist versus generalist be resolved? What teaching practices are most effective with middle grades students? How can teachers help students grow as individuals yet ensure that they learn mathematics?

- **School organization and its relation to the teaching and learning of mathematics.** How does the study of mathematics fit into the "house" concept? What are the characteristics of school structures that promote mathematics learning? Are cross-disciplinary teams compatible with vertical articulation? What are the effects of school organization, scheduling, and philosophy on the mathematics program?

- **Research.** How can the knowledge gained from research be used to improve teaching and learning of mathematics in the middle grades? How can an agenda for continued research that builds on the state of the field as well as moves the thinking forward be framed? What help do teachers need to translate research into practice? How might teachers become researchers themselves as

they reflect on their practice and on ways to improve?

These issues contribute to the challenge of improving mathematics education at the middle grades. Change in schools and in teaching practice has been slow to occur. Evidence is mixed about the effects and directions of efforts to improve mathematics education. Engaging the community at large in conversation about their goals and perspectives is a critical step to help the nation raise the bar and maximize opportunities for all middle grades children in its schools. The dialogue and shared visions that occurred at the Convocation—plenary sessions, panels, and small group discussions—can set the stage for making a difference.

REFERENCES

National Center for Education Statistics. (1996). *Pursuing excellence: A study of U.S. eighth grade mathematics and science teaching, learning, curriculum, and achievement in international context.* Washington, DC: Author.

National Council of Teachers of Mathematics. (1989). *Curriculum and evaluation standards for school mathematics.* Reston, VA: Author.

National Council of Teachers of Mathematics. (1991). *Professional standards for teaching mathematics.* Reston, VA: Author.

National Council of Teachers of Mathematics. (1995). *Assessment standards for school mathematics.* Reston, VA: Author.

Reese, C.M., Miller, K.E., Mazzeo, J., & Dossey, J.A. (1997). *NAEP 1996 mathematics report card for the nation and the states.* Washington, DC: National Center for Education Statistics.

Contents

Mathematics Education in the Middle Grades

Letter from the Program Steering Committee

As representatives of the co-sponsoring organizations and the education community, we would like the Convocation to be viewed as the first step in a continuing dialogue. In particular, we hope that the essence of the Convocation will be replicated by states and regional groups affiliated with the parent organizations. To support such state and regional groups, the thinking and structure we used to design the program is described below. The intent was to contrast the perspectives brought by each of the sponsoring organizations and their constituencies, to raise issues about these perspectives, to promote interaction, and, through small discussion groups, to engage participants in reflecting on their own role in middle grades mathematics education. To reinforce the points illustrated by the plenary speakers, the small group discussions involved participants in an analysis of a "site of practice," grounding the conversation in what teachers and students actually do in classrooms. Discussion group leaders were given instruction and direction for working with their groups following the opening plenary session and were provided with complete packets of materials for use with their groups over the two days. Before the conference, participants were given materials as background reading and to help them begin to focus on the issues framing the Convocation. (See page 5.)

The Convocation began with speakers who presented teaching middle school mathematics from two points of view: teaching mathematics with a focus on the subject matter content or teaching mathematics with a focus on the whole child and whole curriculum. The purpose of this session was to set the stage for thinking about middle grades mathematics classrooms from these two perspectives and to stimulate thinking throughout the rest of the Convocation about teaching and learning mathematics through these different lenses. Within this framework, the Convocation was organized around three central themes with a set of organizing questions for each theme:

- content and learning in middle grades mathematics;
- middle grades mathematics teaching; and
- organization of middle grades instructional programs and their impact on mathematics teaching and learning.

Each of these themes was introduced with a plenary session, where individual speakers or a panel described some part of the landscape. Discussion groups that addressed the issues in terms of an activity selected from the actual practice of teaching followed the first two plenary sessions. The discussion groups were composed of ten or fewer participants that by design represented a mix of three groups: classroom teachers, teacher educators and university representatives, and those in some way responsible for a system including administrators, representatives from state and local systemic initiatives, and curriculum supervisors. In addition, time was provided for district teams to meet and address their concerns in light of the Convocation conversation. The teams were configured differently depending on the needs of the system they represented, with some team members from a given school district while other teams were a blend of teachers and university mathematics educators with common goals for a district.

THE CONVOCATION THEMES

Middle Grades Content and Learning Issues

The plenary session on content and learning mathematics in the middle grades focused on the questions:

- What developmental considerations are important in thinking about middle school students as learners? as learners of mathematics? Are these compatible?
- What do we know about middle school students' capacity for learning? for learning mathematics?
- What are important ideas in mathematics for the middle grades and how are these related to developmental learning considerations?

There were two speakers, one presenting a middle grades perspective about learning, including comments about thematic units and integrated curricula, and the second addressing how students learn certain mathematics concepts in the middle grades from the perspective of mathematics education research. The discussion group participants worked through Marcy's Dots (see page 58), an algebraic reasoning problem from the 1992 National Assessment of Educational Progress, then reflected on student strategies (Appendix 4, page 240) in light of their own thinking. This was followed by a discussion about learning mathematics based on the middle grades algebra section from the 1998 National Council of Teachers of Mathematics *Principles and Standards for School Mathematics: Discussion Draft* using the lens of the child and the lens of content.

Middle Grades Teaching Issues

Two videos about the practice of teaching were the focus of the plenary session on teaching. In the first video, students discussed the nature of mathematics teaching and how they had learned mathematics through the actions and beliefs of their teacher. The second featured an eighth grade class during a lesson on algebraic thinking. The audience was asked to view the videos in light of the following questions:

- What are the important characteristics of effective teaching in the middle grades? of effective teaching of mathematics in the middle grades?
- How can instruction in middle grades classrooms be organized to maximize learning? How can we tell when learning is happening?
- What tools and strategies will make a difference in how middle grades students learn mathematics?

Following each video a panel composed of a middle grades teacher, a mathematician, and a mathematics educator reacted to the three questions. The comments and reactions of the panel within the framework of the focus questions were used to shape the participant discussion sessions.

Middle Grades School Organizational Issues

How middle grades are organized and the impact of that organization on the teaching and learning of mathematics was the theme of a panel discussion in this plenary session. Panelists were asked to consider:

- What are the important characteristics of school organization and mathematics programs that support teaching and learning meaningful mathematics in the middle grades?
- How can the schedules of teachers and students be organized to implement what we know about effective teaching and learning in the middle grades?
- What are the issues surrounding specialists vs. generalists? What kind of teaching assignments maximize program effectiveness in mathematics?

Following the panel presentation, the panelists were asked to address specific questions raised during the Convocation with questions and reaction from the audience. The chair of the Steering Committee gave a closing summary of the issues and challenges raised during the Convocation.

It is our hope that this overview will be useful for the reader to both understand the nature of the Convocation and to think about the design as one that might energize other communities to structure a similar venture.

Executive Summary

As an initial step to address national, state, and local issues of teaching and learning mathematics in the middle grades, the Mathematical Sciences Education Board (MSEB) of the National Research Council's Center for Science, Mathematics, and Engineering Education (CSMEE), the American Educational Research Association (AERA), the National Council of Teachers of Mathematics (NCTM), and the National Middle School Association (NMSA) co-sponsored a National Convocation on Middle Grades Mathematics. The Convocation was held at the National Academy of Sciences in Washington DC, on 25-27 September 1998 with support from the U.S. Department of Education and the AERA. The goals of the Convocation were to

- challenge the nation's mathematical sciences community to focus its energy and resources on the improvement of middle grades mathematics education and
- begin an ongoing national dialogue on middle grades mathematics education, bringing together those with different perspectives and

responsibilities to jointly consider the issues.

The Convocation consisted of plenary sessions attended by all of the participants and small focused discussion groups. Over 400 participants including mathematicians, mathematics teacher educators, state and district mathematics education policy makers, national policy makers, mathematics education researchers, classroom teachers, curriculum developers, and school board members attended the Convocation. Some of the attendees came as individuals. Many others were members of the more than 50 district teams that addressed the issues in terms of their own communities and needs.

Prior to the convocation, attendees reviewed the following background materials:

- a paper commissioned for the Convocation, "What is 8th Grade Mathematics: A Look from NAEP" by John Dossey,
- the abridged version of *Turning Points* from the Carnegie Council on Adolescent Development,

- *This We Believe* from the National Middle School Association,
- an article from the *Kappan Articles online*, "Speaking with One Voice, a Manifesto for Middle-Grades Reform" by Joan Lipsitz, Hayes Mizell, Anthony Jackson, and Leah Meyer Austin, and
- "Middle Grades Mathematics Education: Questions and Answers" a paper prepared by Andrew Zucker for the U.S. Department of Education

On the first evening of the Convocation, Dr. Bruce Alberts, President of the National Academy of Sciences, welcomed the group and spoke of the need to invest ourselves in improving education and to be open to new ways to meet the challenges of the task. He was followed by the Honorable C. Kent McGuire, Assistant Secretary, Office of Educational Research and Improvement, who brought greetings from the U.S. Department of Education. The Convocation Program Steering Committee Chair, Edward Silver, University of Pittsburgh, offered brief remarks about the goals of the Convocation and set the stage for the rest of the activities. Two presentations followed, each representing a different perspective. Glenda Lappan, Michigan State University, discussed the importance of laying a firm foundation for understanding mathematics during the middle years.

She noted the dual goals of respecting the developing capabilities of middle school students while engaging these energetic adolescents in learning mathematics for their own future. Rather than listing a set of topics, she proposed a strand approach to the mathematics students should learn that would be central to further study of mathematics or to being a good and productive citizen. Thomas Dickinson, Indiana State University, then used "small stories" as a way to characterize successful middle schools. He discussed development in the context of the child as well as development and its connection to teaching. He gave several examples of teachers teaching individuals, and teachers teaching mathematics where development was placed within a context of individuals and the individuals in a context of learning.

CONTENT AND LEARNING ISSUES

After greetings from Luther Williams, Assistant Director, Directorate for Education and Human Resources, National Science Foundation, the first focus of the second day of the Convocation was on content and learning mathematics at the middle grades. Nancy Doda, from National-Louis University, spoke of a crossroads in middle school reform. She noted the need for a reexamination of the fundamental philosophy of the middle school concept to understand what is needed to ensure academic success for all children. Doda contended that in many cases, middle schools have been more successful in altering aspects of climate and structure than of the curriculum and instruction. There is now a pressing demand to refine the elements of the middle school concept to build an exploratory curriculum that is also intellectually demanding.

Kathleen Hart, the University of Nottingham, based her remarks on projects from the United Kingdom. Middle grades are recognized as the time students should move from the concrete to the abstract, but the transition must be carefully developed so that understanding emerges. She gave examples where the children she studied did not connect concept development with formal work with algorithms, often due to the fact that teachers did not make strong connections between the two. She noted how important it is for teachers to understand where mathematical ideas are leading and to be ready to build on the different pieces of knowledge individual children take away from a lesson.

Following the plenary session, participants engaged in a mathematical task in small discussion groups (Marcy's dots, see page 58). They were asked to reflect on the mathematics involved and to analyze student responses as a backdrop for their discussion about content and learning mathematics in the middle grades.

TEACHING ISSUES

The afternoon sessions were focused on teaching in the middle grades. In the plenary session, participants viewed two video clips. Nanette Seago, California Mathematics Renaissance Project, showed a videotape of an eighth grade class during a lesson on patterns in algebra. The viewers considered how listening to conversations among students enables teachers to learn about student understanding. Groups discussed the decisions the teacher made as she pursued the lesson and reflected on the impact of these decisions on the outcome of the lesson.

Linda Foreman, Portland State University, showed a videotape of middle grades students making a presentation at the 1998 National Council of Teachers of Mathematics Annual Meeting in Washington, DC. The students spoke about what they had learned in mathematics and what their teacher had done to enable that learning to happen. In particular, the students recognized and supported the notion that learning did not take place without some "disequilibrium" and that struggling with learning was a natural part of the process. These students had been taught by Foreman for four years, and she suggested that structuring learning so students and teachers stay together over time is one way to create a successful community of learners.

A panel consisting of Hyman Bass, a mathematician from Columbia University, Deborah Ball, mathematics educator from the University of Michigan, and Sam Chattin, a middle grades teacher from William H. English Middle School in Scottsberg, Indiana, reacted to each videotape. Bass observed the blend of algebra and geometry in both videos and noted that use of video might be an appropriate tool to help bridge the gap between mathematics as content and mathematics in practice. Chattin's comments related to the environment established by the teacher in each case as evidenced by the kinds of questions and answers and by the confidence students displayed about their work. Ball framed her remarks around the interplay between the mathematics to be learned and the role of discussion where the teacher's decision about how to frame a question and how to respond drives what students learn. In the small group discussion session that followed, the participants were asked to reflect on teaching issues raised by the videotapes as well as on the use of videotape as a means for stimulating reflection and discussion.

ORGANIZATIONAL ISSUES

The last theme of the Convocation was the organization of schools for middle grades students and its relation to teaching and learning mathematics. A panel presentation framed the issues for discussion. Craig Spilman, a principal from Canton Middle School in Baltimore, MD, emphasized the need to make intelligent use of data to promote articulation among elementary and middle grades teachers to understand where students are in their learning. The design and implementation of programs should be flexible enough to accommodate students as they grow. He spoke of the need for principals to communicate with and counsel teachers to ensure that their mathematics instruction is centered around student learning.

Mary Kay Stein, a research scientist from the University of Pittsburgh, hypothesized that the developmental approach—teaching mathematics with a focus on the whole child—and the subject matter approach—teaching mathematics with a focus on the content—each have flaws. She proposed a middle school organization and structure that is jointly informed by subject matter and developmental concerns. Stein argued that the mathematics for middle school students should take into account the developmental needs of adolescents. For this to happen, professional development should be part of the day-to-day administrative functioning of the school.

Robert Felner, National Center on Public Education, University of Rhode Island, spoke about project work that focused on high performing learning communities. A key finding was that if educational improvement efforts do not attend to the full ecology of the setting, they will ultimately fail. Although some schools have success in raising student scores for a time, the success is not sustainable, and, in fact, according to this research, raising student achievement over time is related to the degree of implementation of key structural changes in the school. He also mentioned that parent involvement that correlates with gains in student achievement is "sending home information about how to work with and talk to your children." In response to questions, panelists pointed out that raising expectations is a critical part of raising student achievement, that structural changes should be accompanied by thoughtful support for teachers, and that even though we continue to improve, the task keeps changing, masking the gains.

CLOSING REMARKS

In his closing remarks, Edward Silver noted the dual commitment of the Convocation participants: to enhancing the quality and quantity of mathematics learning in the middle grades and to addressing other needs of young adolescents. He suggested a major concern is how to make mathematics interesting and important to young adolescents. Silver pointed out that the examples presented during the Convocation indicated students can be interested in the mathematical tasks we give them, in the mathematics itself, or in the process of struggling with the tasks, and that the role of the teacher is to cultivate this interest. He challenged the audience to contrast their own view of algebra with the algebraic ideas that were presented in the Convocation sessions and to reflect on what it means to say that students are learning algebra and what it would mean for all students to learn algebra. He advocated a systematic examination of different instructional and curricular arrangements designed to have all students learn algebra. His closing comments addressed the issue of using the generalist/specialist notion as a way to set up a false dichotomy and called for thinking about ways to form a community with a joint identity that moves the Convocation agenda forward.

ACTION CONFERENCE ON THE NATURE AND IMPACT OF ALGEBRA AT THE MIDDLE GRADES

The agenda for the Action Conference was designed to bring attention to different possibilities for algebra in the middle grades and to the issues involved in implementing any of these possibilities. Discussion was framed by six questions presented by the Conference organizer, Hyman Bass, a mathematician from Columbia University. The questions covered the following topics: attention to subject matter vs. attention to students; algebra as the language of mathematics; real world contexts vs. generalization and abstraction; covering mathematics vs. uncovering mathematics; situating algebra in the mathematics curriculum; materials, design, selection criteria for mathematics curriculum. Jim Fey from the University of Maryland suggested that the important aspects of algebra are the concepts and techniques for reasoning about quantitative conditions and relationships. With this as a theme, Fey claimed that moving high school algebra into the middle grades will not be sufficient. Al Cuoco, Director of the Center for Mathematics Education at EDC, presented a view of algebra that relied more on symbols and problems from the world of mathematics, with an emphasis on the ways of thinking that can emerge from reasoning about calculations and about operations. Bass suggested that Fey's and Cuoco's approaches were two different aspects of the same thing. Orit Zaslavsky, a mathematics education researcher from

Israel, postulated that learning is about constructing meaning that can change over time, across learners, and across contexts. Learning algebra in the middle grades is just a beginning, where examples play a critical role and the issue of representation is inherent.

The second day of the conference featured approaches to a middle grades algebra curriculum from the Connected Mathematics Project, University of Chicago School Mathematics Project, Mathematics in Context, and Saxon Mathematics in which the presenters described the nature of their algebra strand and what works in practice. As part of a panel on general implementation issues, Anne Bartel, from the Minnesota project SciMath, pointed out that many of the issues are tied to people's belief systems about whether algebra is focused on skills or thinking and about what "algebra for all" really means. She closed with a discussion of the characteristics of effective professional development, including the need to make the algebra content and corresponding instructional strategies explicit. Vern Williams, Gifted and Talented Coordinator from a Virginia middle school, emphasized that some children need more than the norm with an emphasis on theory, structure, and problem solving. These students need to be challenged every day, and a gifted and talented course in algebra opens the universe of mathematics for them. Nancy Doda, National-Louis University, disagreed with Williams and advocated that all students needed to be challenged and raised issues of equity. In closing, participants discussed algebra in relation to mathematics content, curricular design, and use of research in the context of a search for guidance on how to scale up promising programs to realize improved mathematics learning for more students.

ACTION CONFERENCE ON RESEARCH IN THE TEACHING AND LEARNING OF MATHEMATICS IN THE MIDDLE GRADES

The focus of the conference was to help define research required to better understand and articulate the assumptions that underpin activities aimed at improving the mathematics curriculum, teaching, and learning in the middle grades. The group was charged with making suggestions to those in the field about what further research is needed and advising the Department of Education and National Science Foundation on where strategic investments in research might be made. Invited talks were organized to move from broad theoretical and practical issues on how to address research to specific research

efforts to the applications of research knowledge to recent curriculum development projects.

From the first perspective, James Hiebert, University of Delaware, described a tension between solving practical problems and doing good research and offered a framework to better understand and resolve these tensions. Alan Schoenfeld, University of California-Berkeley, responded to Hiebert by arguing for a stronger theoretical base for and through research. Mary Kay Stein illustrated how research can grow from attempts to solve problems of practice. Richard Lesh, Indiana University–Purdue, commented on how thinking can be changed over time and the need to be explicit about the big ideas in the middle grades curriculum. James Fey, University of Maryland, and Koeno Gravemeijer, Freudenthal Institute, the Netherlands, described ways that the extent research on rational number and proportional reasoning shaped design decisions in their respective curriculum projects. Judy Sowder, University of California-San Diego, discussed ways to deepen teachers' knowledge of mathematics. The participants made recommendations in three areas: teaching and teacher learning; student learning; and communicating with a variety of interested constituencies.

ACTION CONFERENCE ON THE PROFESSIONAL DEVELOPMENT OF TEACHERS OF MATHEMATICS IN THE MIDDLE GRADES

The Action Conference was designed to afford an opportunity for participants to examine promising approaches to professional development by creating an analytic and practical conversation about the sorts of opportunities in professional development most likely to lead to teachers' learning and improvements in their practice. Deborah Ball, University of Michigan, conference organizer, framed the discussion from the vantage point of teacher educators considering sites through which teachers might most profitably learn mathematics content needed in teaching, based on tasks which teachers regularly do as part of their teaching. Participants discussed what is known about professional development, teacher learning, and the improvement of practice. As an initial example of how teachers use knowledge of content to shape their teaching, Ball together with Joan Ferrini-Mundy, Center for Science, Mathematics, and Engineering Education engaged participants in reformulating a mathematical task and considering the mathematical knowledge used to create and evaluate these new tasks.

Margaret Smith, Pennsylvania State University, involved the participants in a case study of student work and discussed how analyzing student responses led to a discussion of the importance of the mathematical knowledge of the teacher. Karen Economopoulos, TERC, posed two questions for reflection and discussion: How might curriculum materials offer professional development opportunities for teachers and how can these materials influence or support teachers' daily decisions? Nanette Seago, Mathematics Renaissance Project, using a video of an eighth grade mathematics lesson, facilitated a discussion of the use of videotape as an instructional medium in professional development. The closing session featured a panel that presented their reflections on the improvement of professional development. Iris Weiss, from Horizon Research, argued for the need to help teachers develop some way to filter and make decisions, and raised a concern about how to scale up professional development models. John Moyer from Marquette University, reflected on professional development with urban, large city middle grades teachers using teacher responses to an observer's comments to promote teachers' reflection on their practice. Stephanie Williamson, Louisiana Systemic Initiative, described the work done to build collaboration among school systems and universities in Louisiana that led to the development of a document used to guide decisions about professional development programs. Participant's comments at the end indicated that the Conference did take seriously professional development as a field and attempted to create a frame for thinking about theoretical, research, and practice-based learning.

Participant Observations

At the beginning of the Convocation, the participants were invited to think about areas of agreement and continuing challenges as they took part in the Convocation activities. Given that the Convocation involved over 400 participants with diverse backgrounds and perspectives, the conversations were far reaching. Mathematics education is a discipline in which it is difficult to find absolutes. Many factors contribute to successful mathematics teaching and learning and what is perceived as convincing evidence from one perspective is not at all convincing from another. The following observations reflect comments made in the reports from the final discussion session during which each group was asked to make statements about areas of agreement and challenges or issues needing more work. The observations are a sampling of the many interesting and important ideas raised.

AREAS OF AGREEMENT WITHIN DISCUSSION GROUPS

The areas of agreements offered by the discussion groups ranged from specific statements about important content to agreeing about a set of challenges faced by the education community as they worked to improve mathematics education at the middle grades. The set below reflect some of the thinking.

- It is important to enhance the quality and depth of mathematics learning in the middle grades and to sensitively address the needs of young adolescents as individuals as well as learners. Participants observed that it is possible to honor these commitments to students and to content simultaneously in middle grades mathematics classrooms, but the intent to do so should be clearly highlighted in the school structure and organization and delivery of learning.

- Participants commented on a clear and compelling need to have higher expectations for all middle grades students. Teachers, schools, and parents should have high expectations for student achievement in mathematics and recognize that to realize these expectations will take renewed effort and commitment from everyone.

- To deliver the kind of mathematics content in ways that respects middle grades students as learners demands a well prepared and motivated teacher. Few existing teacher preparation programs meet this need, and certification requirements do not support adequate content and pedagogical preparation.
- To achieve the kind of instruction that will maximize learning for all students in middle grades, the issue of on-going professional development activities in which teachers focus on their practice and become part of a community with shared goals must be addressed. Teachers in such a community take time to reflect on their teaching and its relation to what students learn and work together to improve what they do in their classrooms.
- The organizational structure of a school system is important but equally as important is the support and commitment for mathematical excellence and for equal opportunities for all. Teachers need adequate time to plan their lessons and work through their curriculum as well as support for staff development.

CHALLENGES RAISED BY DISCUSSION GROUPS

The improvement of mathematics education in the middle grades faces curricular, pedagogical, and contextual challenges. The following are some of the challenges and issues highlighted by the discussion groups in their final reports.

- Good curriculum and pedagogy may be insufficient if policy and political issues are not taken into consideration. Because public perception of a quality mathematics program at the middle grades may be in conflict with the goals of mathematics educators, success in implementing new programs depends on building public understanding of the changes. Families should be informed about the content expectations of the overall program and specific grade levels within the program. District level policy makers should understand the nature of the program and provide support within the system to make changes. Mathematics education researchers should be convinced to investigate questions around reform issues and to produce data that will help the public understand that schools and districts are making informed decisions about teaching and learning mathematics.
- Both internal articulation within school systems and external articulation within states are critical. Mandates concerning assessment, standards, and curriculum often signal different messages about what is

important in mathematics at the middle grades. When the mathematical content for the middle grades is not clearly delineated, there is overlap and confusion about content, particularly in the areas of number and algebra. In teaching students about number and operations, the curriculum can become repetitive contributing to the "mile wide, inch deep" characterization of the middle grades curriculum by TIMSS. On the other hand, the emphasis on algebra in the middle grades has raised articulation issues about high school credits in middle grades, or students repeating content at the high school level with no recognition of their work in the middle grades.

- The practice of grouping students by perceived ability can appear to be in direct conflict with the goal of providing the same mathematics for all students. While many teachers support heterogeneous grouping in theory, in practice they find it difficult to implement. The need to simultaneously provide remediation and acceleration in large classes can prove overwhelming, yet separating students for different academic programs raised questions for the teachers about equitable mathematics opportunities for all students.

- The nature and role of algebra at the middle grades raises curricular

questions as well as articulation issues. Too much emphasis on algebra comes at the expense of other important mathematical topics. For teachers to be successful with algebra embedded throughout the curriculum, they should have a high level of mathematical knowledge, for which many have not been prepared. Implementing a program that teaches algebra only to a select set of students inhibits organizing students into houses, a typical middle grades approach, or forces an arbitrary ability grouping layer on the housing structure. Acceleration for some can lower expectations for others.

- It is important for middle grades students to see the connections among mathematical topics, their lives, and what they learn. The challenge, however, is to achieve a balance between student needs and content; integration should not happen at the expense of mathematics. An overemphasis on developing students as individuals can result in a loss of instructional focus on content. Students should come to understand that while mathematics is not taught in a vacuum, it is a discipline of its own. Unless carefully constructed where the mathematics is not just added on when seen as useful, thematic units can be a detriment to a coherent and complete middle grades mathematical curriculum. Many middle grades teachers do not have mathematical backgrounds and find it difficult to make links with mathematics.

- Communication among the diverse audiences involved in middle grades mathematics programs is problematic. The term "developmentally appropriate" is not well understood by many in the broad education community. Some questioned what it meant to characterize a mathematical concept as developmentally appropriate for a student. Integrated mathematics means different things at the high school level where it indicates blending of mathematical topics with no clear demarcation between algebra and geometry and at the middle grades where it usually refers to blending of content from different disciplines, mathematics with science and literature, for example. To have productive conversations there has to be an attempt to develop a common language.

Convocation Papers and Discussion Summaries

Teaching and Learning Mathematics at the Middle Grades
Setting the Stage

The emphasis on "teaching the whole child and the whole curriculum" advocated by some can be seen as opposed to the emphasis on "teaching mathematics content area" as advocated by others.

MATHEMATICS IN THE MIDDLE: BUILDING A FIRM FOUNDATION OF UNDERSTANDING FOR THE FUTURE

Glenda Lappan, University Distinguished Professor, Department of Mathematics, Michigan State University.

THE MIDDLE SCHOOL LEARNER: CONTEXTS, CONCEPTS, AND THE TEACHING CONNECTION

Thomas Dickinson, Professor of Curriculum and Instruction at Indiana State University.

Mathematics in the Middle
Building a Firm Foundation of Understanding for the Future

Glenda Lappan
University Distinguished Professor, Department of Mathematics,
Michigan State University

What makes mathematics in the middle grades so important? There are factors that have to do with adolescent growth and development. Others have to do with the subject matter itself, its increasing complexity, and its increasing importance as a foundation on which science, mathematics, and technology literacy is to be built. Each of these factors that influence mathematics' importance in the middle years will be elaborated individually and as they interact with each other.

Students in the middle grades go from pre-adolescence to adolescence at different rates. At the beginning of the year in grade six, students may all look much as they did the year before in grade five. By the end of this year or the next, most students, both girls and boys, will grow several inches. Students' reactions to these rapid changes in their bodies are, of course, quite varied. But for all students these changes are accompanied by emotional challenges. Students are faced with getting to know a new self, including a new body, with new emotions. Strong among these new emotions is a need to be like others, to belong. Parents are no longer the center of the world. Peers are now the focus for what is "cool" and for emotional support or crushing rejection. At the same time, a student's intellectual capacity to reason is expanding rapidly.

Students in middle grades are growing in their ability to reason abstractly. They become capable of generalization, abstraction, and argument in mathematics. This signals the need for programs that give students the opportunity to expand their experiences with "doing" mathematics, with controlling variables and examining the consequences, with experimenting, making conjectures, and developing convincing arguments to support or disconfirm a conjecture. Taken together, these changing intellectual capacities and the fragile emotional state of these vulnerable middle grade students call for very carefully crafted mathematical experiences that allow students to satisfy their social needs as well as their intellectual needs. The following section looks at the mathematics of the middle grades, its challenges and its fit with these emerging adolescents.

MATHEMATICS OF THE MIDDLE GRADES

As students encounter mathematics in the upper elementary grades, the emphasis changes from a focus on the additive structure of numbers and relationships to the multiplicative structure of numbers and relationships. This means that the students are faced with new kinds of numbers, fractions and decimals that rely on multiplication for their underlying structure. These numbers are useful in making new kinds of comparisons that rely on two measures (or more) of a phenomena. For example, which is best, 5 cans of tomatoes for $6 or 8 cans for $9? A simple subtraction will not resolve the issue. A comparison that takes into account both the quantity of cans and the prices is called for.

These new mathematical ideas contain intellectual challenges for the students that are as conceptually difficult as anything anywhere else in the K-12 mathematics curriculum. Many of these mathematical ideas will not reach their full maturity in the middle years, but it is in the middle grades that the firm foundation for understanding is laid. It is here that students have time to experiment, to ponder, to play with mathematical ideas, to seek relationships among ideas and concepts, and to experience the power of mathematics to tackle problem situations that can be mathematized or modeled. It is also here in the middle years that the serious development of the language of mathematics begins.

It is easy to make a laundry list of topics in mathematics important in the middle years. Here is such a list:

- Number theory, factors, multiples, division, products, relationships among numbers and among operations
- Rational numbers, integers, irrational numbers
- Fractions, decimals and percents
- Ratios, rates, proportions, quantitative reasoning and comparison
- Variables, variables changing in relation to each other, rates of change among related variables
- Representations of related variables in tables, graphs, and symbolic form
- Slope, linearity, non-linear relationships, families of functions
- How things grow in both an algebraic and a geometric sense
- Maximum and minimum

- Shape and shape relations, similarity, symmetry, transformations
- The Pythagorean Theorem
- Chance and reasoning about uncertainty
- Prediction using probability and statistics
- Measurement systems and measurement of attributes such as length, area, volume, weight, mass, angle, time, distance, speed
- Visualization and location of objects in space
- Representation of three-dimensional objects in two-dimensional drawings and vice versa

The real challenge is to help students see these ideas in their relationship to each other. This requires a different way of bringing mathematics and students together. Rather than see these ideas as a series of events to be covered, good middle school curricula are finding ways to help students engage in making sense of these ideas in their complex relationship to each other. Symbolic representations of patterns in algebra are seen as related to symbolic representations of transformations, slides, flips and turns, in the plane. In other words, we need to think about how we set students' goals for mathematics. Rather than expounding a list of individual ideas to be "cov-

ered," goals need to help a teacher and a student see what is to be learned, how the ideas can be used, and to what the ideas are connected.

What follows is an argument organized around strands of mathematics and important related ideas within those strands for thinking about what is important for students to learn in mathematics in the middle years. In each of these sections an argument for inclusion is based on the universality of the ideas in the strand no matter what the future ambitions of the students will be. Whether students will enter post-secondary educational institutions or the world of work directly after high school, the following ideas are key. They are mathematics that is central to being able to manage affairs as an adult and to be a good citizen who makes good decisions based on evidence rather than persuasive rhetoric. They are also mathematical ideas that have their roots in the middle years.

RATIONAL NUMBERS AND PROPORTIONAL REASONING[1]

One area of mathematics that is fundamental to the middle grades is rational numbers and proportional

---

[1] This strand argument is taken from a paper I presented at the Fourth International Mathematics Education Conference at the University of Chicago in August 1998 entitled *Preparing Students for College and the Work Place: Can We Do Both?*

reasoning. This includes fractions, decimals, percents, ratios, rates, proportions, and linearity, as well as geometric situations such as scales and scaling, similarity, scale factors, scale modeling, map reading, etc. Another important aspect of this mathematics is that it gives a powerful way of making comparisons. Having two measures, rather than one, on attributes that we are trying to compare leads us into the world of derived measures that are often per quantities or rates. This is a core of ideas that relate to quantitative reasoning or literacy and connects directly to science. Almost everything of interest to scientists is a quantity, a number with a label. Study of mathematics involving quantitative reasoning invariably means reasoning about mathematics in contexts. Part of what makes mathematics so powerful is its science of abstraction from real contexts. To quote Lynn Steen (p. xxiii, 1997):

> The role of context in mathematics poses a dilemma, which is both philosophical and pedagogical. In mathematics itself.... context obscures structure, yet when mathematics connects with the world, context provides meaning. Even though mathematics embedded in context often loses the very characteristics of abstraction and deduction that make it useful, when taught without relevant context it is all but unintelligible to most students. Even the best students have difficulty applying context-free mathematics to

problems arising in realistic situations, or applying what they have learned in another context to a new situation.

This is an argument that works for students headed for the workplace as well as college. Clearly applications, but even more so, mathematics skills, procedures, concepts, and ways of thinking and reasoning taught through contextualized problem situations, help students of all kinds and ambitions learn mathematics. The modern high-performance workplace involves problems that require sophisticated reasoning and yet often only the mathematics of a good middle school education. The high level of reasoning that empowers a student to use these ideas in new and creative ways is not complete by the end of middle school but requires continued experiences in the high school curriculum.

DATA ANALYSIS, REPRESENTATION, AND INTERPRETATION

Another aspect of mathematics that pervades our modern life is data, or as statistician David Moore calls it, numbers with a context. In the workplace, in jobs at all levels, employees are dealing with the problem of either reducing or understanding the reduction of large quantities of complex data to a few numbers or graphical representation. These numbers or statistics are expressed in fractions, decimals and percents. Thus, knowing something about data analysis and interpretation and rational numbers is important to all students. The society in which we live has become quantitative. We are surrounded by data.

To handle our money, to make transactions, to run our businesses, as well as to do almost any job well, we need mathematics that is underpinned with a high level of reasoning and understanding. As Iddo Gal puts it, "There are no "word problems" in real life. Adults face quantitative tasks in multiple situations whose contexts require seamless integration of numeracy and literacy skills. Such integration is rarely dealt with in school curricula" (Gal, 1997, p. 36). But, it should be! Using contexts that show the world of work help make mathematics more authentic to students regardless of their future career goals. Data analysis, representation, and interpretation are an important and rich area for such examples.

GEOMETRIC SHAPES, LOCATION, AND SPATIAL VISUALIZATION

Whether we are talking about an intending calculus student or an employee at a tool and die shop, geometry, location, and spatial visualization are important. Just as a calculus student needs to visualize a curve moving to form the boundary or surface of a solid in space, a tool and die employee uses such skill to set a machine to locate and cut a huge piece of steel to specifications that truly exceed our imagination. Here again is an area of mathematics that has application in the workplace and should be a part of the education of all students. This is also a part of mathematics in which strand or areas intersect. While I have labeled this area geometric shapes, location, and spatial visualization, algebra becomes a tool for specifying both location and shape. Even the spatial visualization aspects of geometry are enhanced by experiences with transformational geometry and its related algebra. This is also an area with connections to measurement which means rational numbers are essential. We cannot talk about any aspect of measurement without being able to deal with a continuous number line where rational numbers and irrational numbers fill in the spaces between the whole numbers. So again we see connections among strands of mathematics. Another area that has much to offer to both the world of work and to higher education is *chance*.

CHANCE

Everyday humans are faced with reasoning under uncertainty. Many adults make wrong decisions as a result of not understanding the difference between random variables, correlated variables, and variables that influence or cause certain behavior in another variable. Probability is an area of mathematics that is important across the board. It is a very challenging subject and involves a practical everyday kind of mathematics and reasoning. Here, as in other strands we have discussed, the rational numbers play an important role. Probabilities are numbers between 0 and 1 that express the degree of likelihood of an event happening. In experimental situations, probabilities can be estimated as relative frequencies—again a use of fractions and proportional reasoning. In other situations, probabilities can be found by analyzing a situation using an area of 1 square unit to represent everything that can happen. This makes a connection to geometry and measurement.

So much of the information with which we are surrounded in our modern world is of a statistical or probabilistic nature. Here the conception of mathematics as a discipline that comes as close to truth as we know it in the modern world and the idea that what mathematics predicts may not in fact happen in every instance clash. Students learn to deal with the notion of random variables and the seeming contradiction that there can be a science of predicting what happens in the long run when what happens in an instance is random and unpredictable. These are hard ideas that take a great deal of experiencing before they seem sensible and useful. I would argue that the study of chance or probability should be a part of the curriculum for all students in the middle grades. It is in these years that students have the interest and we can provide the time to experiment with random variables. Students need to collect large amounts of data both by hand and with technology simulations, to see that data can be organized to build models that help predict what happens in the long run, and our own theoretical analysis of situations can help us build predictive probability models. Now an argument for one last area—algebra.

ALGEBRA AND ALGEBRAIC REASONING

I think it is pretty clear that few workers meet a quadratic equation to solve on a daily basis, or for that matter few ever meet higher degree polynomial equations to solve. But they do deal with formulas on a regular basis that are quite complex. Figuring the exact amount of a chemical cocktail to inject into a cancer patient demands complex measures and uses of formulas. The consequences of a mistake raise the stakes a great deal. There are so many examples of such in the world of work that a strong case can be made that all students do need algebra, both from a functions point of view and a structure or equation solving point of view. In fact algebra that integrates with other areas of mathematics and that uses applications as a driving force can reach all students no matter what their career goals. For the future mathematician or scientist, algebra is fundamental. For the future office worker, algebraic thinking can mean the difference between remaining in a low-level job and advancing to much higher-paying, more demanding jobs.

I do have to express one caveat. If this is the dry memorized algebra of the past, then it is as likely to damage middle school students as help them. However, an algebra strand that at some grade levels has a real concentration on algebra and algebraic thinking can benefit all students. This means that the ideas will develop over time. This means that applications will drive the learning of algebra, not just be the problems that you try after you memorize the types of problems in the section of the book. This means that the fundamental ideas of algebra will be taught in such a way that students have a real chance of developing deep understanding as they develop technical proficiency. It should also be an algebra that takes full advantage of calculators and computers as tools to explore ideas and to carry out procedures.

Rather than belabor my point, let me just make it outright. We need to develop a set of mathematical expectations during the middle years that are for all students. At some stage of high school, students can benefit from options of continuing in a statistics, discrete mathematics direction or toward calculus and more formal mathematics. These should be real choices, equally valued and equally valuable depending on the post-secondary directions a student aims to take. But in the middle years, we need to develop curricula that preserve student's options for those future choices. However, such a curricula alone will not make an excellent mathematics experience for all students. Teachers and teaching matter. What teachers do with the curricula, what the expectations are for students, how students are expected to work, what conversations are expected and how these are conducted matter. Teaching in the middle grades requires knowledge of the subject matter and also of students at this age.

TEACHING MATHEMATICS IN THE MIDDLE GRADES

What are the challenges associated with teaching mathematics in the middle grades? Not all students reach the same levels of cognitive growth at the same time. This means that the middle school mathematics classroom teacher has the challenge of creating an environment that supports students' mathematics growth at many different levels. Since middle school students are at many stages of cognitive, physical, and social development, the teacher needs to understand where students are in their mathematical growth. Typical paper and pencil computation driven tests give little specific understanding of student's thinking. Thus, an additional challenge for the teacher is creating and using many opportunities for assessing student understanding. Teachers are experimenting with many new forms of assessments varying from partner or group tests or performance tasks to projects or student portfolios.

Middle grades students have many social, emotional, and physical challenges with which to deal. In order to capture their attention and direct their growing cognitive powers on mathematics, the mathematical tasks posed for students must be focused on things they find interesting and important. Things that we as adults think of interest to middle school students are not always on target. This argues for opportunities for choice within the mathematics classroom. Choice of project topics, choice of problems of the week to work on, and even dealing with problems that

allow different strategies for solution, are ways of allowing students to feel the power of choice. In addition, the kinds of problem settings used for tasks need to take into account the interests of students at this level.

In order for students to make sense of concepts, ways of reasoning, productive procedures, and problem solving strategies in mathematics, and to develop skill with number and symbolic operations and procedures, they must be engaged in exploring, investigating, inventing, generalizing, abstracting, and constructing arguments to support their ideas and conjectures. New mathematics materials for the middle grades are problem oriented. Interesting contexts for investigation are posed. Within these contexts students bump into mathematics that they need but do not yet have in their tool kit. This need drives students to invent, to create strategies for solving their problems. Out of these student ideas come the conversations that, with the teacher's guidance, help make the underlying mathematical ideas, concepts, procedures, skills, and arguments more explicit for the students. As you think of the socialization of the middle school level, there is a natural match between the mathematical need to deeply understand ideas and the social need to interact with ones peers around tasks that are of interest. We can use this energy and need to socialize to advantage in mathematics by refocusing our instruction to be more on mathematics as an experimental science where seeking to understand why is the major quest. Another tool that we have available to us in teaching mathematics is technology.

Technology is engaging to students. It also allows access to mathematics that could not be explored in the past. It helps to create environments in which students can see change, can engage in a dynamic way with mathematical conjecturing. It allows students to tackle real problems with messy data. It allows students control over different forms of representation of mathematical relationships. It allows students to invent new strategies for tackling problems; it allows students to reason through problems in ways that are different from the strategies we would use. Again this freedom to experiment and to create makes mathematics of greater interest to many more students. It connect mathematics to the real world and to the interests of these emerging adolescents.

SUMMARY

While mathematics in the middle years is cognitively demanding, it is suited to the developing capabilities of middle school students. New forms of classroom interaction, more emphasis on experimentation, on larger, more challenging problems, on seeking to understand and make sense of mathematics and mathematical situations, on using technology as a tool—these are the ways in which new middle school curricula are seeking to engage these social, energetic, developing adolescents in learning for their own future. Mathematics can be a key to opening doors or to closing them for students. Our goals has to be to help preserve future options for our students until they reach a level of maturity to understand the consequences of their decisions. We cannot do this unless we can make mathematics interesting and relevant to our students.

REFERENCES

Gal, I. (1997). Numeracy: Imperatives of a forgotten goal. In L.A. Steen (Ed.), *Why numbers count: Quantitative literacy for tomorrow's America* (pp. 36-44). New York: College Entrance Examination Board.

Steen, L.A. (1997). Preface: The new literacy. In L.A. Steen (Ed.), *Why numbers count: Quantitative literacy for tomorrow's America* (pp. xv-xxviii). New York: College Entrance Examination Board.

The Middle School Learner
Contexts, Concepts, and the Teaching Connection

Thomas Dickinson
Professor of Curriculum and Instruction, Indiana State University

SMALL STORIES[1]

Successful middle schools have small stories "because the school has time for small incidents before they become large" (Lipsitz, 1984). I have one such story to share.

It was one of those early spring days that promised clear skies and warm weather for weeks to come. School had just let out, and I was sitting at my desk, grading papers. Wrapped up in the process of marking and recording, I didn't immediately see the small figure at my door. "Mr. Dickinson, are you busy?" the voice asked and my grading reverie was broken. It was Amy Bounds, a seventh grader in my homeroom and a student in one of my social studies classes. Amy was one of those students that make up the bulk of our classes, best described by phrases such as "good student" or "neat kid," one of those individuals that we honor with the label of "nice to have in class."

The question repeated itself, "Mr. Dickinson, are you busy?" I shook my head and waved her on into the room where she took the seat next to my desk. "What are you doing here Amy? You should be outside on a day like this." I told her. Her reply abruptly changed the detached mood I was in. "Mr. Dickinson, I've got a problem."

I attempted to fight off my immediate adult questions—what kind of problem could Amy have? And as my mind raced with possibilities, it didn't slow down with her next comment. "You're a man, Mr. Dickinson, so you'll understand my problem." Gathering my strength, I

---

[1] "Small Stories" was originally published, in an expanded version, in the November 1988 issue of *Middle School Journal*. Used with permission.

asked Amy, "What's the problem? How can I help?"

"Well," she said, "where do you get your ties?"

"My ties?" I asked, trying to put two and two together, unsuccessfully. "My ties?"

"Yeah, your ties. My father's birthday is tomorrow and I'm not going to let my mother buy my present for him. I want to buy him a tie like the ones you wear. And I've been saving my lunch money. Do you think I have enough?"

And with that Amy extracted from her backpack a plastic bag stuffed with change and plopped it on my desk.

Amy Bounds was growing up. She was, to use her phrase, "no longer a baby." And this translated most immediately into a problem with her father's birthday. She wanted to buy her father a present, an appropriate present, and she wanted to do it herself. But who could she talk to, who could she ask? Not her father. It was his birthday, and she wanted very much to surprise and impress him. Not her mother. She might not understand, or she might try to interfere. So I was chosen, partially because I was her homeroom teacher, partially because I was a man, and mostly because she liked the ties I wore.

Before we did anything we sorted the money and talked about her father. I asked about his taste in clothes, colors, and fabrics. Amy could answer all my questions because she'd checked his closet, several times. During our talk Amy related that she didn't have a regular allowance, that she had been saving "extra" from her lunch money for the last three months. She'd also been lugging it around in her backpack since she didn't want to risk it being discovered at home. She also knew better than to trust her hall locker. And once a day she'd been handing it over to her best friend for safekeeping while she took gym. Most interesting to me was Amy's revelation that she'd been counting it every night, hoping that she'd have enough before her father's birthday.

We talked ties for quite a while—rep stripes, paisleys, solids, Italian silks, and knits. She had a list of the ones I wore that she liked, and we went through her list and discussed all the possibilities. Finally Amy decided on something silk, something blue or blue/grey, and something with a small conservative pattern. And then she asked her original question again, "Where do you get your ties?" I had been buying clothes from one men's store ever since I'd had my own money. I drew a map for Amy of where the store was located. Would she be able to find it? She nodded with a quiet "yes." Did she want the present gift wrapped? They would do it for free, but she had to ask. Did she have a card already? No, well, there was a card shop two doors down.

And then everything was settled and in place. She left with a grin and a quick thank you. After she was gone I went to the office to make a telephone call. The next day I had a note on my desk at the start of homeroom—"Everything is set. Thanks." That evening I received a telephone call from Amy's mother. Years later I only remember her "Thank you." What I do remember as if it were yesterday was the grin on Amy's face as she came into homeroom the next day and her comment, "He wore it this morning, and it looked terrific!"

DEVELOPMENT IN CONTEXT: THE CHILD, THE SCHOOL, AND SOCIETY

You teach Amy. Or you teach teachers about Amy. Or Amy may sit across from you at your dinner table. Amy is an individual. She is a human being. She is a person. She is not a list of developmental characteristics. She is not a "typical" young adolescent (there aren't any). She is instead, Amy. And that is enough, if we would but see and acknowledge it.

I began with a story about a young adolescent—not in a mathematics context—on purpose. That purpose was so that all of us would see development for what it is: a natural and normal process, bounded by general psycho-

logical guidelines, but embodied in individuals. And this embodiment is bounded, shaped, and influenced by a range of contexts—the individual context of self, that mixture of heredity and randomness; the context of family, street, neighborhood; the larger social context, which today includes an overwhelming and disturbing mass media context that impacts young adolescents at their every turn. (Half of all young adolescents spend three hours or more each day watching television.) The average young adolescent is exposed to the mass media a total of about four hours per day. Only sleeping and attending school occupies more time. I won't even go into the content—if you'd like, watch MTV for an hour, or flip through the latest issue of any popular magazine.

To try to understand development for young adolescents we have to frame these contexts with their individuality. To put it bluntly, we have to understand the individual to understand their development. Good middle schools try to do just this. They try to understand and teach individual children, not types or categories of children, but individual children themselves. This is what *This We Believe: Developmentally Responsive Middle Level Schools* (National Middle School Associations, 1995) talks about. It's what *Turning Points: Preparing American Youth for the 21st Century*

(Carnegie Council on Adolecscent Development, 1989) recommends. And it's what I've been seeing in a small school in San Antonio, Texas.

DEVELOPMENT AND THE TEACHING CONNECTION

Donna Owen looks out over the overhead projector at a sea of khaki and white and asks "What's my rule?" and points to the bright yellow poster on the board. Two columns of numbers lie waiting for her young charges:

IN	OUT
3	11
5	15
0	5
10	25

The students are already at work on this daily ritual. These are 6th graders, in uniforms (that's the khaki and white) at the American Heritage School, an Outward Bound Expeditionary Learning (ELOB) school-within-a-school that is part of Edgar Allen Poe Middle School in San Antonio, Texas. The vast majority of students are Hispanic. Their school, a new building, stands in stark contrast to its neighborhood surroundings.

Kids, seated in pairs, are tackling the problem—some with charts of their own, others with series of problems trying to arrive at a formula that works for all of the four pairs, one student using a number line. Around the room there is a rich riot of color—number lines, bought and teacher-made posters with vocabulary lists and mathematics operations, and two computers (still not hooked up to the internet—it's November when this is being written) in the back of the room by the teacher's desk. The kids continue to work—focused, on task, quiet.

What first drew me to this teacher is outside. On one side of the hall is a large gallery (think about that word as opposed to a "bulletin board"), maybe 15 feet long. On it are student charts and graphs. But not *just* charts and graphs, but charts and graphs about the students. In preparation for the team's first "expedition" where the topic was the Americas, studied through the lens of the focus question "How is the good life in the Americas nurtured and challenged?" Donna had her sixth graders work on charts and graphs by collecting data on *themselves*. Working in pairs the students queried their teammates, recorded the data and graphed or charted it, and then wrote narrative explanations of their findings. There were bar graphs, line graphs, pie charts. And the topics of the charts and graphs were wide ranging:

- the males and females in the class
- the numbers of letters in students' names
- the days of the week students were born
- the right- and left-handedness of students
- the number of lima beans that each student could pick up with one hand (!)
- the height of individuals in the class, in centimeters
- the circumference of individuals' heads, also in centimeters

And all this work was displayed (and graded too). The accompanying narratives demonstrated:

- a sense of audience (especially in their detail and completeness)
- a concern for language, structure, and correctness
- an appreciation of self and others (peers) as a source of information that could be used in mathematical understanding

Donna Owen was teaching individuals. She was also teaching mathematics. And she was also helping students understand themselves. She was placing development within a context of individuals and those individuals within a rich and involving context of learning, in this case mathematical understanding. And if you're wondering about this marvelously insightful teacher, here's the bio: she is late to teaching; at 29 she went off to get a degree after serving as a teacher's aide in a classroom where she was getting more and more responsibility because of her talent, insight, and drive. Encouraged by her teacher and principal to pursue a degree and teaching license, she did just that and became the first of seven children (she's the oldest) to go to college. And she did her degree in three years, cum laude, taking 18-21 hours of course work at a time, arranged on three days a week so that she could continue to do her aide work. By the way, Donna has taught middle school English and journalism for the past ten years. She thought she needed another challenge so she got licensed in mathematics and is in her second year of teaching that subject. Last year, her first teaching mathematics, 91% of her students passed the Texas Assessment of Academic Skills.

I'm back in the classroom again. The second expedition is under way. Students are working on problems involving space travel. Along one entire wall, probably 40 feet, is a swath of purple paper, floor to ceiling, with the sun at one end and off on the other side of the room (actually on the back of the door), Pluto. This is the entire solar system, to the scale of 1" = 10,000,000 miles. And the sizes of the planets are to scale as well. The students are working on estimated travel time in hours to the planets. It's another example of "What's my rule" where the kids are deriving the rule from data. I watch, amazed at the degree of engagement. At the end of the class my notes summarize the lesson:

- focus on reading directions
- finding necessary information
- using available data
- drawing conclusions from data
- working in cooperative groups
- recording information accurately
- doing basic mathematical operations
- working alone
- making choices to investigate individually

I could tell you all the developmental psychology connections here, but I hope you see them. I know my readers, being mathematically skilled, can see what's happening here mathematically. This is another "small story." And like most small stories in good middle schools it goes relatively unnoticed, except by the teacher and students who are growing and changing together, as individuals.

REFERENCES

Carnegie Council on Adolescent Development. (1989). *Turning Points: Preparing American Youth for the 21st Century.* New York: Carnegie Corporation.

Lipsitz, J.S. (1984). *Successful schools for young adolescents.* New Brunswick, New Jersey: Transaction Books.

National Middle School Association. (1995). *This we believe: Developmentally responsive middle level schools.* Columbus, OH: Author.

Content and Learning Issues in the Middle Grades

The sessions on content and learning mathematics in the middle grades focused on the questions:

- What developmental considerations are important in thinking about middle school students as learners? As learners of mathematics? Are these compatible?
- What do we know about middle school students' capacity for learning? For learning mathematics?
- What are important ideas in mathematics for the middle grades and how are these related to developmental learning considerations?

REFLECTIONS ON MIDDLE SCHOOL MATHEMATICS

Nancy Doda, Professor of Education, National-Louis University.

MATHEMATICS CONTENT AND LEARNING ISSUES IN MIDDLE GRADES MATHEMATICS

Kathleen Hart, Chair of Mathematics Education (retired), University of Nottingham, United Kingdom.

SUMMARY OF SMALL GROUP DISCUSSION ON CONTENT AND LEARNING ISSUES IN MIDDLE GRADES MATHEMATICS

Reflections on Middle School Mathematics

Nancy Doda
Professor of Education, National-Louis University, Washington, DC

OVERVIEW

Young adolescence is a remarkable and challenging time in human life not always appropriately appreciated nor well understood. In 1971, Joan Lipsitz published a review of research on the middle grades child and learner in which her chosen book title, *Growing up Forgotten*, was essentially her most provocative conclusion—that young adolescents were American education's most neglected and least well understood age group (Lipsitz, 1971). Since this seminal work's debut, there has been without question a steady cacophony of hearts and minds that have joined to recognize, celebrate, and better understand and serve this unique age group. Indeed, several decades of reform initiatives now stand before us, yielding wisdom to guide future efforts to improve schooling for young adolescents (Lipsitz, 1981; George and Shewey, 1994).

While we are fortunate to have this rich history of middle grades reform, with its now well-documented dividends (e.g., Felner et al., 1997), it is nonetheless clear that the dividends of greater student learning and achievement are still more illusive than we might have hoped. There still remain enormously stubborn achievement gaps between white children and children of color; between poor children and financially advantaged children, between girls and boys. If asked the question, "How are we doing in the U.S. with regards to student achievement?", the truthful answer would be, "That depends on which children we are discussing." And in the case of our focus here, perhaps it also depends on which subject we are examining.

We face a crossroads in middle school reform. One that calls upon us to reexamine not only the fundamental philosophy of the middle school concept, but the beliefs and practices that remain as potential deterrents to our gravest challenge—that of ensuring academic success for all our children. There is an urgent need to dig deeply to understand what is needed in the reform conundrum, particularly with student learning in mathematics. Student success in middle school mathematics remains the great equalizer or divider, as it were, and our students' individual and our collective futures depend upon it.

CHANGING THE IMAGE— CHANGING THE CURRICULUM

While the contemporary dialogue about the nature of young adolescents has often been delivered with affectionate humor, such humor often highlights the least dignifying portrait of the young teen. I have often quoted Linda Reiff's comments to evoke an affirming chuckle from most middle grades educators or parents. She wrote:

> Working with teenagers is not easy. It takes patience, humor and love. Yes, love of kids who burp and fart their way through eighth grade. Who tell you "Life sucks!" and everything they do is "Boring!" Who literally roll to the floor in hysterical laughter when you separate the prefix and suffix from the word "prediction" and ask them for the root and what it means. Who wear short, skin-tight skirts and leg-laced sandals, but carry teddy bears in their arms. Who use a paper clip to tattoo Jim Morrison's picture on their arm during quiet study, while defending the merits of Tigger's personality in Winnie-the -Pooh. Who send obscene notes that would make a football player blush, written in pink magic marker, blasting each other for stealing or not stealing a boyfriend, and sign the note, "Love, _____ P.S. Please write back." (Reiff, 1992, p. 90-91)

In their light-hearted intent, such comments can spur teacher camaraderie, but they also can serve to remind us of how easily this unique stage of development might be misconstrued. In fact, caution is in order since for a variety of reasons beyond such language, the intellectual character and energy of young adolescents have often been underrated. Most certainly we have nearly eliminated reductive images portraying young adolescents as "hormones with feet," and yet the achievement question ought to call upon all of us to make a more deliberate effort to acknowledge and celebrate the incredibly powerful intellectual character of this age group.

As I travel around the nation, I have had the delightful opportunity to dialogue with many young adolescents, and I'd like to share with you that our young people, from all ethnic and cultural affiliations, from all levels of income and from all levels of school competence, repeatedly demonstrate that they are immersed in one of the most intellectually pivotal times in human development. I ask young people to share with me the questions and concerns they have about the world. Their musings should remind us at how phenomenal our educational opportunity is during the middle school years. Let me share a few of their recurring questions and concerns:

- Will there ever be world peace?
- Can we clean up the environment?
- Will men and women ever be equal?
- Will there ever be a black President?
- What happens when you die?
- Why do people hate each other?
- Are millions of people in the world really starving?
- Why is there so much hatred and violence?
- Why does anyone have to be poor?
- How can we cure AIDS and cancer?
- Is there life in outer space?
- Why are we here?

Young adolescents are philosophical, investigative, reflective, hypothetical, and skeptical. They love to debate, query, conjecture, moralize, judge, and predict. They are filled with the joy of self-discovery and the inevitable disillusionment of world discovery. They are paradoxical. While plagued with self-doubt, they are armed with a heroic invincibility (Elkind, 1984). In sum,

these young people are developmentally ripe for intellectual growth.

But when they enter our middle schools every day, not many find in their classrooms a match for the intellectual intensity their questions reflect. For too many, curriculum is not seen as exciting, useful, meaningful, or helpful. In numerous and lengthy focus group interviews with students, I have found their responses quite telling. I asked one energetic sixth grade student what he was learning and why. He responded dutifully, "Latin America." I then asked, "Why are you studying this? What's really important about this topic?" He was equally honest and said, "I have no clue, but I think it's in the curriculum." His peer offered, "I think we need to learn it cause we might need it later on." Another added, "No, I don't really think so because my father is very smart and successful, and I know he never uses this stuff." Something huge is missing in how students are experiencing curriculum.

We shouldn't presume that it is only those struggling students who raise serious question with our curriculum. I asked a group of honor roll students in a middle school to tell me about what they had learned from the fall until January. They couldn't recall much. In considering their plight of failed memory, one eager student perked up with some sense of enlightenment, "I think I know why we're stumped. We were in the accelerated program and we went so fast, we don't remember much." In the very least, his comments affirmed my often nagging notion that much of what we define in schools as accelerated is merely more content taught faster, more homework done hastily, and not much more learned deeply. Clearly, the TIMSS findings (Silver, 1998) illuminate this "mile wide and inch deep" curriculum problem that challenges our pedagogy.

That curriculum in all fields of knowledge in middle school must be more meaningful, challenging, and engaging is unquestionable. When observing students and teachers at work, I discover that many of our students are often not engaged in challenging learning experiences. I watched extremely bored students sit in a well managed classroom listening to a litany from peers who were to each report to the class on the content of an individually read current event. This was an entire class period of high disengagement and notable disenchantment. This is where an urgency for reform should be felt. This still happens far too often.

THE REFORM PICTURE

While the middle school movement's thirty year history has secured a place on the reform map and has contributed greatly to the overall improvement of many middle level schools, the movement's reform recommendations and efforts have, I believe been more successful in altering the climate and structure of middle level schools than the curriculum and instruction our young people have experienced (Felner, et al., 1997). Organizing smaller, more personalized learning communities, commonly called teams, creating teacher scaffolding and support for all students, emphasizing interdisciplinary planning and teaching, and creating more flexible schedules liberated from tracking, have without question, raised teacher efficacy, encouraged professional dialogue, reduced school anonymity, improved school climate, and even in some pockets, raised school achievement. They have not always resulted in the dramatic shift in teaching and learning that was I believe a bold hope of the middle school movement's many advocates and champions.

Perhaps the simplest explanation that draws nods from many is that the middle school movement has devoted too much of its energy and attention to reforming the organizational character of our middle level schools. James Beane (1998a) would suggest that such a situation with the state of reform in middle school teaching and learning was inevitable since we never fully achieved consensus on the goals and purposes of the middle school curriculum. Likewise, some speculate that three decades of work devoted to the creation of more humane schools has resulted in soft attention to the intellectual development of our young people. Others argue that achievement, particularly in mathematics, has been short-changed by our advocacy and implementation of thematic teaching which often highlights social studies and language arts or disparagingly, reduces mathematics to labeling correct measurements on an interdisciplinary exhibit. Still others I might say, quite legitimately, have argued that misguided interpretations of progressive instructional methods have yielded sloppy attention to intellectual development and authentic and substantive student learning.

Regardless of the complex puzzle of causes that we are now facing, the TIMSS results in mathematics are not surprising. In the last three decades of classroom practice, approaches to mathematics instruction in middle schools have not changed as consistently and dramatically as some of us might have hoped following the publication of the NCTM standards. The islands of excellence are simply too few.

None of the recommendations for middle school structural reform are void of underlying theory about their relationship with student learning. While not always clear to the public nor consistently conveyed in professional development, we should not be too quick to blame the current achievement conundrum in mathematics or any field on the middle school concept.

Interdisciplinary teaming, for instance, remains at the core of middle school reform, in large part because of its research credibility to raise teacher sense of efficacy—a key element in high performing classrooms. Team organization has also been associated with reduced school anonymity and teacher collegiality, additional features in safe and productive schools. Moreover, attempts at increased personalization, in the form of Teacher Advisory programs and similar middle school initiatives, were fundamentally grounded in the belief that the quality of teacher-student relationships greatly impacts student motivation and performance. That learning is a social endeavor, embedded in relationships is not an assumption unique to middle school philosophy (Glasser, 1992). That curriculum was intended to be exploratory was not meant to suggest that it could not also be demanding. That middle schools were intended to be humane and caring places was not intended to be antithetical to serious mathematics education. Indeed, there is a tremendous need to pursue and refine these elements of the middle school concept as we engineer a new plan towards higher performing middle schools with greater learning for all.

MIDDLE SCHOOL MATHEMATICS— SEARCHING FOR SOLUTIONS

The standards movement is accompanied by a wave of achievement panic that threatens to diminish the focus on learning in the middle grades. In this panic context, the TIMMS data suggest to some that classrooms have failed to conduct sufficient skill and drill work. Others cast the blame on thematic teaching or detracking. Fortunately, there are several themes that are recurring in current conversations among middle school advocates and those interested in mathematics reform which, when united, bring clarity and perspective to some of the more emotional attacks. Both groups call for a curriculum that is challenging and engaging for young people, offers connections across disciplines, challenges students to apply knowledge, putting mathematics to use, emphasizes problem-centered learning, provides opportunities for collaboration, and seeks to end inequitable practices like tracking (Beane, 1998b).

The earnest call to engage more young adolescents in meaningful mathematics has led exemplary districts and schools to pilot new programs and test their own results. In Corpus Christi, Texas, where standards-based reform is ongoing, all but one middle school has extended the invitation to take algebra to all eligible 6, 7, 8 graders. Eligibility is still the sticky issue since *algebra for all* does not mean all students are guaranteed exposure to algebra concepts by the 8th grade. In fact, while it opens the door to early maturing, frequently advantaged young people, it still fails to embrace the very young people we have missed all along.

In that same district one lone middle school has employed Connected Mathematics, a program developed out of Michigan State University, and the student engagement and learning success they are observing are inspiring. The manipulative and collaborative nature of this curriculum approach finds a place for varying levels of readiness in a way I have not observed with traditional pre-algebra and algebra approaches. Their story and the story of other schools engaged in reflective practice and study will continue to offer promise to our steady search for solutions.

I am frequently asked, "Should all middle school students take algebra before moving on to the high school?" I might begin by posing a clarifying question, "As it is most often taught?" If the response is "yes," then I am compelled to answer, "no." We recognize that many of our young adolescents are not formal operational thinkers with a strong logical-mathematical intelligence and that algebra has traditionally been taught to them as if they were. I am not sure, however, that that is the right question to ask; rather, shouldn't we be asking, what kind of mathematics should all young adolescents be learning to enhance their understanding of the world and the role mathematics plays in it?

Algebra as a course is problematic. Middle school algebra for high school credit is even more problematic. The presence of algebra as a select course with eligibility and teaching certification requirements faithfully diminishes a middle school's chances at academic equity. When students are grouped for mathematics instruction, they are divided as well by race, economics, and learning orientation. As middle schools organize in small learning communities to ensure the noted benefits of teaming, students are grouped by mathematics levels in ways that can result in tracking and the reduction of mathematics learning for non-algebra students. These students deemed less ready or able, travel apart from algebra students, and may spend an entire year relearning mathematics concepts many already know, while they wait to enter "the algebra course."

For young adolescents, meaning is everything. In fact, human learning involves meaning making, does it not? Should we tell our young teens to endure our current version of algebra because they will increase their chances of going to college or because then we can outperform our international partners?

If we are eager to embrace more learners in mathematics education, these suggestions will hardly inspire the tentative. The same students with involved parents or from advantaged homes will be at our college doors while those who wonder if there is life after middle school or hope in life at all will remain out of reach. Even among supported students we still must go further as not one of my son's 8th grade friends, all in 8th grade algebra, can explain to me why or how algebra is or even could be useful in the world. Perhaps it is time for a bold step to move towards creating in middle schools, mathematics for life—far more challenging and meaningful than what many currently experience in algebra? Perhaps what all middle school students should experience is the kind of foundation algebra that few of us received—the kind that would make it possible today for you to identify the many ways in which algebra is at work in the world. Perhaps we might even be able to recognize when we use it? Few of us who do not teach mathematics can do this well.

What really stands in the way of true reform in middle school mathematics has less to do with education, however, and more to do with politics. Mathematics is a subject area with social status. To suggest that algebra not be taught as a course reserved for "capable learners," is to invite a public relations disaster of epic proportions (Beane, 1998a). In fact, in James Beane's work with mathematics teachers who have had success in teaching mathematics in the context of curriculum integration, many have begun to schedule their mathematics as one of the separate subjects in their programs, not because they think it is sound educational practice, but because they would lose the rest of their programs if they did not.

These questions also reflect the major points of deliberation such as whether international test scores should shape curriculum goals, whether all mathematics must be taught as a separate subject, and to what extent higher expectations ought to involve vertical acceleration through mathematics areas or application of knowledge to increasingly sophisticated problems.

I believe we have answers to what constitutes best mathematics education. Perhaps the really critical question we need to address is how can we make the rhetoric of best practice a reality for more of our young people. In answering this question, we in fact push ourselves towards a vision of mathematics education that offers great hope for equity and academic excellence.

JOINING FORCES

We do have many important questions to consider: what is the purpose of the middle school curriculum? Is it to prepare students to be academic scholars? To understand themselves and their world? To make our students score higher than students from other countries and with what assurance that it translates into benefits in life and work? To decide early who will take what path in schooling?

REFERENCES

Beane, J. (1998a). The middle school under siege. Paper presented at the National Middle School Association's annual conference, Denver, CO.

Beane, J. (1998b). Paper prepared for Middle Grades Mathematics Convocation, September, 24-25, 1998. Washington, DC.

Elkind, D. (1984). *All grown up & no place to go*. Reading, MA. Addison-Wesley.

Felner, R. D. Jackson. A.W., Kasak, D., Mulhall, P., Brand, S., Flowers, N. (1997). The impact of school reform for the middle years. *Phi Delta Kappan*, 78(7), 528-532, 541-550.

George, P.S., & Shewey, K. (1994). *New evidence for the middle school*. Columbus, OH: National Middle School Association.

Glasser, W. (1992). *The quality school: Managing students without coercion.* New York: Harper Perennial.

Lipsitz, J. (1971). *Growing up forgotten: A review of research and programs concerning early adolescence.* New Brunswick, NJ: Transaction Books.

Lipsitz, J. (1984). *Successful school for young adolescents.* New Brunswick, NJ: Transaction Books.

Reiff, L. (1992). *Seeking diversity: Language arts with adolescents.* Portsmouth, NH: Heinemann.

Silver, E.A. (1998). *Improving mathematics in middle school: Lessons from TIMSS and related research.* Report prepared for the U.S. Department of Education, Office of Educational Research and Improvement.

Mathematics Content and Learning Issues in the Middle Grades

Kathleen Hart
Chair of Mathematics Education (retired), University of Nottingham, United Kingdom

In the United Kingdom compulsory schooling starts at the age of five and continues until 16 years of age. The provision of free education continues for another two years. The structure of the school system varies and children can proceed through infant school (age 5-7), junior school (8-11) and secondary school (11-16/18) or through a system in which they change schools at 9 and 13 years of age. So in England a child in the middle grades is probably changing (or has just changed) schools. In the first schools, the teacher is a generalist and probably teaches all the subjects the child meets during a week. For the pupil, being promoted to a secondary school (or even a middle school) means that there are many teachers to face in any one day. These teachers tend to be interested in only one curriculum subject. In the primary school, it is likely that the teacher has tried to present the curriculum through project work, which might mean that the intention was to exploit a topic (e.g., The Vikings) for its possibilities to illustrate English, geography, religion, art, science, and mathematics. In the secondary school, these subjects are allotted separate time slots, and the teacher only teaches that subject.

The institutional life in school changes to a greater focus on formal learning, and in mathematics the concentration is on competencies and skills and their application. Often assumptions are made concerning the repertoire of skills the child already possesses, and she may lose confidence when it is shown her repertoire is limited. Add to this the changes in children's physical makeup and the new interests which occupy them, and it is a wonder that they learn anything.

FORMALISATION—MANIPULATIVE LINK

The influence of Piaget on educational theory has meant that much of the child's primary education has been imbedded in the idea that pre-11 years of age the child is operating at the concrete level. Mathematics educators for many years have interpreted this stage as one which requires concrete embodiments or manipulatives to promote what are essentially abstract mathematical ideas. The chasm between the manipulatives and the abstraction has not been addressed very thoroughly. The research project "Children's Mathematical Frameworks" (CMF) sought to investigate the transition made by children when moving from "concrete" experiences to a formula or mathematical generalisation. Teachers who were pursuing a masters' degree in mathematics education enrolled for a module which required them to:

a. Identify a topic which they would normally introduce with the use of manipulatives, which experience was to lead to a formula, algorithm or other mathematical generalisation.

b. Prepare a series of lessons and teach them to a target class.

c. Allow the CMF research team to interview six children, before the teaching started, just before the formalisation took place, just after it, and three months later.

d. Alert the researchers to when the "formalisation" lesson or acceptance of the rule would take place and allow the lesson(s) to be observed and tape-recorded.

e. Interview two other children in the class and report on the responses. Additionally, an analysis of the tape recorded lesson would be written (the transcript of the recording being supplied by the researchers).

Topics which were included in the study, fulfilling the description of concrete embodiments leading to formalisation, were area of a rectangle, volume of a cuboid, subtraction of two and three digit numbers with decomposition, the rule for fractions to be equivalent, the circumference of a circle, and enlargement of a figure.

The advice given to teachers in teaching manuals etc., often describes the experiences the children should have and then implies (or even states) that "the children will come to realise" the formula. In practice, it seems that a few children in a class might come to the realisation, and the rest be encouraged to accept the findings of their fellows. The teacher feels that time is short, and the class must move on. Part of the three month follow-up interviews was to ask the pupils for the connection between the two experiences, concrete and formal. Only one of the interviewees (out of 150) remembered that one experience led to the other and provided a base for it.

Most of the replies are summed up by the girl who said "Sums is sums and bricks is bricks." The forgetting would be unimportant if the concrete experience (which is often arduous and time consuming) had resulted in a successful use of the formalisation, but it had not. The observations of lessons and analysis of the transcripts of what the teacher said brought to light how very disparate were the views of teacher and pupil. The teacher knew the mathematics, knew the formula or rule, and had devised a set of "manipulative" moves to convince the child of the truth of the rule. The child did not know where the manipulations were leading and to him/her a red brick made from two centimetres of wood was exactly that. The teacher might refer to it as "x, 2, 4" and could even say "let us pretend it is 17."

Figure 1. Terence's Diagram for Equivalence

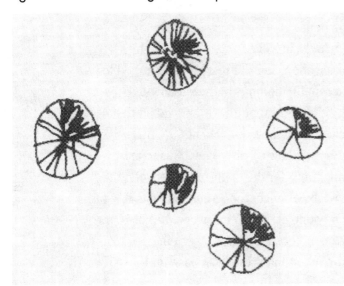

JOINING THE GROWN-UPS

From the observations in CMF (and some subsequent research), it was plain that teachers and children embarked on a voyage of discovery to a place well known to the teacher. None of the teachers observed (some 20 experienced practitioners) explained why the pupils would want to abandon bricks, naive methods, and even invented child-methods in favour of the formalisation. Nobody explained the power of the new knowledge. The nearest statement to a reason for its adoption was "you do not want to carry around bricks for the rest of your life." The teacher's attitude was one of friendly guidance, more in the sense that the lessons were a review of something we already knew rather than an introduction to the complete unknown. Consider how few teachers draw on the board accurate subdivisions when partitioning a circular disc into equal fractional segments. The illustration is produced free-hand and quickly split into sections. Little wonder that Terence produced this set of diagrams when he was trying to convince the interviewer that $9/27 = 3/9$ (Figure 1).

Andrew was in a group learning subtraction when the teacher produced a three digit subtraction which resulted in zero in the hundreds place. The ensuing conversation with the class of eight pupils was as follows:

(Note: **T** = Teacher; **P** = Pupil):

P: And that would be one hundred take away one hundred is nothing.

T: Is nothing, so do I put that there?

P: No.

T: Shall I put that there? Who thinks I should put that there? Who doesn't think I should put that there? Well, I mean, you can, but if I was to ask you to write down 99 . . . in your books, just write down 99, you wouldn't write down 099 would you?

P: No.

T: You would just write the 99, wouldn't you? So we don't really need to put that there. 1 take away 1 leaves you with an empty space, so we might as well leave an empty space, okay?

Andrew's attempt at 304–178 gave the answer 2 and his argument went as follows:

A: Say if you said, four take away 8, it's 4. You've got 4 and you can't take 8 from 4, so there's nothing there and . . . nothing take 7, you can't do that and 3 take away 1 gives you 2.

T: I see. So take 4 away 8 I can't do, right. So do I write anything underneath there or do I not bother?

A: Not bother.

He had absorbed the "don't bother" but not when to use it. There were other instances in the interviews of children selecting a specific part of a teacher's statement and generalising incorrectly or of remembering the one erroneous statement the teacher had made.

FRACTIONS AND DECIMALS

The middle grades are the years when the elements of arithmetic cease to be exclusively whole numbers, and much energy and time is spent on the study of fractions and decimals. There has been a lot of research on children's understanding of these "new" numbers. Generally most eight–nine year olds can recognise and name a region as 1/2, 1/4, 1/3, 1/8; fewer recognise that a region split into twelfths can also be labeled in sixths. Far fewer children can successfully carry out operations on fractions. The model for introduction currently in most of our textbooks is that of regions (square, circle, line). This enables us to talk of shares, but the result is a tangible amount (slice of pizza, cube of chocolate) which does not neatly fit within the operations of addition, subtraction, multiplication and division. How can you multiply two pieces of pizza? The other meanings of a/b are often not addressed separately in school textbooks, and the child is expected to infer division or ratio from the same region model. The result is confusion and a heavy reliance on rote-learned rules. Many children reject the whole idea of noncounting numbers and attempt to deal with secondary school mathematics without them. The research project "Concepts in Secondary Mathematics and Science" (CSMS) obtained data by both interviews and tests. A representative sample of 11-16 year olds was asked to give the answers to various division questions, and they were told that if the question was "impossible" they should say so. Table 1 shows some results.

A parallel test had required pupils to write a story to illustrate $8 \div 4$ and $128 \div 8$. Very nearly all the responses involved the sharing of sweets among friends. This interpretation of the division sign is in conflict with $16 \div 20$ as there are obviously not enough sweets for the friends to share. Do teachers redefine the operations to accommodate fractions and decimals? The middle grades is when children are trying to graft new concepts on hopelessly inadequate foundations put in place for counting numbers. Algebra is likely to be introduced during these years and viewing it as generalised arithmetic seems fraught with difficulties. In algebra, we need to spell out all connections among the numbers now represented by letters, and in arithmetic the aim is to carry out the operations and to obtain a result as quickly as possible. "$x + y$" stays as such and cannot be processed to become xy whereas we find it unwieldy to work with $5 + 3$ and replace by 8 as soon as possible. Collis (1975) described a level of algebraic understanding as "Allowing Lack of Closure" (ALC). When a child can accept and even work with $(x + y)$, a significant step has been taken.

Table 1. CSMS Results to Division Questions

Large Survey Results

Divide by 20		1.2	1.0	1.4	1 rem 4	Impossible
(i) 24	(n=170) 11-12 yr	9%	7%	8%	12%	15%
	(n=240) 14-15 yr	34%	1%	15%	3%	6%
		0.8	0.0	0.16	0 rem 16	Impossible
(ii) 16	11-12 yr	7%	2%	4%	–	51%
	14-15 yr	36%	–	6%	–	23%

MATCHING THE MATHEMATICS TO THE CHILD

It has long been known that from any class lesson, the child participants take away very different pieces of knowledge. In CMF a group of eight pupils, all thought by the teacher to be "ready" for subtraction and all taught in the same way, were found to have very different paths to success. A child's success depends on what was known before (how many of the pre-requisite skills are in place?); how much of the current content matter is understood; his attention span (was he even in school, absences matter) and the confidence with which the mathematics is approached (does the child feel in control of the mathematics content or is it magic?). A child cannot be confident if all the mathematics exercises he does are marked incorrect. By the middle grades it is likely that any group contains a number of "low attainers" who, without positive action, are unlikely to become even "average attainers."

The curriculum development project "Nuffield Secondary Mathematics" was designed to provide suitable material for all attainment levels in the secondary school (ages 11-16 years). The books were: a) Topic books; short "content" orientated material in four sets— Number, Space, Probability and Statistics, and Measurement; b) Core books; books of problems for an entire year to allow groups of mixed attainment to work together applying their mathematics; and c) Teachers guides; very full information for teachers. To find where to start the Number strand, children in primary school (some 100 pupils), including some who were identified as displaying "special needs" were tested with items that researchers had previously used with six year olds. Follow-up interviews disclosed that there were pupils about to enter secondary school, who had very limited number skills. A list of pre-requisite skills was drawn up, and we stated that to start on the Number books, children had to demonstrate that they could do the following:

- Arrange cards showing configurations of dots for 1 to 6 in order.
- Give the number before and after a written two-digit number.
- Count on (rather than count from 1) when given two strips of stamps.
- Write correctly two-digit numbers when they are read out (oral).
- Put written numbers, less than 25, in order (written).
- Interpret the words "more" and "less" when given two sets of dots
- Count a pile of coins (less than one pound) accurately, taking account of the different face values.
- Choose the correct single coin for a purchase of 45p.

Practising secondary school teachers during in-service courses were shown the contents of Level One Number and asked if they had pupils who could only "do this." Usually they assured us that none of their pupils knew so little, but later we were bombarded with requests for the material at this level. In the trial schools there were usually about ten 11-12 year olds who needed it. We only found one pupil in a normal school for whom the work was too difficult. The material was put through several, well regulated trials and re-written if it proved too difficult for the pupils using it. The intention was that the child should experience success and so become confident in mathematics, no matter how limited. An early result was that although the first book took perhaps three months to complete, the second took much less time. As confidence built, so did the speed with which the child worked. The classes using this early material were usually small, and the pupils worked in pairs or groups of three with a lot of teacher help. No child progressed to the next book until he/she had demonstrated that the content of the previous book had been absorbed by passing a test at the 80% (or better) level. No test was given until the teacher was sure that the child would pass because all the book had been understood. Failing a test helps neither teacher nor child. This concept was very difficult for some teachers because they assumed there would always be failures. We were closely involved in all the trials and often marked the tests. In one school, the teacher agreed that the reason six children had not reached "mastery" level in the test was because they had not covered the entire book but only part of it. This must perpetuate a situation which is bound to be deficient—half learned mathematics grafted onto holes in knowledge. The teacher explained that she could not wait for these pupils.

CONSTRAINTS AND BELIEFS

Running parallel to any new curriculum effort, and having an unseen but powerful influence on it, are the constraints and beliefs of the general populace, politicians, headmasters, publishers, and even classroom teachers. Some of these are listed here:

1. There are certain topics which every child should be taught.
2. There are specific topics that every child should have learned before a certain time in his/her life.
3. A certain amount of time spent in school on mathematics lessons is sufficient.
4. A certain amount of material (books, worksheets or scheme) is enough.
5. Mathematics is difficult.

We should be wary of these beliefs because they are very strongly held and usually backed up by appeals to "raising standards." In the UK during the summer of 1998, the Minister of Education boasted that the number of pupils passing the school-leavers' examination in mathematics had fallen, in order to claim that standards had been maintained. The expectations the community has of pupils vary from country to country and what may seem obvious to a Japanese writer, is not obvious to an Italian observer. Howson (1991) published a list of ages at which specific mathematics content was presented to pupils.

An excerpt is shown in Table 2. There is obviously no "obvious" age for the introduction of a topic.

CONCLUSION

Mathematics in the middle grades is still "Mathematics for All," although the move is towards a formalisation of the subject. Failure to understand destroys the child's confidence so any introduction of new concepts, such as numbers which cannot be used for counting objects, must be built up carefully and with few assumptions on the part of the teacher. Learning mathematics is a series of leaps, so it is good to know that the ground from which you take off is solid.

Table 2. Age of Introduction of Content (adapted from Howson, 1991)

	Belgium	France	Italy	Japan	England
Decimals	9	9-11	8-11	8	9
Negative numbers	8	11-12	11-14	12	9
Operations on these	12	12-13	11-14	12	13
Fractions	7	9-11	8-11	8	11
Use of letters	12-13	11-12	11-14	10	13

REFERENCES

Cockcroft Committee of Inquiry Into The Teaching of Mathematics in Schools. (1982). *Mathematics counts.* London: HMSO.

Collis, K. (1975). *Cognitive development and mathematics learning.* Chelsea College, P.M.E.W.

Hart, K. (Ed.). (1981). *Children's understanding of mathematics: 11 - 16.* London: John Murray.

Howson, G. (1991). *National curricula in mathematics.* Leicester, UK: The Mathematical Association.

Johnson, D.C. (Ed). (1989). *Children's mathematical frameworks 8-13: A study of classroom teaching.* Windsor, UK: NFER-Nelson.

Summary of Small Group Discussion on Content and Learning Issues in Middle Grades Mathematics

Working through a problem in the role of student can serve as a springboard for a discussion of the issues around content and learning mathematics. Contrasting student solutions with adult solutions (Appendix 4) further grounds the conversation in a situation—reading student responses—that is in fact, part of the practice of teaching. Marcy's Dots (Figure 1) from the 1992 National Assessment of Educational Progress grade 8 test provoked a variety of responses ranging from concern over the clarity of directions to surprise at the many and diverse ways students found their solutions. Common themes that emerged from the group discussions are described below.

Figure 1. Marcy's Dots Problem from the 1992 National Assessment of Educational Progress

A pattern of dots is shown below. At each step, more dots are added to the pattern. The number of dots added at each step is more than the number added in the previous step. The pattern continues infinitely.

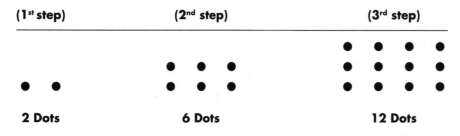

| **(1ˢᵗ step)** | **(2ⁿᵈ step)** | **(3ʳᵈ step)** |

2 Dots   **6 Dots**   **12 Dots**

Marcy has to determine the number of dots in the 20ᵗʰ step, but she does not want to draw all 20 pictures and then count them. Explain or show how she could do this *and* give the answer that Marcy should get for the number of dots.

Note: See Appendix 4 for sample student solutions and the guiding questions for the discussion.

STUDENT WORK

"Student work helps teachers think about how students learn mathematics and about the depth of their own understanding." (Participant comment) Studying how students come to learn mathematics by using a "site of practice," an activity that is something teachers do as part of teaching, led some discussants to conclude that the richness of student thinking about a problem accompanied by student solutions can be buried in the raw statistics reporting student achievement. The variety of strategies used by the students in their solutions—charts, recursive rules, formulas, listing all of the cases, drawing diagrams—paralleled the strategies used by the adults. Discussing how students used their understanding of the mathematics to select an approach led to a discussion about the reasoning used by the adults, and in fact, led to some stimulating mathematical discussions. In some cases, there was concern over the lack of consistency between the work students did and their description of what they did. This was attributed to a lack of communication skills on the part of the students, although learning to communicate is an important middle grades topic.

An effective strategy to promote student learning could be to have students themselves learn by using other student work. The question of quality answers vs. quality thinking became an issue, however. How do teachers reward and reinforce correct thinking even though the desired solution is not presented? Groups identified non-mathematical causes for student errors, answering the wrong question, not reading carefully, or jumping to conclusions, as well as mathematical reasons such as identifying the wrong pattern. A side effect of the analysis of the diversity in the student work was a reminder to the teachers not to impose their solution method on their students.

THE MATHEMATICS

The question of teacher knowledge and capacity to deal with problems such as Marcy's Dots is a serious one. There was a strong feeling that many middle grade teachers do not have the necessary background to deal with some of the broad mathematical and algebraic concepts involved in the problem: variables and an introduction to symbols, functional relationships, linearity, sequences and series, recursion. The problem links algebra and geometry, is multi-step involving logical thinking, and leads to making generalizations. The perception that teachers are not prepared to teach this kind of mathematics was reinforced by studying the algebra portion of the draft version of the revised National Council of Teachers of Mathematics standards: *Principles and Standards for School Mathematics: Discussion Draft.* The issue of certification for teaching mathematics in the middle grades, the nature of preservice programs, and professional development were repeatedly identified as critical in helping teachers move beyond their comfort with number to other mathematical strands that should be part of the middle grades curriculum. There was also strong agreement that content knowledge is not enough; teachers must learn how to help students bridge from the concrete to the abstract.

ALGEBRA IN THE MIDDLE GRADES

The issue of whether all eighth graders are developmentally ready for algebra and how to position algebra in the learning environment of the child raised more questions. There was a consistent belief that the study of patterns was important, but there was tension over how to move from the specific to a

generalization with all students. The nature of the problem allowed students with different abilities and understanding to find a solution, an important feature for good problems. It is important for students to see each others work and then come to consensus on an effective way to solve the problem at the most abstract level that the students are developmentally capable of understanding. Common beliefs were that the use of a problem without a context lacks motivation for students and that problems should be relevant and real to engage students. Students should be able to see where a problem is going and how it connects to other areas they are studying. They need to understand why formulas and generalizations are important, as well as how to think about and use them appropriately.

ORGANIZATIONAL ISSUES

Two organizational issues surfaced as barriers against practicing teachers approaching any such problem in a thoughtful and analytic way: the lack of time during their school life to engage in this kind of thinking and the current emphasis on testing, where most of their energy is concentrated on what is being tested or the need for accountability.

Teaching Issues in the Middle Grades

The sessions on teaching issues in the middle grades focused on the questions

- What are the important characteristics of effective teaching in the middle grades? Of effective teaching of mathematics in the middle grades?
- How can instruction in middle grades classrooms be organized to maximize learning? How can we tell when learning is happening?
- What tools and strategies will make a difference in how middle grades students learn mathematics?

USING VIDEO OF CLASSROOM PRACTICE AS A TOOL TO STUDY AND IMPROVE TEACHING

Nanette Seago, Project Director, Video Cases for Mathematics Professional Development, Renaissance Project.

PANEL REACTIONS TO THE "CINDY VIDEO"

TEACHING AND LEARNING MATHEMATICS IN THE MIDDLE GRADES: STUDENT PRESPECTIVES

Linda Foreman, President, Teachers Development Group, West Linn, Oregon.

PANEL RESPONSE TO FOREMAN STUDENT VIDEO

SUMMARY OF SMALL GROUP DISCUSSION ON TEACHING ISSUES IN THE MIDDLE GRADES

Using Video of Classroom Practice as a Tool to Study and Improve Teaching

Nanette M. Seago
Project Director, Video Cases for Mathematics Professional Development

A newly-funded NSF project,[1] which I direct, is focused on developing video cases as tools for use in mathematics professional development. Currently, staff are in the process of hypothesizing, testing-out, analyzing, and revising working theories around the use of video as a tool to promote teacher learning. There is limited knowledge in the field about how and what teachers' learn from professional development experiences. It is mostly uncharted territory. Not much is known about what teachers learn from professional education (Ball, 1996), especially as it pertains to the effect on teachers'

practice. Even less appears to be known about how and why teachers develop and use new understandings in their own contexts. Conversations with colleagues,[2] experiences of classroom teachers, and experiences of professional developers responsible for teacher learning are the basis of our current knowledge.

Reflecting on the practice of teachers and teachers of teachers, I have developed some "working hypotheses" (Ball, 1996) about the use of video to promote teacher learning. These frame the design, development and formative evaluation[3] of my current work:

[1]National Science Foundation; (ESI #9731339); Host Institutions: San Diego State University Foundation, West Ed

[2]I would like to acknowledge my colleagues Judy Mumme, Deborah Ball and her research group at University of Michigan, Magdalene Lampert, Deidre LeFevre, Jim Stigler, Joan Akers, Judy Anderson, Cathy Carroll, Gloria Moretti, and Carole Maples for their on-going help in thinking about these ideas.

[3]Joan Akers is the formative evaluator of the VideoCases Project; Deidre LeFevre is a graduate student of Magdalene Lampert and Deborah Ball at the University of Michigan and is using the developmental process of our project to research the impact of different forms of video case facilitation on teacher engagement and learning around issues of pedagogy, student learning, and mathematical content.

- teachers' mathematical and pedagogical learning is greatly enhanced by connecting learning opportunities to classroom practice—to the actual work of teaching.
- video cases of teaching can afford teachers' opportunities to learn mathematics *as well as* pedagogy;
- video cases of teaching can afford teachers' opportunities to study and learn about the complexities and subtleties of teaching and gain analytic tools; and
- video case materials cannot stand alone; the facilitation process is as critical to what teachers learn as teaching is to what students learn.

This paper is organized around some questions to explore in the attempt to understand how video can be used to promote effective learning: What is the work of teaching? What do teachers need to know and be able to do in order to do the work of teaching well? How can video cases be used effectively to develop teacher learning? Putting forth working hypotheses and questions invites others responsible for teacher education to make explicit the teacher learning theories or working hypotheses that guide and frame their own work so that the community can engage in critical professional discourse and inquiry into practice as professional educators responsible for teacher learning. Educational researchers can use this work across multiple and varied contexts to research why and how teachers learn from professional education experiences—whether it is using video or other practice-based materials such as student curriculum, student work, or written cases.

Teaching is thinking, intellectually demanding work. Teaching is complex and involves the interactive relationship between content, students, and teacher (Figure 1). Typically in professional development we tend to isolate and separate this relationship which can pull apart and oversimplify the work of teaching. What gets left out

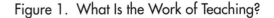

Figure 1. What Is the Work of Teaching?

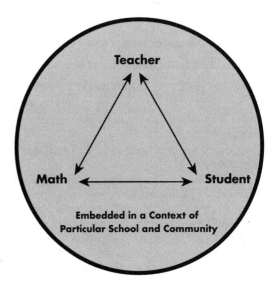

when this happens is the actual role of the teacher in the thinking work of teaching. For example: we spend time doing mathematics because understanding mathematics is crucial to teaching mathematics for understanding and interpreting student thinking. But learning mathematical content in and of itself hasn't helped teachers deal with figuring out the mathematical validity in students' thinking, to recognize the validity in partially-formed and inadequately communicated student thinking, or to analyze mathematical misconceptions. But this kind of mathematical analysis is a large part of the mathematical content needed in teaching for understanding.

Another example of professional development is the examination of student work and student thinking. This is a critical part of the work of teaching but not sufficient to help teachers deal with the work of figuring out what to do with student thinking once they have it. Are there certain strategies or solutions that the teacher ought to highlight in whole-class discussion? Does the order in which solutions are shared matter in creating a cohesive mathematical story line? How does one use individual student thinking and alternative approaches to further the collective mathematical learning of the whole class? Does a teacher stop and pursue every child's thinking, always, in

every lesson? How does context factor into the decisions?

Other efforts focus on teaching strategies such as use of cooperative groups, manipulatives, or writing in mathematics separate from mathematical learning goals and student learning. Does one always use cooperative groups? Are there advantages or disadvantages in terms of student learning? For what mathematical learning can manipulatives be helpful? Do they ever hinder learning? Are some manipulatives more helpful than others? If so, why? Does how they get used make a difference? These are just some of the recurring dilemmas teachers face without sufficient help in acquiring the skills and knowledge necessary to make intellectually flexible decisions.

The work of teaching involves more than "in-class time." It involves acts of professional practice before, during, and after the moments of face-to-face teaching. Some examples of the kind of work teaching entails are:

Before

- Setting mathematical learning goals
- Choosing/analyzing tasks and curriculum in relation to goals and students
- Figuring out various student approaches and possible misconceptions
- Learning about students
- Planning a mathematical story

During

- Figuring out what kids are thinking/understanding—the mathematical validity of student thinking on-the-spot
- Figuring out what to do with student thinking once you have it—seize or not to seize? For what mathematical learning goal?
- Balancing between individual student and whole class mathematical thinking and learning—analyzing and deciding
- Building a mathematical story
- Budgeting time
- Learning about students

After

- Figuring out what to do tomorrow based on today
- Analyzing student work
- Learning about students

PURPOSES FOR USING VIDEO

When most people think of the purpose for using video with teachers, they think of models, exemplars, or illustrators of a point. The question this poses is one worth researching. What is being modeled or exemplified? What is it that teachers learn and use in practice from viewing models or exemplars? Teachers approach new learning in the way in which they were taught by following the procedure in an example. Using this familiar "way of learning," they watch the video in search of procedures to follow or features to copy. This can create barriers to a deep level examination of teaching, for it often keeps the focus on surface and superficial features of classroom practice.

Video can be used with a different frame, an analytic frame which focuses on the *analysis* of teaching practice, gaining the awareness necessary to analyze and interpret the subtleties and complexities involved in the relationship between knowledge of content, students, learning, and teaching. Analysis involves studying the same video episode through multiple lenses, as well as the comparative study of multiple and varied videos through the same lens. It involves examining the details and specifics of practice—in this instance, in this context, under these circumstances, and perceiving the subtle particulars (Schwab, 1978) in classrooms while recognizing how these together form a part of an underlying structure or theory of teaching. Analysis involves supporting and disputing assertions or conjectures with evidence or reasoning.

Taking an analytic stance in framing the use of video creates a set of teacher learning issues for teacher educators/professional developers to consider. Gaining awareness of the subtleties and complexities of practice does not happen easily. We exist in a strong culture of quick fixes, definitive answers, and oversimplification of the practice of teaching. It will take purposeful teaching of analytic skills (Ball and Cohen, 1998) in order for teachers to use analytic skills. This means it will also take the study of how teachers develop and use those skills over time to understand how to help teachers acquire them.

Developing a culture where teachers can learn to critically examine the practice of others as well as themselves will be no easy task either, for there currently exists a strong culture of being nice. Teacher struggles and challenges need to be seen as opportunities to learn rather than secrets to hide. Teachers need to be active members of an intellectual professional community that values risk-taking, diversity of opinion, critical debate, and collaborative analysis. This has implications for the teachers of the teachers, for they will be responsible for developing this culture—a culture foreign to most U.S. teachers.

Video can be used for educative purposes (Lampert and Ball, 1998), as opposed to a more open-ended "what do you think?" approach. Open-ended discussions can be useful in gathering data on what teachers attend to, are

aware or unaware of, or how they think about teaching, learning and mathematics in practice, but for teaching something such discussions are not usually effective. Often the conversations become unfocused and scattered. When viewing video, there is so much data that sorting through it needs focused guidance and structure. An educative point of view means to plan and focus on specific goals for teacher learning. What can teachers learn from this particular video and how can they best learn it? The mathematical and pedagogical terrain of the video needs to be mapped out in relationship to what each episode offers teachers to learn about mathematics, teaching, and learning. An educative point of view explores the question, *how can we go beyond this particular video or set of videos to learn the big ideas of practice? the big ideas of mathematics?*

HOW DO WE USE VIDEO TO PROMOTE TEACHER LEARNING?

What might it mean to plan and orchestrate professional education that is guided by analytic and educative purposes? What are the implications for the work of teaching teachers? Just as the practice of teaching is complex and involves the interactive relationship between teacher, students and content, the practice of teaching teachers involves the interactive relationship between professional educators, teachers, and teaching content (Figure 2).

While there is no one right way to plan and facilitate a video session, purposeful planning around three key areas is helpful: (1) the content of the video segment(s), (2) the learning goals of the session and (3) audience (or learners). A discussion of the planning and facilitating these three areas using the Cindy video as a context for analytic and educative purposes in the work of teaching teachers follows.

THE CONTENT OF THE VIDEO

The Cindy video clip lesson begins with Cindy posing the problem, If you lined up 100 equilateral triangles in a row (shared edges), what would the perimeter be? This is the first part of the larger mathematical problem of the lesson: if you lined up 100 squares, pentagons, hexagons in a row, what would the perimeter be? Can you generalize and find a rule for the perimeter of any number of regular polygons lined up in a row? Figure 3 shows a graph of Cindy's lesson with an arrow marking the point in time that we drop in with the video clip.

Figure 2. Teaching Teachers

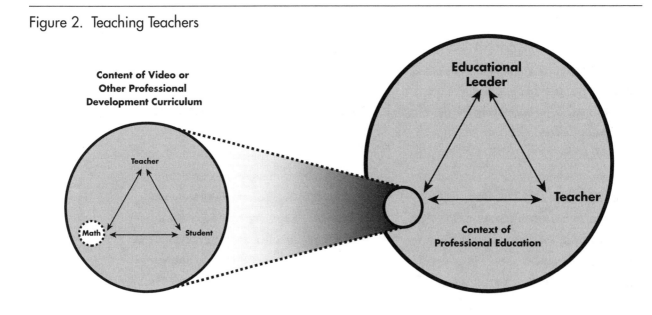

Just as teachers need to know the content of tasks they pose to their students, teacher educators need to know the content of the material they are using as tools for educating learners. Analyzing the material means to analytically examine the terrain of the video. What opportunity does it offer to learn about mathematics? pedagogy? students? learning? In what ways can it be used to learn new professional habits of mind? How can it be used to develop skills in analysis and develop dispositions of inquiry? The Cindy video has been used to:

- **Learn mathematics.** The mathematical content allows for teachers to learn about multiple algebraic representations of a geometric relationship in non-simplified forms. It offers the opportunity to examine and learn about recursive and relational generalizations. The role of mathematical language and definitions are also embedded opportunities for working on mathematics within this video.

- **Learn about student thinking/ reasoning.** Focusing on student conversation and responses (Nick, Chris, and Lindsey) provides the opportunity to learn what we can or cannot tell about the student's apparent understanding. Nick may have

Figure 3. Cindy Lesson 1. Overview of whole lesson (50 minutes)

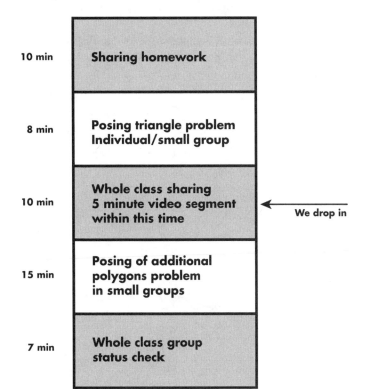

the beginnings of making sense of the geometric relationship by viewing the whole of each individual polygon's perimeter multiplied by the number of total polygons, and then subtracting out the inside shared edges: (*n* represents the number of polygons; *s* represents the number of sides of each polygon).

Nick's Response
Total Number of Sides – Shared Sides: $p = ns - 2(n - 1)$

ns is the number of polygons multiplied by the number of sides of each polygon.
$2(n - 1)$ is the number of shared sides, i.e., sides of the polygons not contributing to the perimeter. The perimeter is the total perimeters of all polygons minus the perimeter of the shared sides.

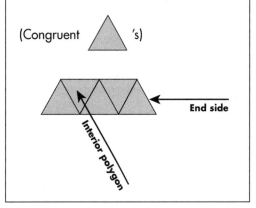

(Congruent 's)

Interior polygon

End side

Chris sees the relationship like Cindy does—tops + bottoms + 2 end sides, where the tops + bottoms are the contribution each polygon makes toward the perimeter of the whole:

Chris's Response
Tops and Bottoms + 2 End Sides: $p = n(s - 2) + 2$

If top and bottom are considered together, each polygon contributes the same amount to the perimeter. Thus, the perimeter equals the number of polygons times the perimeter contributed by each polygon plus the two end sides.

Lindsey may be trying to make sense of the relationship by taking out the end polygons, counting the outside edges of each and dealing with the middle polygons separately.

Lindsey's Response
Interior Polygons + End Polygons: $p = (n - 2)(s - 2) + 2(s - 1)$

$(n - 2)$ is the number of interior polygons

$(s - 2)$ is the amount contributed to the perimeter by each interior polygon

$(s - 1)$ is the contribution of each end polygon to the perimeter

The perimeter equals the number of interior polygons times the amount contributed to the perimeter by each interior polygon, plus the contribution toward the perimeter by the two end polygons.

Examining students' thinking can provide opportunities to work on mathematics. It also offers the opportunity to examine the teacher-decisions around each student's thinking. What appears to be the teacher thinking and reasoning for the decisions around each student's thinking? For what mathematical learning goals would she seize individual student thinking, when would she not? When and why might she slow things down? or speed things up? Veronica introduces a recursive pattern she sees from the table. Examining the table and being able to generalize the pattern is an opportunity that can be utilized.

- **Learn about teacher decision-making.** While it may seem obvious that teachers make constant conscious or unconscious decisions while planning and orchestrating discourse, this is not typically recognized and critically examined by teachers and administrators. In order to analyze teacher decision-making in light of content and students, one first needs to become aware such decisions even take place. You can't analyze and interpret what you can't see. It is the work of the facilitator to "lift the veils so that one can see" what isn't normally seen (Eisner, 1991). Using this video over multiple sessions helps to move the learning from awareness of decisions to the level of analysis of decisions in light of content and context. When focusing on teacher decisions, the opportunity exists to push at the current tendency for teachers to be definitive in their claims around teacher decisions. Pushing for alternative possibilities, alternative possible reasoning or conjectures with supporting evidence and arguments over time can create the necessary dissonance for learning new norms and practices.

- **Learn about the uncertainty in teaching.** These video segments offer the opportunity for participants to learn about the uncertainties involved in a complex practice (McDonald, 1992), especially the recognized uncertainties involved in the moments of not knowing if a student's reasoning has mathematical validity (Lindsey and Nick). It can highlight the recurring teacher dilemma of figuring out what a student is thinking and offer the opportunity for teachers to gain multiple tools for dealing with these uncertainties themselves. This learning can create a tension for the facilitator between not wanting teachers to leave with the notion that all of teaching is uncertain and on-the fly nor with the notion that one can always predict what will happen with certainty. The learning focus is to gain understanding of the importance of planning for possible student approaches as well as gaining tools for better decisions in their own moments of uncertainty.

GOALS FOR TEACHER LEARNING

It is important to decide on goals for teacher learning when using a video case. Why are you using this case? What outcomes do you seek from the video case experience(s)? A case can be used and facilitated for a number of purposes, so it is very important to be clear in your own mind about your purpose (Miller and Kantrov, 1998). It may be that you have multiple goals for using this video case, but you should be clear about what they are. Do you want participants to extract principles from the specifics of the video case? Pedagogical principles? Mathematical principles? Cognitive principles? In other words, can you abstract bigger ideas about the practice of teaching mathematics? If so, does a facilitator bridge from the concrete and specifics of the video case experience to larger, more abstract ideas? Your decision needs to be informed by what you know about the group's expectations, past experiences, and interests. As in teaching, figuring out how to begin with the learner's experiences and bridge to new learning is part of your work as a facilitator in planning and orchestrating video case experiences for learning.

THE AUDIENCE (LEARNERS)

It is important for the facilitator to learn as much as possible about the audience who will view the video case session. This will enable the facilitator to anticipate possible reactions and ways of viewing the video. While people will attend to the things that they themselves find important, spending time thinking of audiences as a whole can aid in planning. This will help bridge from the audience's world to a new learning that may be outside the experience of the group. It will also help engage the participants by identifying an entry point (a best guess determined by what is known of the group). Since the Cindy Case is complex and offers a number of possible entry points, it is important both to know the case and what it offers as well as knowing the participants in order to make an educated guess as to what part of the case is an attractive entry point for the participants. While this may be very different from the way in which the facilitator connects to this video case, reaching the participants means the facilitator has an understanding of where the participants will enter the video case.

Some entry points into the Cindy video include: student thinking—specifically Lindsey and plus 4; teacher questioning—specifically all of the questions Cindy asked in the segment; the role of the table in furthering/hindering student learning; classroom environment; and the role of mathematical understanding in teacher decision-making around student thinking.

It is also important to spend some time thinking about possible audience barriers to analysis. These are things that can get in the way of analyzing the video segment. It helps to come up with strategies for dealing with these barriers. Some barriers might be:

- **The mathematics.** Gaining awareness of the task helps participants to see more in the video than possible without mathematical access. In some cases doing the problem with the squares first helps to highlight the relationship and multiple representations while moving to the triangles prior to viewing the segment(s). Anywhere from 20 minutes to 45 minutes can be spent on the mathematics depending on the time available and the audience. Pushing to get the three ways of representing the relationship out has proven helpful in participants' ability to recognize the alternate ways that Nick and Lindsey use to making sense of the relationship.

- **Judging Cindy as good or bad.** Spending some time up front framing the session as the analysis of one moment in time without enough data to judge Cindy as good or bad helps, but it will probably be necessary to seize seemingly judgmental comments and go underneath them—asking for specific evidences in the video and why that is important to them. Figuring out how to use evaluative statements as entries into analysis is something for which strategies are not

yet well-defined. Comparing this to analyzing student thinking is helpful. The point is not to judge the student as good or bad but to analyze the mathematical thinking and reasoning. In this way, we are examining teacher work—analyzing the mathematical and pedagogical thinking/reasoning. An analogy that is sometimes helpful is an archeological expedition—concentrating on what can be learned from each layer of artifacts, analyzing the relationship between content, students, and teacher decisions.

- **"This class does not look like mine!"** Cindy's class is in an upper-middle class suburban community. The ethnicity of the class is not representative of the national population of students. It might help to raise this issue up front, acknowledging the fact that it is different from many contexts—asking that the video be viewed from what can be studied and learned about mathematics, teaching and learning even though it is situated in a context different from one's own. This issue can emerge when other grade levels view and discuss this video as well. The notion that we can learn from situations like our own as well as those not like our own might be a worthy goal in an initial session. It may also be that this particular video may not be a good first experience if it presents too much of a barrier to the analysis of practice. This raises the important issue of providing opportunity to use many video cases to analyze through the same lenses, so learners have a chance to bump up against the big ideas of practice in multiple and varied contexts.

- **Too many things to pay attention to.** There are multiple things to pay attention to when viewing the complexities of classroom practice. While participants can be asked to focus on one aspect (i.e., student learning, teacher decision-making, mathematics), a group will pay attention to multiple and varied things—what they care about as individuals. It is helpful to recognize this up front and to plan for at least two viewings—the first to get out on the table the things they will pay attention to anyway and the second to focus using a particular lens. Asking that viewers choose individual students to follow and figure out their apparent thinking along with the apparent teacher decisions and possible reasoning around that thinking is a helpful task in learning to focus.

In planning professional education experiences, time is a necessary consideration. Do you have 2 hours? 4 hours? Multiple sessions? Consider how variables of time, goals, and number of participants interact. What can be done in advance? Can readings help? What about after the session? If you have multiple sessions, what can participants do between sessions? Think about what can be done realistically in the time available. Using some time up front to access the mathematics of the task is worthwhile. This time is not intended to mine the task for all of its mathematics but rather to get enough experience to access the video case for analysis. The viewing and discussion can offer more opportunities to examine the mathematics with purposeful questioning by the facilitator.

Video of classroom practice offers potentially powerful resources for the professional education curriculum. Video and surrounding contextual material constituting a video case study can provide much needed tools for professional developers to use with teachers for observing and analyzing complex practice. Increasingly accessible and affordable technologies create exciting possibilities for the use of video in teacher development. Yet, the most powerful, well-designed, and technologically advanced tools will do little to improve teaching in this country by themselves. As good as the curriculum may be, it can't teach. Teaching matters in what students learn; teaching teachers matters in what teachers learn.

REFERENCES

Ball, D.L. (1996). Developing mathematics reform: What don't we know about teacher learning—but would make good working hypotheses. In S. Friel and G. Bright (Eds.), *Reflecting on our work: NSF teacher enhancement in K-6 mathematics* (pp. 77-111). Lanham, MD: University Press of America.

Ball, D.L., & Cohen, D.K. (1998). Developing practice, developing practitioners: Toward a practice-based theory of professional education. In G. Sykes (Ed.), *The heart of the matter: Teaching as the learning profession.* San Francisco: Jossey-Bass.

Eisner, E.W. (1994). *The educational imagination: On the design and evaluation of school programs* (3rd ed.) New York: Macmillan.

Lampert, M., & Ball, D.L. (1998). *Teaching, multimedia, and mathematics: Investigations of real practice.* New York: Teachers College Press.

McDonald, J.P. (1992). *Teaching: Making sense of an uncertain craft.* New York: Teachers College Press.

Miller, B., & Kantrov, I. (1998). *A guide to facilitating cases in education.* Portsmouth, NH: Heinemann.

Schwab, J.J. (1978). *Science, curriculum, and liberal education: Selected essays.* In I. Wesbury & N. Wilkof (Eds.). Chicago: The University of Chicago Press.

Panel Reactions to the "Cindy Video"

Hyman Bass, a mathematician from Columbia University in New York, spoke from the perspective of a mathematician about his observations on mathematics and the teaching of mathematics after viewing the video. He pointed out that in his experience, the mathematics preparation of teachers comes from a list of topics that have been incorporated into the design of a course. Either the teachers do not learn what is taught at all or they learn the content, but see no connection to what they will do in their classrooms. He indicated that the use of a video might be an appropriate tool to help bridge the gap between mathematics as content and mathematics in practice.

From his perspective, although the video was framed as an algebra lesson, he found it hard to think of it that way. The lesson covered functions, data, patterns, graph, but algebra as he thinks about it was not dominant. He noted that the teacher had navigated through measurement and the topic of unit and that some students moved past symbolic patterns to use geometry to solve the problem. There was also some mathematical tension because using $T+2$ to find the perimeter seems on the surface to conflict with the fact that the perimeter increases by increments of 1. What the expressions $T+1$ and $T+2$ each mean in the context of this problem, as well as how they map onto each other, are crucial mathematical issues in this lesson, according to Bass.

Choices made by the teacher indicated that she was on unfamiliar territory in some respects and approached some of the topics with uncertainty. While some teachers would have been insecure in this role and moved toward something they understood, Cindy was a courageous teacher willing to move into unfamiliar terrain to explore the mathematics. He noted that the important analysis is not just about the mathematics but also about how that mathematics is begin taught.

Deborah Ball, a mathematics educator and researcher, addressed the video from the platform of teaching and framed her observations in the context of conducting a lesson by discussion. She pointed out that it is much simpler if the teacher does the talking because the teacher then has control. In discussion situations, the teachers and students are jointly authoring the text and if the teacher has a goal in mind, it can be difficult to reach the goal with this joint authoring. She raised four points, and in each, indicated that there were two ways to approach the situation and there were costs in choosing either. Her first point was the mix of Cindy's reactions to student responses. Some were open and elicited student ideas, "What do you think?" and some closed off discussion, "That's right." When teachers elicit responses, they leave what they hear to chance, not knowing what kind of input they will get. When they close off discussion, they don't have access to student thinking but can be sure they direct the lesson in ways to finish within the class period. Ball indicated it would be interesting to analyze what Cindy's choices in this respect meant for the learning that went on in the class. In handling student errors teachers make the same choices. In one case, Cindy moved the student past an error to the right vocabulary and in another instance asked the class what they thought of the statement, again either closing off any discussion or opening it up and taking a chance on hearing something unexpected.

Ball's second point was to examine who was being called on to respond. Teachers make choices based on a variety of considerations knowing what a student is likely to say, who is likely to

be having problems, and so on. These are complicated decisions and the way teachers make them contribute in significant ways to creating lessons out of discussions.

Her third point was that the lesson contained very little praise. Japanese teachers use praise and reinforcement in ways much different from teachers in the United States. Praise can be motivating and a clue to students that they are on the right track, but too much reinforcement increases student reliance on the teacher and makes them less self directed. The clues about whether the class was doing well in the video seemed to be embedded in the content. The students seemed to feel they were thinking appropriately although there were very few verbal clues.

Ball's final point was to emphasize the relation between the ability to ask questions and the teacher's understanding of the mathematics in the problem. She commented that it strikes her as particularly unhelpful in professional development to talk about good questioning techniques absent a content base. The teacher has to have the ability to hear students and to keep an eye on where she is going with the discussion. She has to have a sense of the mathematics and of the students she is teaching to make the right decisions about the questions she will ask.

The final remarks came from Sam Chattin, a middle grades science teacher. Chattin began with some comments on the TIMSS video of an eighth grade Japanese classroom that he had viewed during lunch. He observed that the Japanese classroom had students in rows, no decorations, the map on the wall was in only two colors, there were no interruptions, and there were two teachers for 36 students. This is a significant cultural difference compared with middle grades classes in the United States. Chattin drew a parallel between this and some other observations about Cindy's teaching behavior. If students were to answer any questions, they had to do it very fast because she moved on. When the students spoke, you could not hear—which is typical because in U.S. classrooms it is often not required that everyone hear student responses. Jenny gave a wrong answer, but it is important to know that you can have wrong answers and still do well. The U.S. culture uses some prompt such as "excuse me" to speed up and move on. The question "Does everyone agree?" elicits no response or just one—everyone knew they did not have to pay attention because she was moving on. Remarks such as "Think about this," are immediately followed by "Okay, no..." with no time to think. Teachers can do all of the changes they are asked to make as teachers but don't have the time to internalize them so they will be useful in the actual process of teaching.

Teaching and Learning Mathematics in the Middle Grades
Student Perspectives

Linda Foreman
President, Teachers Development Group, West Linn, Oregon

In the spring of 1994, I spent six weeks teaching mathematics to a heterogeneous class of 4th and 5th graders so that I could field test several activities I was developing for the *Mathematics Alive!* curriculum.[1] Working with these students informed my writing in remarkable ways, and since my assignment was to create a complete four-year curriculum, this six-week project extended to four years. During this time, a few students moved away and a few were added, but most of this group remained, receiving their only mathematics instruction for three or four years in my classroom.

In the spring of 1997, I read several excerpts from the TIMSS report to my class. The students responded strongly to descriptions of "typical" American and Japanese classrooms and suggested they would like an opportunity to share their ideas about what is possible. Hence, they applied and were invited to present at the 1998 annual meetings of the National Council of Teachers of Mathematics and the National Council of Supervisors of Mathematics in Washington, DC. Each of the students identified a "big idea" related to teaching and learning mathematics, wrote a two-page paper about the idea, and based a 3-4 minute presentation on that paper. Included below are excerpts from five students' papers/presentations. Although students received input and

---

[1] *Mathematics Alive!* is a comprehensive mathematics curriculum for grades 5-8, written by Linda Cooper Foreman and Albert B. Bennett, Jr., and developed with support from the National Science Foundation.

support from one another as they read each other's drafts and practiced their presentations, each student's ideas and work are original.

Please note that I did not begin this project intending to do research or expecting the students to share stories as they have. Rather, I chose a school that was convenient to get to and from so I could test ideas and maximize my writing time. I chose the class because the teacher had been thoughtful about assuring a heterogeneous mix of students (interestingly, the students' achievement levels were very diverse in the beginning but grew to be very similar, e.g., by the end of their 8th grade year, they averaged in the 92nd percentile on the statewide standardized test). With this in mind, I encourage you to set aside the concerns you have about ways these students may differ from yours or others you know, and simply consider the issues and possibilities prompted by these young mathematicians' comments.

As you read their papers, you might speculate about the nature of the classroom instruction and culture that enabled the students' views about learning, teaching, and mathematics. While these students are explicit in their recommendations, are there implicit messages about teaching and learning in the middle grades? What can you "read between the lines" about their mathematics experi-

ence? In particular, what thoughts do the students' comments and work samples prompt about the following:

- What are the important characteristics of effective teaching in the middle grades? Of effective teaching of mathematics in the middle grades?
- How can instruction in middle grades classrooms be organized to maximize learning? How can we tell when learning is happening?
- What tools and strategies will make a difference in how middle grades students learn mathematics?

ERICA—QUESTIONING

Ben: "Ms. Martin, I am stuck on this problem. How do I figure out the area of a triangle? Can you help me get started?"

Teacher: "Sure, Ben. First, here's what you need to do. Think about what a triangle looks like. Now where would you find the formula in your book for determining the area?"

Ben: "Okay. I've got it. It's $\frac{1}{2} bh$."

Teacher: "Good job. Now what is the base measurement? What is the height measurement? Do you see how to plug in those measurements for base and height to get the right answer?"

Ben: "Thanks! I really understand now!"

No way!! I don't think Ben really understands. This dialogue is an example of what I call ineffective questioning by a well-intentioned teacher. This type of questioning leads a student to a certain way of thinking instead of having them figure it out on their own. … Also, using questions like this only generates one method, focuses on the answer not the process, and stops the student from thinking very much….

Ineffective questions do not allow the students to explain anything that they have done or thought about. If students don't have the chance to explain their thoughts, then the teacher can't know if they really understand the problem. Students may have the answer, but that doesn't help them in the long run.

… I know how powerful it is to come up with an answer all by myself. My teacher might help me get started, but I prefer to solve a problem myself. Once I find an answer I am intrigued to continue thinking of other possible methods. Also, when I find the answer, I am more likely to remember how to do that problem, or ones like it, than if I am told the solution by a teacher or a book….

Some examples of effective questions to ask a student or a group of students are:

- "What do you think?"
- "What if _____?"
- "Is there another way to think about that problem?"

- "What are some observations you can make?"
- "Can you explain your thinking?"
- "Can you predict what might happen next?"

…Being asked questions that didn't lead me right to the answer was hard to adjust to at first. I wasn't used to finding more than the answer. Eventually the whole class got used to being asked these open-ended questions. Then we asked the same type of questions that the teacher had asked us, but to each other….

In the beginning dialogue, Ben was led to his answer by the teacher and he wasn't able to feel the joy of finding a solution on his own. Sooner or later he may realize that he really doesn't understand the mathematics concept; he just figured out the answer by plugging into a formula without thinking. Ben would have had a greater understanding if the questions his teacher had asked had been something like this instead….

Teacher: "First, tell me what you understand about area."

Ben: (explains his thinking)

Teacher: "Can you tell me what you already know about the triangle from the picture?"

Ben: (describes what he "sees")

Teacher: "What do you think you need to know in order to find the area of a triangle?"

Ben: "Can you give me a clue?"

Teacher: "Sure. What if you build the triangle on a geoboard to help you see it in a different way?"

Ben: (explores and invents a formula for the area of the triangle)

Teacher: "So now you have a formula that works for the area of that triangle. Do you think it will work with a right triangle? ...an equilateral triangle? ...any triangle? Why don't you investigate that?"

JULIE—WORTHWHILE ACTIVITIES

In order for a mathematics class to be worthwhile, I believe that the teacher needs to provide the students with worthwhile activities. For example, when we explain our thinking out loud, make posters of our work, draw diagrams, work in groups, and use manipulatives, we are more productive and therefore learn more.... To determine if an activity is worthwhile, some helpful things to ask are:

- Will it make students stretch their thinking?
- Will it branch off to other topics?
- Is there more than one way to solve the problem?
- Will it help students' understanding of the idea?
- Will it cause some disequilibrium?

... The best activities to do are ones for which the teacher can say "yes" to all of the above questions. Teachers can't expect the students to work well in groups if they give them a problem like, "Find the sum of twenty-eight and seventeen." Better questions to ask would be, "Can you find more than one way to solve the problem twenty-eight plus seventeen?" or "Can you invent an algorithm for adding any two digit numbers?" ...

As you read on, look for evidence in Lindsay's, Joel's, and Kyle's papers that effective questioning and worthwhile activities are/are not elements of their instruction. What questions and/or activities might have prompted the mathematical thinking that Lindsay, Joel, and Kyle demonstrate in their examples?

LINDSAY—VISUAL MODELS

Working with models for mathematics ideas helps me have a better understanding of mathematics concepts which leads to confidence and success in mathematics. Visual models don't just help me find an answer, they help me understand why the answer works. When I use visual models, I have more confidence in my thinking, and I have a stronger grasp of the mathematics ideas. When I can find an answer by myself, and see why it works, it makes me feel confident and that makes mathematics more fun for me.

Models help guide me to the invention of formulas. Visual models also help me reinvent ideas. If I forget a formula or concept, all I have to do is go back to the model and I can reinvent the proof. For example, if I forget how to find the area of a trapezoid, different formulas just pop right out to me in the model. Before I was able to invent the following formulas, I invented formulas for the areas of triangles, rectangles, and parallelograms.

In diagram 1, I divided a trapezoid into 2 triangles. I found the area of both triangles and added them together. That gave me the area of the trapezoid.

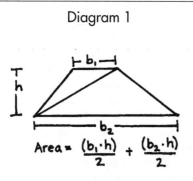

Diagram 1

$$\text{Area} = \frac{(b_1 \cdot h)}{2} + \frac{(b_2 \cdot h)}{2}$$

In diagram 2, I took 2 trapezoids and "smooshed" them together to form a parallelogram. I found the area of the parallelogram and then divided it by 2. In diagram 3, I divided the trapezoid into 2 triangles and a rectangle. I

"smooshed" together the 2 triangles, forming a larger triangle. Then I found the area of that triangle and added it to the area of the rectangle.

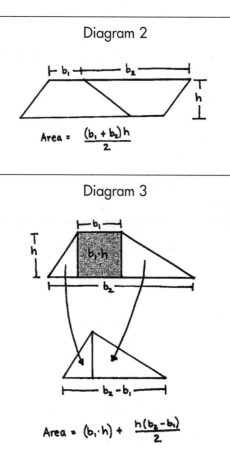

Diagram 2

$$\text{Area} = \frac{(b_1 + b_2)h}{2}$$

Diagram 3

$$\text{Area} = (b_1 \cdot h) + \frac{h(b_2 - b_1)}{2}$$

…There are many advantages to using visual models. They help me produce work more efficiently, and give me a better understanding of mathematics concepts because I can actually "see" the why behind a concept. Most importantly, these models enable me to be confident in myself as a mathematics student and know that I really do have an inner mathematician.

JOEL—RECORDING IMPORTANT IDEAS

As we work on different problems, we come across "big ideas" that seem to keep coming up, even in seemingly unrelated topics.... This is where our journals come in. They allow us to record our thoughts and processes so that we may look back later and work through our thought processes again.

Each student's journal is different, as a journal is a place for records of personal struggles, discoveries, and insights that help illustrate what we have been working on in class.... I have chosen a few excerpts from my journal to help demonstrate how we record important ideas and look back later if we are stuck.

It is by coming across examples such as this that we have learned that it is very important to record the important mathematics ideas we come across, and to try applying methods we came up with earlier, even if at first look it seems as though the methods have nothing to do with the idea we're examining. In this way, new ideas make sense and are easier to understand....

Figure 1. Journal excerpts 1 and 2

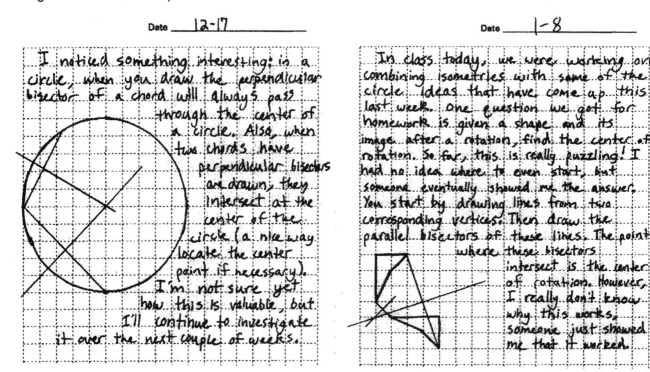

Date ___12-17___

I noticed something interesting: in a circle, when you draw the perpendicular bisector of a chord will always pass through the center of a circle. Also, when two chords have perpendicular bisectors are drawn, they intersect at the center of the circle (a nice way locate the center point if necessary). I'm not sure yet how this is valuable, but I'll continue to investigate it over the next couple of weeks.

Date ___1-8___

In class today, we were working on combining isometries with some of the circle ideas that have come up this last week. One question we got for homework is given a shape and its image after a rotation, find the center of rotation. So far, this is really puzzling! I had no idea where to even start, but someone eventually showed me the answer. You start by drawing lines from two corresponding vertices. Then draw the parallel bisectors of these lines. The point where these bisectors intersect is the center of rotation. However, I really don't know why this works, someone just showed me that it worked.

Figure 2. Journal excerpt 3

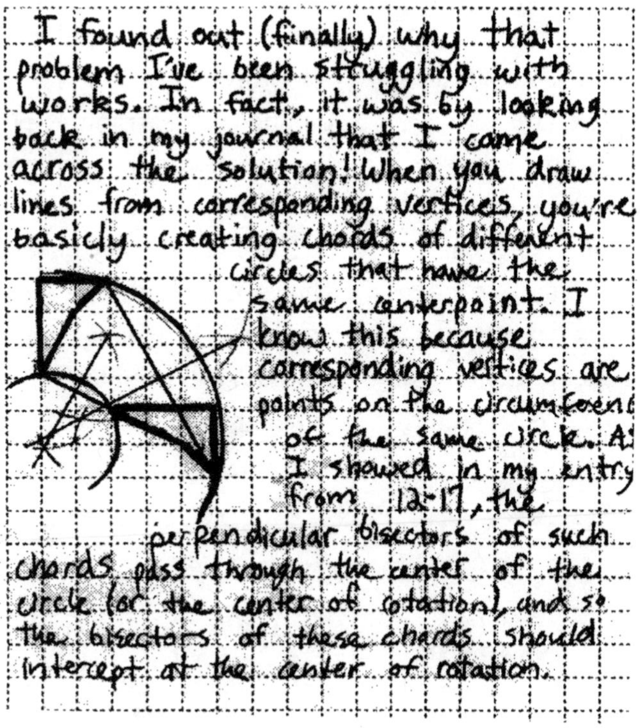

I found out (finally) why that problem I've been struggling with works. In fact, it was by looking back in my journal that I came across the solution! When you draw lines from corresponding vertices, you're basicly creating chords of different circles that have the same centerpoint. I know this because corresponding vertices are points on the circumference of the same circle. As I showed in my entry from 12-17, the perpendicular bisectors of such chords pass through the center of the circle (or the center of rotation), and so the bisectors of these chords should intercept at the center of rotation.

KYLE—MATHEMATICAL TRUST

Learning mathematics is a journey. … Our teacher trusts us as capable mathematical thinkers who can find our own way…. That is, she believes there is a mathematician within each of us. Therefore, she does not lead, show, or guide us in our journey… .

A teacher that does NOT have mathematical trust in her students may:

• Show a best way to solve a problem,
• Ask a leading question that looks for an expected answer,
• Answer a question without letting the students get involved,
• Not allow students to invent their own procedures,
• Not allow students to feel disequilibrium.

The above actions discourage the use of new ideas and different approaches. They also take away the student's opportunity to feel the joy of learning and doing mathematics. I have noticed that when someone tells me how to solve a problem, my thinking stops. On the other hand, when someone allows me to wrestle with an idea, I find myself inventing more strategies and I get a stronger grasp of the idea. Solving a problem myself helps me clarify my understanding of the mathematics and leads to important conjectures.

Last year our class invented the strategy "completing the square" to solve quadratic equations. This fall, when the idea came up again, we felt certain we could solve any quadratic equation. So, our teacher said, "Just for fun, if $ax^2 + bx + c = 0$, what is x?" After

the first day of exploration our teacher asked us if we wanted clues. We protested and ended that day and the next day of class in disequilibrium. Finally, after three days of building models, cutting and rearranging pieces, debating and discussing, and no clues, we found the value of x.

The journal entry on the left below shows how I solved a specific quadratic equation. The journal entry on the right shows how I used that idea to generalize about any quadratic equation.

Figure 3. Journal entries

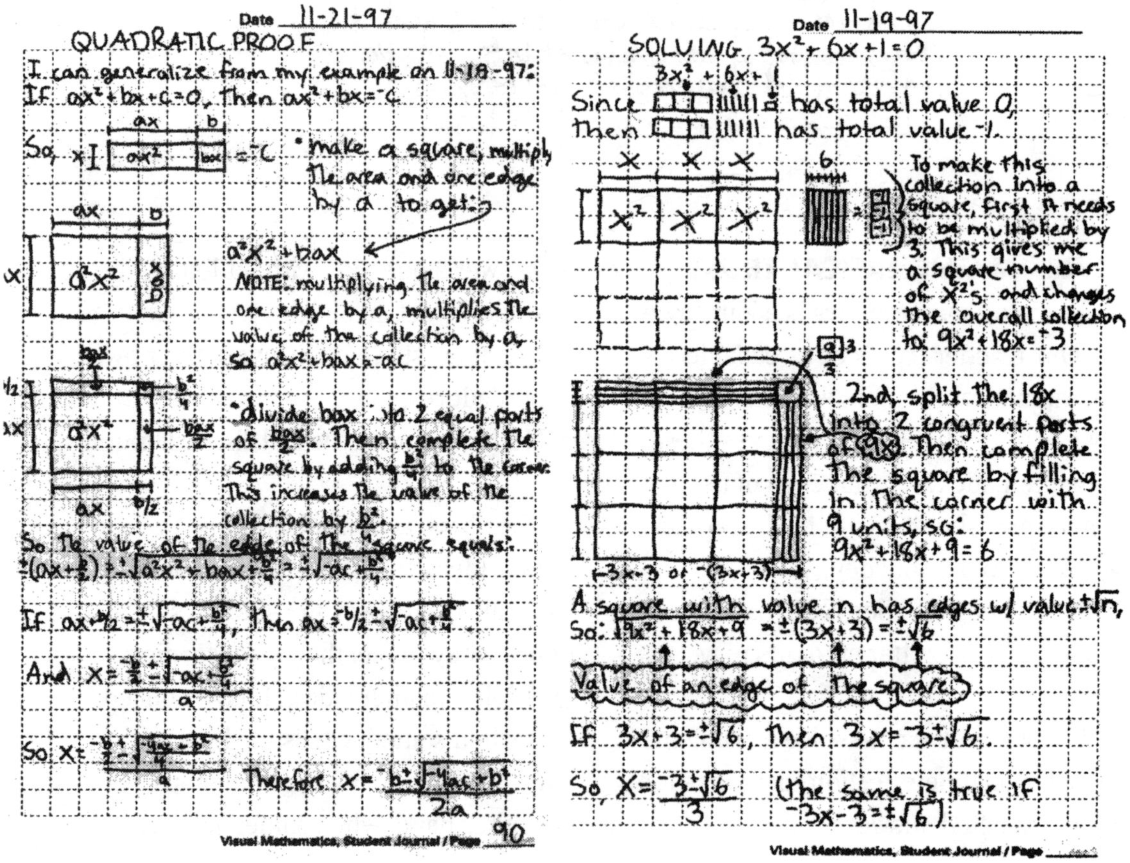

Because our teacher trusted us and we trusted ourselves, we invented an algorithm for solving any quadratic equation (later we found out that other mathematicians had also invented that algorithm).

Learning is a journey. Mathematical trust keeps us going and allows us to travel in new directions without worrying about getting lost or taking the routes that others do.

CONCLUSIONS

Working with these students for four years has stirred my thinking about learning and teaching and enabled my growth as a writer. More importantly perhaps, it has left me with food for thought about teaching mathematics. Following are a few ideas on my mind, prompted by the students' comments and work and by the Convocation panelists and participants. Perhaps they will provide thought or discussion starters for you, and/or perhaps you have other ideas to add to the list.

- It is possible to form a remarkable mathematics community and classroom culture when youngsters and their teacher stay together over time. How can this model be adapted to work in the mainstream middle school setting?

- We teachers and curriculum developers can impose artificial limits on students by the questions we don't invite or pose and by our own conceptions of learning, teaching, and mathematics. How do we learn to recognize this in our actions and work?

- While it is the case that Lindsay, Joel, and Kyle each went on to explore applications of the area of a trapezoid, center of rotation, and quadratic formula, their papers suggest it was the mathematical ideas themselves that were engaging. What motivates students to engage in thinking about mathematical ideas? What makes a problem "real" for students? What is meaningful context?

- If one agrees that these students provide evidence that it is possible to cultivate interest in serious mathematical content, what are the instructional practices that are most influential in cultivating such interest?

- What is important and relevant mathematics for middle grades? What is worthwhile mathematical activity? Note: deriving the quadratic formula was not a part of my original lesson plan; however, as Kyle pointed out, the class spent 3 days wrestling with the challenge. What may have been gained or lost by taking this mathematical excursion? It seems to fit Julie's criteria for worthwhile activities. What are other criteria to add to Julie's list?

- Many teachers were educated in a system that promoted the notion that only certain people can do mathematics. Can students come to recognize and nurture their "inner mathematicians" if the teacher does not believe every student has a capable mathematical mind? What professional development experiences are necessary for teachers to develop a sense of "mathematical trust" in their students?

- Contrary to many common descriptors, doing mathematics *is* an emotional experience, and those emotions can be positive ones, e.g., empowerment and passion for the subject matter, pride in discovery and invention, respect for disequilibrium, and joy over solving challenging problems. What teacher actions best facilitate the development of such feelings about mathematics?

- When students are called upon to communicate mathematically, they learn the language of mathematics as they learn to speak any language—simultaneously using invented language (e.g., smooshing) and formal language (e.g., disequilibrium, transformations). It can be uncomfortable for teachers as they strike a balance between accepting students' invented language and teaching formal mathematical language.

- As Erica pointed out, teaching that focuses on how students think about mathematics has a powerful influence on students' learning as well as their views of themselves as mathematicians. It also provides the teacher rich information about the extent to which students understand and are able to integrate mathematical ideas and processes into their own way of thinking. For example, in Lindsay's and Joel's explanations of their thinking, their use of transformations provides evidence of their sense of geometry as a process; and we see evidence of Lindsay's and Kyle's sense about the integrated nature of algebra and geometry by their use of algebraic symbols to represent the geometric and algebraic relationships they could "see" in models. Because teaching that centers on how students' think is so different from the mathematics instruction most teachers and parents have experienced, it is particularly challenging to shift away from practice that emphasizes telling students what to think. Long term professional development and a curriculum that emphasizes students' mathematical thinking are essential for teachers to make this shift.

The examples given in this paper provide a glimpse of what is possible when students are immersed over time in a Standards-based curriculum; however, it is important to keep in mind the fact that this project lasted for four years. Just as implementing reform is a challenge and requires long-term support for teachers, the benefits of reform-based teaching are not immediately apparent in students. Had these students written their papers even a year earlier, some students would have expressed doubts about how and what they were learning (they kept close tabs on activity in their peers' more traditional classrooms—the media, and even some mathematics teachers, told them they would never learn what they needed to know); there would have been more disequilibrium about certain mathematical ideas that are described with confidence here; their parents may have expressed doubt due to the uproar about mathematics reform in the local news; and their teacher would have been a little less secure in her conviction to maintain high expectations, trusting everyone's disequilibrium was a sign of new learning about to occur.

Panel Response to Foreman Student Video

Three panelists were invited to comment: Hyman Bass, a university mathematician, Sam Chattin, a career middle grades teacher, and Deborah Ball, a researcher on teaching and teacher educator. Sam Chattin, who does not teach math, reacted to the video thinking about middle grades students in the context of social groups. He observed that the students in the video had formed an effective social group and seemed to have made a conscious choice to stay in the group, probably because of the affirmation they received about their ability to do mathematics and be successful. The teacher had clearly done some modeling about learning mathematics and about group behaviors. He noted that a strong commitment to the social group was evident in the students' willingness to raise money to travel to Washington, DC. The body language of the students making their presentations indicated they felt very secure, and it was clear that adults had made them that way, free to make mistakes with no censure. They used their own words (e.g., "smooshed"), an indication they felt free to translate what they knew to their own world. Probably the most significant observation for the audience was his remark that the audience laughed when the students were the most serious. Chattin pointed out that it is hard for adults to recognize just how serious middle grades students are.

Hyman Bass described himself as a university mathematician "infected" with observing elementary teaching and thinking about how students learn mathematics. He shared Sam's impressions and saw in the students a reflection of the teacher's practice: attitude towards content, classroom culture, philosophy, and principles of teaching. Bass felt the students saw themselves as mathematicians with the pride of discovery when they realized they were part of history. The mathematical topics covered algebra and geometry, which in his view have been excessively separated in the standard curriculum. Particularly nice was the use of transformational geometry, cutting and pasting to find the area of the trapezoid (which preserves area), and in one of the presentations the use of rotations and the center of rotations as a way to approach the problem. He observed that some of the methods of teaching were obvious in the student presentations, such as keeping a journal of mathematical ideas. When one of the students was given a problem about using perpendicular bisectors of chords to find the center of a circle, although he had the answer, he returned to his records in the journal and made the connections with the mathematics he had recorded to learn why his answer worked. According to Bass, the tape revealed products of enlightened teaching where the students were able to communicate about mathematics and had a passion for the subject.

Deborah Ball noted the challenge of commenting on teaching when teaching was not visible on the video segment. However, she said, several key observations were possible about what the teacher must have done for students to be able to do the things displayed on the video. She framed her remarks around the conjecture that this teacher had actively held and communicated high expectations for students. She said that teachers can move children if they hold expectations that students can learn and do not take refuge in "Most (or my) kids can't do this." Ball's first point was that the teacher in this case had to teach her students how to use her questions as a way to learn; they had to learn to make sense of the way she teaches. Second, the teacher had to cultivate interest in the mathematics. Thinking students are not interested is the static view; the teacher had done something to make these students interested and involved. A third point was that the teacher had to cultivate a language within which the class could work. She had taught them some formal words that were not part of their vocabulary (e.g., "disequilibrium") but she also accepted their words ("smooshed"). And finally, she must have created some incentives for students to learn to work this way. The students had been given high incentives to engage in mathematically sound work.

Summary of Small Group Discussion on Teaching Issues in the Middle Grades

Using the videos and panel observations as a backdrop, the discussion groups addressed the following questions: What are the important characteristics of effective teaching in the middle grades? Of effective teaching of mathematics in the middle grades? How can instruction in middle grades classrooms be organized to maximize learning? How can we tell when learning is happening? And, what tools and strategies will make a difference in how middle grades students learn mathematics? What are the important characteristics of effective teaching in the middle grades? Of effective teaching of mathematics in the middle grades?

The answers to the first question clearly reflected the middle school philosophy, with an emphasis on a safe learning environment where students work in a social caring classroom and learning mathematics is treated as a social activity. There was strong support for student-centered classrooms and reinforcement of student ideas and work. Some caution was voiced about using praise to reward less-than-adequate performance. As the groups struggled to identify effective mathematics teaching, many mentioned that "quiet discomfort" signals new learning and that a sense of disequilibrium is essential to learning, reflecting the message from one of the videos. A clearly identified characteristic of effective middle grades mathematics teaching was the need for strong content knowledge on the part of the teacher. This was particularly significant when mathematics was viewed from the perspective of a challenging middle grades curriculum that goes beyond computational skills. The groups identified the following characteristics of effective middle grades mathematics teachers. Effective middle grades mathematics teachers:

- have high expectations for their students
- have students who are involved in active learning situations and engaged in communicating mathematics
- design their lessons with well defined

goals and a coherent message making connections within the course and the curriculum

- are able to build understanding from concrete models, knowing how and when to bring the ideas to closure
- understand the importance of asking the right questions in ways that promote thinking and allowing sufficient time for students to respond
- listen to their students' responses so they know where those students are in their mathematical understanding and use this knowledge to develop student learning
- are flexible yet have created a familiar structure and routine for their classes
- provide models for student learning by the way they teach.

How can instruction in middle grades classrooms be organized to maximize learning? The groups stressed the critical role of the school administration in creating a structure and support for student learning, from setting the school environment to ensuring that class disruptions were minimized. The groups also consistently mentioned the need for time for teachers to work together developing lessons and thinking through the curriculum, for flexible blocks of time (not necessarily block scheduling), for manageable class sizes, and for clear articulation between grades. Over a fourth of the groups

supported "looping"—having a teacher remain with a class of students over several years. There was strong support for using teams as a way to create a community of teachers.

How can teachers tell when learning is taking place? Students provided such evidence when they were engaged and able to explain the mathematics they were learning to others. Students who understand can apply mathematics to solve problems and have the ability to revise their thinking based on their investigations.

What tools and strategies will make a difference in how middle grades students learn mathematics? Manipulatives, calculators including graphing calculators, and computers all were referenced by the discussants as important tools to help students learn mathematics. Assessment as a tool to enhance learning was suggested, as well as engaging students in writing and projects. Strategies for helping students learn mathematics included creating a warm and open environment, where there were clear and consistent policies among the team members. Parents should be informed and involved. Mentoring and building a community of teachers were reoccurring themes. Teachers should be working with other teachers on lessons, visiting classes, and designing professional development activities around the context of the content teachers were teaching. Teachers should be engaged in posing questions and debating answers to stimulate student thinking. Attention should be paid to the developmental levels of students, although questions were raised about what the term developmentally appropriate meant and how teachers would understand this in terms of their students.

The comment was made that "We are not taught to teach, only about teaching." Video as a way to initiate a discussion of teaching was perceived as both positive and negative. The initial tendency to criticize can overtake the discussion. There was concern that viewers might not recognize good teaching. The risk of going public as a teacher and standing for inspection was too great to make this a useful medium. Those who found viewing actual instances of teaching useful, appreciated the different thinking that can result from talking about actual practice. A video allows a situation to be viewed repeatedly from different lenses. The groups did agree, however, that the viewer should have a well defined focus in order to make the viewing and ensuing discussion useful.

Organizational Issues in the Middle Grades

The sessions on organizational issues in the middle grades focused on the questions

- What are the important characteristics of school organization and mathematics programs that support teaching and learning meaningful mathematics in the middle grades?
- How can the schedules of teachers and students be organized to implement what we know about effective teaching and learning in the middle grades?
- What are the issues surrounding specialists vs. generalists? What kind of teaching assignments maximize program effectiveness in mathematics?

THE ORGANIZATION AND STRUCTURE OF SCHOOLS AT THE MIDDLE GRADES: A PRINCIPAL'S PERSPECTIVE

Stephen O. Gibson, Patapsco Middle School, Ellicott City, MD.

THE ORGANIZATION AND STRUCTURE OF SCHOOLS AT THE MIDDLE GRADES: THE ROLE OF DEVELOPMENT, SUBJECT MATTER, AND TEACHER PROFESSIONAL DEVELOPMENT

Mary Kay Stein, Learning Research Development Center, University of Pittsburgh.

IMPROVING ACHIEVEMENT IN THE MIDDLE GRADES IN MATHEMATICS AND RELATED AREAS: LESSONS FROM THE PROJECT ON HIGH PERFORMANCE LEARNING COMMUNITIES

Robert D. Felner, National Center on Public Education and Social Policy, School of Education, University of Rhode Island.

PANEL DISCUSSION ON THE ORGANIZATION OF SCHOOLS AT THE MIDDLE GRADES

The Organization and Structure of Schools at the Middle Grades
A Principal's Perspective

Adapted from the Transcript of Remarks by Stephen O. Gibson
Patapsco Middle School, Ellicott City, MD

The key word in the three questions we were asked to consider is "meaningful." At the middle level, principals and administrators often fall into a trap of offering programs that many do not consider meaningful. To ensure that we are looking at meaningful mathematics programs, we have to represent a full scope of the types of mathematics that we offer within middle schools. We need to look at the individual needs of students as opposed to placing everyone into a nice box starting here in mathematics in sixth grade and ending there in eighth, knowing that our students do not come to us like that.

One of the major key issues is the examination of data. All too often, our students come to us from elementary schools with testing that has gone on in first, second, third, fourth and fifth grades. They arrive at the middle level, and very few people review that data.

The students are placed into an area and do not move. They stay within that functional mathematics program, or they stay in a designated mathematics program without any flexibility. In that regard, it is very important to look at the different levels that we can give to students. We see students who come into the classroom who are not achieving well in mathematics. One of the things that you do is to ask some questions and start examining behind the picture. Then you see there are just fundamental flaws in small areas that have prevented them from having achieved at the highest level. We need to use data effectively to be able to get that done.

Within that structure, we must also make sure the schools are organized well so that articulation can take place. A fundamental flaw that we have within the K-12 system is that levels do not articulate among each other. Students come to middle school. The middle schools have really never talked to anyone at the elementary school to see how these students are doing in mathematics. What are the basic premises that we need to teach them? When students are not achieving and are not doing well in that first few weeks of school, all too often what we want to do is to point a finger at the grade level before and say, "You did not teach them. You did not give them the capabilities, the skills to prepare them for middle-level mathematics." Conversely, the same thing happens when those students go on to high school, and our high school teachers say they are not ready or prepared for the rigorous mathematics they need to be competitive with people across the world.

We need to set up a process for articulation. It is important that we talk to fellow colleagues at the elementary level and set up those times where middle grade teachers can speak to the elementary teachers of mathematics because elementary teachers have the toughest job in the world. They are trying to deliver multiple skills and sometimes skills that they are not even prepared for as well. Articulation will give us a better picture. Also, we need to make sure we are taking a look at the assessments that we give students so that we are getting a real feel for where students are as far as understanding and skills.

If we can build a program where we are utilizing data, data that tells us a lot, then we will start to build programs that allow us to have multiple levels that actually work. Schools need to be organized so they are not afraid to be risk takers. Schools can modify assessments. They can look at assessments that fit their particular building. We have a middle-level TT-type program. It is not taking our students two levels above, but one level above. How do we get students into that program? Is it by feel? Is it by guess? When we do that, we short-change youngsters. We set them up so they cannot succeed. You can develop assessments that actually match students and content knowledge, and when students are put into those programs, it works better.

A major flaw in what we are doing with students is not utilizing technology that is out there. There are students who, given the right tools, can be successful. I have a daughter who does tremendously well if you give her the calculator as a tool. If you take that tool away, she is going to struggle. She knows the systematic way of doing things, but she may not always know how to do it correctly. She gets frustrated to the point where she can't put the calculations together. We have computer technology that has not been utilized within our schools. It is probably the biggest shame in American education. Principals and others will admit to having 100 computers in their building. When you ask them how they are used instructionally, there are frowns on people's faces because they really don't know.

Students are using computers at home all of the time. They come to school, their parents ask did you use computers today, and the answer is no. Are computers in the building? Yes. In visiting a school that was in reconstitution, I had the distinct privilege of looking at a school that had four brand new computer labs, and nobody knew how to use them. We need to question whether or not the technology is there, whether it is being used, and how we effectively train our teachers to use it.

Moving on to the other questions, students' schedules need to be put together so that they have opportunities to be able to move, to match those schedules effectively with other issues. Mathematics is not taught in a vacuum. Mathematics is part of a larger course of teaching; if mathematics is not used effectively across the different subject matters, then it is not going to be really learned well. It must be integrated into other things that are going on. We must utilize schedules that enable students to see the relevance of mathematics across multiple discipline areas. Mathematics

can be used all the time.

Writing, conversely, can be used the same way in mathematics. We have to make sure the students know the old fundamental question. How do I use algebra? How do I use geometry? How do I use calculus? There should be places for students to be able to see and maximize the use of that understanding in terms of their learning environment.

If effective teaching is really going on within a building, teachers can collaborate and talk across subject lines and see how it all fits together for the relevance of the student going to school. When students were two, three and four years old, all of the things they put together were relevant to one another. They could figure out why they matched. We get to school, and all of a sudden everything is in an individual subject compartment or area.

Perhaps the main issue in all of this is looking at the last one in the set of questions—of generalists versus specialists in teaching mathematics. Some generalists are outstanding mathematics teachers, and they call themselves generalists. However, if you watch them and sit in a classroom with them, they are no longer generalists—they have worked exceptionally hard; they have taken course work; they have studied their materials. They have pushed themselves to a new level, and they are no longer generalists. They have become specialists in their areas. Perhaps the flaw in that is taking the teacher and then moving them around year after year and having them feel they can teach this mathematics or that mathematics. So they no longer become a specialist. They are a generalist again.

There are teachers who are trained as specialists who are in the same realm. They are pushed around. They do not get a chance to acquire the knowledge and the skills to be able to teach courses effectively. We must put together schedules that make things work for teachers. We should not put teachers into a bind of every year returning back to school, looking at a master schedule, and finding themselves scheduled to teach something different. They are, therefore, in a trap and a vacuum, starting day one off along with the students. It is a huge flaw. It is a problem that we create for teachers sometimes.

As principals and effective leaders of the building, we have to be able to sit down and communicate with our teachers, to understand their skills and know the support that they need to succeed. We need to push them along. We need to counsel them to push their classes. We need to observe their classes, ensuring that mathematics instruction takes place, where students actually learn, where students can ask questions, and where students can succeed.

Every student coming into the sixth grade or the seventh grade or the eighth grade can learn very quickly if given the proper tools, given the proper training, and, perhaps the most important thing of all, given a caring, nurturing environment that says instructionally, academics are first and that we are going to make it work. But we are going to support you as an individual in an academic environment so that you can find success.

The Organization and Structure of Schools at the Middle Grades '
The Role of Development, Subject Matter, and Teacher Professional Development

Mary Kay Stein
Learning Research Development Center, University of Pittsburgh

Middle school scholars and mathematics educators agree on the broad goals for middle school reform: High-performing schools for young adolescents should be developmentally responsive, academically excellent, and socially equitable (Lipsitz, Mizell, Jackson, & Austin, 1997). Despite this broad agreement on goals, however, these two groups have tended to advocate different strategies for reaching those goals. Middle school advocates favor a developmental approach, while mathematics educators favor what I will label a subject matter approach.

The developmental approach to middle school reform is based on a well-established literature which asserts that the imperatives of adolescence are too powerful to be ignored. Therefore, school practices must be adapted to meet these needs. In large part, the response of reformers has been to initiate organizational and structural changes aimed at creating small, consistent communities of learning for students. The subject matter approach, on the other hand, is driven by the imperatives of mathematics, particularly by the new ways of conceptualizing the teaching and learning of mathematics which have been recommended by the National Council of Teachers of Mathematics Standards (NCTM, 1989). At the middle school level, these standards call for the broadening of topics beyond the typical review of general arithmetic, and, at all grade levels, for more student-centered forms of pedagogy, more cognitively challenging mathematical tasks, and greater diversity in pedagogical practices (e.g., the use of extended projects, small workgroup settings, and a variety of representations).

In this paper, I suggest that each of these approaches is inherently incomplete and propose a third approach—one that attempts to build on and integrate the two. The proposed approach to middle school reform joins professional development for teachers and administrative functions giving rise to a new middle school organization and structure that is jointly informed by subject matter and developmental concerns.

THE DEVELOPMENTAL APPROACH

The developmental approach to middle school reform builds on our knowledge of the social, emotional, physical, and intellectual characteristics of students in their early adolescent years. Socially, we know that adolescents have great needs for peer affiliation, while at the same time struggling to establish a personal identity. Emotionally, adolescents are often torn between attempts to assert their independence, and feeling the need for adult support and guidance. Physically, adolescents are experiencing changes in the size and shape of their bodies, changes which are associated with anxiety and the need for physical activity. And, last but not least, adolescents are growing intellectually. The expansion of their cognitive capacities to include formal operational thought and the ability to entertain "the

possible" is a well-documented phenomenon of this stage of life.

In response to these characteristics, middle school reformers have set into motion a variety of structural and organizational changes that have resulted in middle schools which look very different from traditional junior high schools. For example, many middle schools have been reorganized into a series of smaller units (e.g., houses, teams, advisory programs, homebase groups, team-based mentorships) that are designed to encourage students to form stable relationships with a consistent group of peers and adults. Many schools have organized their faculty into interdisciplinary teams in order to better teach integrative and exploratory forms of curricula that are meant to challenge adolescents' expanding cognitive capabilities. Some reforms even extend beyond the physical walls of the school building by setting up home-school partnerships, liaisons with community organizations, and comprehensive guidance services.

Over the past decade as these organizational and structural changes have taken hold, we have seen considerable progress in the creation of a new middle school climate, one that is discernibly warmer, more respectful, and more encouraging of adolescent development. Unfortunately, this improved climate has not been accompanied by increases in student achievement in the content areas. A variety of state, national, and international studies—not just in mathematics—but also in reading and science, suggest that the performance of middle grades students can be characterized by academic stagnation (Lipsitz, Mizell, Jackson, & Austin, 1997)

Why is this so? The theory was that the above changes would set the conditions for strong academic learning. If students felt secure, respected, and intellectually stimulated, it was argued, they would be motivated to engage with the cognitively challenging academic work before them. One hypothesis for the lack of academic progress is that the organizational rearrangement and resulting climate changes have not been nearly as widespread as is often reported; this argument goes on to suggest that in those schools in which the changes have been successfully installed, students are showing learning gains (see Felner, this volume).

Another hypothesis, however, is that middle schools, across the board, have been overly focused on organizational and climate variables. While houses may promote a stable sense of community and rearranged schedules may permit students to have steady access to consistent mentors, all of these efforts, positive as they are, will not—in and of themselves—lead to improved student learning. School principals and teachers must progress to the next step: the critical examination of their instructional programs. What is actually being taught and learned inside the classroom door?

The failure of organizational changes to impact student achievement is not a new problem, nor is confined to middle schools. Throughout history there has been resistance to making profound, lasting changes in the educational core, that is, in "how teachers understand the nature of knowledge and the student's role in learning, and how these ideas about knowledge and learning are manifested in teaching and classwork" (Elmore, 1996, p. 2). Most of what passes for reform is the rearrangement of structures at an organizational level which—although well intended—is not robust or potent enough to induce, let alone sustain, real improvements in classroom teaching and learning.

If the second hypothesis is accepted, the problem of the middle school reforms of the last decade can be recast as a problem of not penetrating the educational core, a core that by definition resides in teaching and learning interactions inside the classroom door and hence needs to be informed by subject matter. Teaching and learning is always about *something*.

THE SUBJECT MATTER APPROACH

The subject matter approach starts at the educational core with questions regarding the nature of mathematics and how it is best taught and learned.

In fact, questions about issues of teaching and learning—What does it mean to know mathematics? How can students develop deep and flexible understandings of mathematics? What is the role of the teacher in a mathematics classroom?—*define* the reform movement in mathematics. With the release of three landmark documents (i.e., the *Curriculum and Evaluation Standards for School Mathematics*, 1989; *Professional Standards for Teaching of Mathematics*, 1991; *Assessment Standards for School Mathematics*, 1995), the National Council of Teachers of Mathematics has steadfastly called for deep epistemological shifts in how these questions are answered. In order to truly "know" mathematics, these documents argue, one must be able to use mathematical concepts and procedures to think with, reason about, and communicate with. In order to develop into mathematical thinkers, students must have the opportunity to construct their own understandings of mathematics. And in order for students to develop in this way, teachers' instructional practice must provide students with the opportunity to engage with cognitively challenging tasks and to learn to think, reason, and problem solve.

Over the past decade, there have been encouraging signs that the "mathematical core" is undergoing, or about to undergo, reconstruction in hundreds of middle school classrooms across the country. Largely through the outreach efforts of NCTM and other professional networks, middle school teachers are beginning to recognize the value of instructional programs and practices that are more student-centered and inquiry based. The signs of progress include increased levels of awareness of the NCTM Standards among teachers (Weiss, 1993), as well as beginning attempts to redesign curriculum, instructional methods, and assessment practices to align with the Standards. In some schools and classrooms, substantial changes in how mathematics is actually taught and learned can be witnessed.

Despite these efforts, however, middle school students' performance on national and international tests of mathematics proficiency has remained at low levels over the past decade. For example, on the Third International Mathematics and Science Study, U.S. 8th grade students' mathematics achievement was found to be below average internationally and lower than that of students in many countries which are our economic competitors (Silver, in preparation). These findings parallel the disappointing middle grades performance on the most recent National Assessment of Educational Progress.

Why is this so? Similar to arguments

that there has not been widespread adoption of the organizational and climate changes advocated by middle school reformers, the extent to which mathematics reform has actually reached most of our country's schools and classrooms has been brought into question. Although there are increasing calls for more widespread, often system-wide changes in mathematics instructional practice, there are few answers for how to do this effectively. It is more typical to find pockets of excellence than it is to see entire schools or districts enacting the mathematics reforms.

Another (related) reason for the lack of progress in student achievement, however, is the ambitious nature of the reform itself. Learning mathematics in this way is very difficult for students who have been socialized into another way of thinking about what it means to know and do mathematics. When speed and accuracy have been the main criteria for successful performance, students are likely to feel anxious (and sometimes resistant) when they first encounter tasks that demand conceptual understanding, problem solving, and communication. In addition, teachers are being expected to teach in ways that they themselves have never experienced and for which they have not been trained. And teachers are the linchpin in any reform effort. Students will not receive the opportunities to learn mathematics well unless their teachers are well prepared and supported.

Seen in this way, low student performances on mathematics assessments is at least partly attributable to a failure on the part of the educational system to adequately educate its teachers to teach in this new and demanding way. Most professional development consists of one-time, pull-out workshops with little or no attempt to transfer what has been learned to teachers' day-to-day working environments (Loucks-Horsley, Hewson, Love, & Stiles, 1998). Frequently, teachers select professional development sessions from a district-generated menu of options, with little or no continuity from one session to the next and little or no connection to the overall goals of their school or district.

Aware of these shortcomings, professional development experts have begun to recommend more focused, continuous, classroom-based forms of professional development. In addition, they point to the need for professional development that connects to the curriculum that teachers are implementing, as well as to their school's overall improvement plan. Given the current structure of the educational system, however, there is little chance of such forms of professional development flourishing in the near future.

In most schools and districts, professional development is organized and delivered as a discrete activity, far from the line of institutional decision making, power, and authority. As such, it is viewed as an optional activity, often with limited resources and little institutional sway. If conflicts arise between the philosophy and needs associated with professional development offerings and the standard operating procedures of a school (as they will), these conflicts are likely to be resolved in favor of maintaining the status quo, if, indeed, they are noticed at all. Without continuous attention from the highest levels of school organization, professional development, the only provision for adult leaning in the educational system, is bound to be viewed as tangential by administrators and experienced as disconnected and unhelpful by teachers.

A THIRD APPROACH

Although some successes can be claimed by both the developmental and the subject matter approaches to middle school reform, to date, neither has led to the level and kind of student performance that one would like to see. Although both approaches could argue that the reason for poor student performance has been the lack of widespread adoption of their recommended practices, I'd like to argue that the alterna-

tive hypotheses (i.e., failure to reach the educational core and lack of appropriate forms of teacher support) also deserve deep consideration.

In the remainder of this paper, I argue for a third approach which has two unique features. First, it calls for the joining of subject matter concerns and developmental concerns into a new definition of *mathematics for the middle school student*. The second feature is the joining of professional development and administrative functions into a new middle school organization that is jointly informed by mathematical and developmental concerns.

MATHEMATICS FOR THE MIDDLE SCHOOL STUDENT

Although middle school scholars and mathematics educators have approached the topic of adolescent learning in different ways, there is considerable overlap in their conclusions regarding the kind of cognitive activity in which adolescents should be engaged. Both agree that young adolescents need to be challenged academically in order to make use of their expanded cognitive capabilities. Both agree that adolescents benefit from working on authentic tasks, tasks which they view as relevant to themselves personally and to the world in which they live. And, finally, there is a great deal of similarity in the kind of cognitive process advocated by middle school scholars and mathematics educators. Both see the need for students to actively engage in the construction of their own knowledge using processes such as exploring, debating, and collaborating with peers. In fact, mathematics educators view these and other cognitive processes (e.g., reasoning and justification) as part and parcel of what it means to "do mathematics." Given the extent to which there seems to be a common framework on which to begin discussions, it would appear as though consensus could eventually be reached regarding the definition of mathematics for the middle school student, a consensus that would take into account the developmental needs of adolescents, as well as reach the subject matter objectives of the mathematics community. This new field could then become a guiding influence on the organization of the middle school—an organization that aims to provide for the learning of students *and* adults. As a learning organization for students, this would involve the creation of organizational structures that would provide the best possible contexts for meaningful, developmentally appropriate forms of mathematics learning. In the remainder of this paper, I focus on what it would

mean for a middle school to be a learning organization for adults.

PROFESSIONAL DEVELOPMENT AS PART OF SCHOOL ORGANIZATION

The urgency of bringing professional development into the organization of schools as opposed to treating it as an afterthought is suggested by the following quotation. After noting that universities exist to nurture the ongoing learning of their faculties, as well as to educate students, Sarason (1998) states:

> If you ask schoolteachers to justify the existence of an elementary, middle, or high school, the answer will be that it is for students; it is not for the learning and development of teachers. Yet if contexts for productive learning do not exist for teachers, they cannot create and sustain that context for students. (p. 10).

Sarason goes on to cite the failure of schools to provide for the ongoing learning of adult professionals as one of the major flaws in our educational system.

How can the continuous learning of adults become a more central function of middle schools rather than something to be done only if there is extra time and funds? Although the commitment to adult learning must occur at the highest levels of the educational system (see, for example, Elmore & Burney's discussion of Community School District 2's management and professional development system, 1997), the integration of professional development into the mainstream of school life has specific manifestations at the school level as well. It is these upon which I will focus.

In order for professional development to become ingrained in the culture of a school, the principal must set the tone as a forceful instructional leader. Rather than focusing primarily on administrative work, principals need to communicate, through their talk and actions, that the continuous improvement of student learning through an unrelenting focus on instructional improvement is the school's primary mission. Daily visits to the school's classrooms, attendance at professional development sessions alongside their teachers, and bringing in and then working with school-based professional developers are just a few of the ways that principals can become deeply involved in their schools' instructional improvement efforts. Observations that my colleagues and I have conducted in schools that attempt to follow this approach (Stein, 1998; Johnston & Levine, 1997) suggest that these kinds of principal activities and attitudes go a long way toward ensuring that teacher support is focused, coherent with school goals, tailored to their needs, and ongoing in a meaningful way.

A second key element in creating a culture of continuous adult learning in a school is the development of a sense of professional community among teachers. Professional communities afford teachers the opportunity to collaborate on a regular basis, plan together, discuss each other's teaching practice, develop consensus on ways to assess their students' thinking, and support each other through difficult points in the improvement process. They also enable teachers to feel a sense of belonging as members of a community. One of the hurdles that must be overcome in building such a community is the deprivatization (or opening up) of instructional practice.

A final (and perhaps controversial) element of this third approach to middle school reform is the melding of accountability and professional development functions. In schools in which expectations for instructional practice and student learning are high, teachers begin to develop their own internal standards for accountability, as well as holding each other accountable. Nevertheless, principals must accept the responsibility for hiring and training new talent, and they also need to encourage the exodus of teachers who are not interested in or capable of meeting the needs of their students. After poorly performing teachers have been given ample opportunity to take advantage of training opportunities and improve their practice, if change is not forthcoming, the principal must be willing to consider options for removing the teachers.

The foundation upon which this third approach to middle school reform is built consists of an unrelenting focus on the educational core. The underlying principle is that issues of teaching and learning must drive the organizational structure, not the other way around. At the student level, for example, it may be decided that the normal 42 minute period is too short for engaging students with complex, authentic problems. At the teacher level, it may be decided that shared planning periods at a particular grade level are needed in order to work through a new curriculum. Impacting the core in a focused and coherent way means looking at each organizational decision from the viewpoint of its influence on the opportunities for continuous learning of students and adults.

These suggestions for bringing professional development into the mainstream of a school's organizational structure bring their own set of challenges. Principals will find it easier to follow such an approach if it is expected and supported by the district. Even then, it requires a tremendous amount of knowledge and stamina on the part of principals. They must understand instruction in the subject areas well enough to critique practice fairly. They must build relationships with their teaching staffs that are both fair and firm. Another challenge is finding time and resources. Both are needed to free up teachers to observe one anothers' classes, to attend professional development, and to put into place a classroom-based staff development model. Sometimes the time demands associated with students' vs. teachers' needs are found to be in direct conflict. Despite these challenges, bringing professional development into the mainstream is a worthwhile undertaking.

CONCLUSION

In this paper I have made a case for middle school reform that targets the educational core and that provides for the ongoing learning of teachers as well as students. I have argued that, in mathematics, the educational core can be described as "mathematics for the middle school student," a field of study that takes into account the developmental needs of adolescents and the mathematical processes and content that students ought to learn. Furthermore, I have suggested that improvements in how the educational core is taught and learned will be dependent on the preparation and support of teachers. By bringing professional development into the day-to-day administrative functioning of the school, the learning of adults will become a critical function of the school organization, leading to an overall improvement in the quality of middle schools and middle school student performance.

REFERENCES

Elmore, R. (1996). Getting to scale with good educational practice. *Harvard Educational Review, 66*(1), 1-26.

Elmore, R., & Burney, D. (1997). *Investing in teacher learning: Staff development and instructional improvement in Community School District #2, New York City.* Paper prepared for the National Commission on Teaching and America's Future and the Consortium for Policy Research in Education.

Johnston, J., & Levine, D. (1997). *The Mary Lindley Murray School, Community School District #2: A case study.* A report to the Office of Educational Research and Improvement. Pittsburgh, PA: Learning Research and Development Center, University of Pittsburgh.

Lipsitz, J., Mizell, H.M., Jackson, A.W., & Austin, L.M. (1997). Speaking with one voice: A manifesto for middle-grades reform. *Phi Delta Kappan, 78*(7), 533-543.

Loucks-Horsley, S., Hewson, P.W., Love, N., & Stiles, K.E. (1998). *Designing professional development for teachers of science and mathematics.* Thousand Oaks, CA: Corwin Press.

National Council of Teachers of Mathematics. (1989). *Curriculum and evaluation standards for school mathematics.* Reston, VA: Author.

National Council of Teachers of Mathematics. (1991). *Professional standards for teaching mathematics.* Reston, VA: Author.

National Council of Teachers of Mathematics. (1995). *Assessment standards for school mathematics.* Reston, VA: Author.

Sarason, S.B. (1998). Some features of a flawed educational system. *Daedalus, 127*(4), 1-12.

Silver, E.A. (in preparation). *Enhancing mathematics teaching and learning in the middle school years: Lessons from TIMSS and related research.*

Stein, M.K. (1998). *The Alfred E. Smith School, Community School District #2: A case study.* A report to the Office of Educational Research and Improvement. Pittsburgh, PA: Learning Research and Development Center, University of Pittsburgh.

Weiss, I.R. (1993). *Mathematics teachers' response to the reform agenda: Results of the 1993 National Survey of Science and Mathematics Education.* Paper presented at the annual meeting of the American Educational Research Association, San Francisco.

Improving Achievement in the Middle Grades in Mathematics and Related Areas

Lessons from the Project on High Performance Learning Communities

Robert D. Felner*, Minsuk Shim, Steven Brand,
Antoinette Favazza, and Anne Seitsinger
National Center on Public Education and Social Policy,
School of Education, University of Rhode Island

In recent years much has been written about the poor performance of America's middle grade students on the International Mathematics and Science Assessments (TIMSS). Of particular concern is that America's young adolescents perform more poorly relative to their counterparts in other countries. Further, they show significantly poorer performance than would be predicted based on the scores and relative ranking of fourth graders in the United States.

This state of affairs has led to a number of calls to address the "vast wasteland" that some see as the American middle school. Key to these recommendations has been the need to have students take more rigorous, challenging, and advanced courses in mathematics and science; one such recommendation is that all 8th grade students be required to take algebra. Proponents of this position often argue that such a stance is at odds with current recommendations for middle level education. They maintain that it is not until those concerned with the schooling of young adolescents shift from their "fuzzy" developmental recommendations to those emphasizing content and high standards that the United States will make gains in these areas.

In this paper we hope to accomplish three goals. The first is to briefly

---

*This paper was presented by the senior author at the Convocation.

clarify the degree to which critics of current recommendations for middle level education are far afield in their *mischaracterization* of current recommendations for middle level education. Our second goal is to provide evidence that directly links more adequate levels of actual implementation of the recommendations for middle level reform to higher achievement and performance by young adolescents in mathematics and related areas. Our third and final goal is to provide some recommendations for more effective ways to address the need for continued improvement in this area than are provided by overly simplistic, blaming, and unidimensional calls to arms.

THE PROJECT ON HIGH PERFORMANCE LEARNING COMMUNITIES

Over the past two decades the senior author of this paper has been engaged in examining the common elements of high performing schools: those schools in which students perform, achieve and display more positive adjustment in social, behavioral, and emotional domains than would be predicted for students from similar backgrounds and environments. These school settings enhance the resilience and competencies of students and others in them far

beyond that accomplished in the typical school. High performance schools are ones that take the stance that we have termed "no acceptable casualties"; that is, they seek, more successfully than most, to help all students succeed and perform at high levels, regardless of the initial level of a student's social or economic disadvantage. They view no student as disposable. They hold the perspective that if schools raise scores by enhancing the performance of some, using tactics that leave out others, their strategies are not effective. And, their practices and outcomes reflect these views.

A core finding of our work has been that if educational improvement efforts do not attend to the full ecology of the setting they will ultimately fail. Even if they "work" by raising scores or the performance of all students for a brief time, the changes will not be sustainable. Here, we view sustainability as a core litmus test for judging recommendations for reform—no matter how transiently successful. Strategies employed must not only provide conditions for all students to succeed and develop at their highest levels; they must in addition assure that improvement will continue, so that schools, students, and teachers do not go through the continuous cycle of dashed hopes and effort wasted that ultimately impedes all future efforts to improve and drives wedges between students, staff, and communities.

An ecological approach is one that is defined by its comprehensiveness and coherence. Separate elements of change cannot be implemented as if they will be effective when they are divorced from other elements in the building. For example, when structural changes such as common planning time for teams, block scheduling, or flexible periods are instituted, it is recognized that they are but parts of a whole whose intent is to provide the conditions in which more effective, integrative, deep, and meaningful long-term instruction may take place. Such a recognition leads to the clear understanding that if these "parts" are provided apart from other necessary elements, such as adequate levels of professional development, teacher buy-in and understanding, and adequate degrees of [instructional] decision-making authority for teachers, the potential of structural, motivational, and resource opportunities for change will go unrealized.

As part of the Project on High Performing Learning Communities (Project HiPlaces) we have had the opportunity to study and conduct evaluations of several major initiatives that focus on transforming middle grades education, as well as reform efforts in a number of states and communities with similar goals. National initiatives we have

studied include the Carnegie Corporation's Middle Grades School State Policy Initiative (MGSSPI), the Lilly Endowment's Middle Grades Improvement Project (MGIP), and the Kellogg Foundation's *Middle Start* initiative. In addition, at various times, schools in the Illinois Middle School Network, the Texas Mentor Networks, the state of Missouri "Outstanding Schools" initiatives, the state of Rhode Island's statewide reform, and the Ewing Marion Kauffman Foundation's *Successful Schools Project* have all contributed to our work and data set. To date we have had more than 1,000 schools, approximately one million students, and more than 60,000 teachers participate in this work.

At the core of the study process is a set of assessment instruments completed by teachers, students, other staff, and parents. These assessments, collectively known as the *High Performance Learning Community (HiPlaces) Assessment*, were developed and selected to examine the degree to which a broad range of recommendations for effective school reform are implemented and manifest in a school as well as to examine more fully their impact on students and staff. Initially, in determining the elements of schools on which to focus we drew from such sources as the work of Seymour Sarason, the developmental literature on human ecology,

Turning Points: Preparing American Youth for the 21st Century, the work of James Comer, the Coalition of Essential Schools, the Accelerated Schools Initiative, other major reform efforts, the empirical literature and Felner's previous work. From these sources we identified a first set of constructs and dimensions of school reform to consider as they would relate to the outcomes with which we were concerned. Over the last two decades we have continuously revised and refined these instruments, based on both the emergence of new recommendations and lessons for reform (e.g., the standards movement, the work of Lauren Resnick, Fred Newmann, Michael Fullen, and others) and on the continuous testing of the model and the measures against their ability to predict and account for gains in student performance, achievement and adjustment on a broad spectrum of indices (e.g., everything from "New Standards" exams to nationally norm referenced tests to teacher provided grades, ratings, and reports of student performance and adjustment).

As a result of this work we have identified nine major dimensions that are characteristic of High Performance schools at the middle level. (Indeed, our work has shown that these same dimensions appear to hold true as characteristic of High Performance schools at all grade levels!)

What should be clear is that each of these dimensions represents a large overarching construct that cannot be directly observed but that is defined by the presence of a number of more directly observable conditions. These observable conditions or "manifest variables" can be grouped into five elements (Table 1), and it is the ways in which the specific school actually does or manifests each of these common elements in a given school that define the degree to which any of nine overarching dimensions is implemented in that school. In turn, it is the degree to which each of the nine dimensions is then implemented across the school that defines the degree of implementation of the recommendations in the model and its potential impact on students and staff. This model is provided in Table 2. Importantly, in different schools and at different grade levels the specific manifestations of a dimension may vary significantly. For example, one school may create a more personalized middle grade environments through teaming and others through self-contained classrooms.

In the remainder of this paper, when we refer to whole school change and "levels of implementation" (LOI) of High Performance middle schools, we are referring to the practices, processes, and conditions that are consistent with comprehensive and integrative gains in

Table 1. Elements that Define Implementation of High Performance Learning Community—
Dimensions in Middle and Secondary Schools and Grades

1. **Structural/organizational characteristics and conditions.** These conditions provide the opportunities for other implementation elements to emerge and change. They are necessary but in and of themselves, as for all of the other elements, they are typically not sufficient.
   Examples include: school/grade enrollment, grade configurations in the building, class size, student-teacher ratios of teams/grades, number of students a teacher is responsible for in a day, instructional grouping, block scheduling, common planning time for teachers, strategic planning time for staff, bell schedules, length of the day, span of classes covered by a team, length of class periods/school day, number of instructional and professional development days.

2. **Attitudes, norms, and beliefs of staff.** Staff buy-in, beliefs, and norms define yet another necessary but not sufficient element of each dimension. For example if staff buy-in to the professional development offered *and* they have the other necessary structural/organization opportunities and supportive climate, they may implement the practices that are addressed in the professional development. But, if they do not, such professional development experiences or content may do little good.

3. **Climate/empowerment/experiential characteristics.** The levels of stress, safety, and support for achievement, and the degree to which teachers and other staff feel empowered to make necessary decisions for effectively implementing that element are critical for a high performance school. Illustratively, teachers who are overly stressed and feel little opportunity for making instructional improvements are less likely to make and sustain changes with any degree of fidelity.

4. **Capacity/skills/professional development.** Simply put, staff and other stakeholders who do not know how to do something will not do it, or at least not do it well. For each of the nine dimensions there is a significant skill and knowledge component needed that requires adequate professional development. Teachers who are not well prepared to engage parents, to provide standards-based instruction, or to participate with community agencies, will not be able to do any of those things well if at all.

5. **Practice/procedural variables.** These are the practices, processes and procedures used in the building for instruction, decision-making leadership, administration, and staff development, parent involvement, and community involvement, building and conveying high expectations, etc. Surprisingly, this element often receives the least amount of attention or is attempted without necessary attention to the other elements. In either case practice and procedures will not change in the desired directions, and schools will fall short of maximum impact on student achievement and learning.

the dimensions and defining elements that are reflected in Tables 1 and 2. There are a number of important features of this model that respond to the critics of current middle level recommendations versus current middle level practice. Most critically, at the heart of all major recommendations for middle level education, including the integrative model we present, are calls for a high quality core curriculum that is rigorous and embedded in high expectations for all students. This stands in stark contrast to the statements of

Table 2. Common Dimensions of High Performance Learning Communities. (R.D.Felner, 1999)

- Small, personalized learning communities
- Deep, integrated standards based-instruction and curriculum
- A continuing emphasis on literacy and numeracy development at all grades and for all students
- High expectations and opportunities that promote success for all students
- Empowered decision-making at each of the appropriate system levels for each of the key stakeholders at those levels (e.g., the district, school, the team)
- Professional development that provides for teachers who are well prepared to teach the subject matter and developmental levels of students on which they focus
- A focus on fostering and addressing health and safety for all student and school-community members
- Engage families in the education of their students
- Strong school-community and school-to-work linkages

critics of middle level education who argue that such high quality instruction is not part of the focus of middle level reform or recommendations. Given this understanding why then do middle grade programs appear to their critics in the ways that fuel alternative views of middle grades as low expectation environments that lack rigor and sound instruction? What must be considered here is the *degree* to which *current practices* in many middle grade programs, whether in elementary schools, in middle schools, or in junior high schools actually reflect what most middle level educators would consider to be the recommendations for best practice at the middle level (i.e., Table

1). Critics of middle level reform argue that it is in the recommendations where the shortcomings exist. By contrast, what we have found in our work is that the deficit is in the implementation, not in the recommendations. The unfortunate reality is that most middle level programs, whatever the grade configuration of the schools they are in, fail to approximate high levels of implementation of the current state of recommendations for best practice by middle level proponents.

So, if we can now put aside the argument that the recommendations for middle level reform are responsible for the "vast wasteland" in education that the middle grades appear to be, the next question is: What happens when the recommendations are actually implemented? If the recommendations are not responsible for the problem, could they be a significant part of the solution? We have come at this question in several ways. We first examined, cross-sectionally, differences in mathematics, science, language arts, and other forms of achievement (e.g., student grades, grade-level performance in core subjects, behaviors, and adjustment), as a function of the degree to which middle grade schools and programs could be categorized at various levels of implementation by the *HiPlaces Assessment*. Next, to further explore the actual association between increasing levels of implementation and increasing levels of student achievement we then examined, longitudinally, with changes within schools (and sets of schools) that were consistent with the nine dimensions and the way that these changes impact subsequent functioning of the inhabitants of the school community (i.e., teachers, students, administrators, parents of students, and other targeted subgroups).[1] Let us briefly turn to a representative set of the findings of these analyses.

In the initial year of the representative study on which we report here, there were 11 schools in the sample. During the following school year, the number of schools was increased by 20 to a total of 31 schools, and we obtained second-year data on the 11 original schools. While the number of schools now in this particular sample has reached more than 90, the results presented below pertain to the 31 schools that were a part of this element of the Project on High Performance Learning Communities from that second year through a fifth year of the Project. Analyses of the larger samples are ongoing and preliminary results are highly consistent with those reported next. The subsample on which we report here was selected for this paper due to the availability and consistency of the achievement measures over time and the degree to which these measures have been found in our work to generalize to other widely employed measures of achievement and performance.

Employing data we had obtained about the 31 schools using the HiPlaces concerning key structures and resources, decision-making patterns, teacher norms, and instructional patterns, each school was classified into one of three levels of implementation (LOI). Briefly, schools classified as being in the highest level of implementation, relative to the other schools in the sample, were those that had accomplished the majority of structural changes "at high levels," i.e., in ways that most reflected the constructs they were intended to manifest rather than simply being present in a checklist sense. For example, schools in which teams had four to five common planning periods per week, relatively small numbers of students on the team (i.e., not more than 120), relatively low

---

[1] Univariate and multivariate correlation analyses, multiple regression procedures, multivariate analyses of covariance (MANCOVA) (and subsequent univariate analyses [ANCOVA]), and structural equation modeling are the primary analytic procedures that serve as the bases for the results reported in the remainder of this paper. They have been conducted to test for nested settings effects at multiple levels (e.g., school, grade, team).

teacher-student ratios (i.e., one teacher per 20-25 students), advisories occurring with relatively high frequency (e.g., four or five times per week), and teacher-student ratios in advisories of 20-22 or less were weighted as having more fully implemented the creation of "small communities for learning." Not surprisingly, these schools also showed critical changes in the school context and in the teaching and learning process. Schools that showed patterns of instruction, decision-making, and teacher norms consistent with the educational practices that attended to the developmental issues of adolescents also were generally included in the highest group.

Schools in the initial "partial implementation" group were those schools that had implemented at least some of the key structural changes at high levels but were not yet showing the levels of instructional and contextual changes that were typical of the high group. The schools in this group had made the structural changes either more recently or at lower levels than those in the most fully implemented group. Finally, those in the "low implementation" group included those schools that were not yet making significant progress on implementation and that looked most like traditional junior high schools in their organization and functioning.

In considering the findings that follow, the reader is again reminded that the assignment of schools to a LOI group was done on the basis of their relative similarity (within groups) and relative difference (across groups), not on the basis of some absolute scale. Moreover, in assigning schools to groups, and, more specifically, in establishing "boundaries" between groups, we also considered sociodemographic characteristics of the schools to maximize comparability of the groups. As a result, there were three sets of schools that, although clearly differing in level of implementation, are demographically comparable in terms of size, percentage of free/reduced priced lunch students served (an indication of family income), and per pupil expenditures. It is not the case, as some might suspect, that the highly implemented group are all affluent, suburban schools and the least implemented are poor, urban schools; rather, each group contains a representative mix of schools reflecting the diversity of schools in the sample.

STUDENT OUTCOMES

Figure 1 shows the average achievement scores in reading, mathematics, and language arts that were obtained by schools in each of these groups. There is a total number of more than 15,000 students and nearly 900 teachers in these schools. The average score for all schools in the State of Illinois on each of these achievement dimensions is 250 with a standard deviation of 50. The data show that across subject areas adolescents in highly implemented schools achieved at much higher levels than those in non-implemented schools and substantially better than those in partially implemented schools. Average achievement scores shown in this and later charts are a composite of sixth and eighth grade scores. The states' achievement tests are constructed so that scores across grade levels are comparable, and can therefore be averaged to create a single school-wide composite, as we have done here. It is important to note, however, that combining sixth and eighth grade scores into a single index is a more conservative test than if only eighth grade scores were used, which some would argue represents a truer assessment of the power of the conditions that appear to influence achievement. Reflecting longer exposure to these conditions, differences between groups when only eighth grade scores are used are substantially larger than with the combined sixth/eighth grade index.

A critical feature of our design is that we have attempted to obtain multiple convergent measures on aspects of both the implementation of reforms and outcomes across related dimensions.

Hence, for these initial LOI analyses there were a number of other student outcomes that were considered including additional indicators of achievement. These indicators included the percentage of students who are performing at grade level and scores in subsets of

Figure 1. Student Achievement Test Scores by Schools' Level of Implementation of High Performance Learning Communities Dimensions

Mathematics Achievement Scores

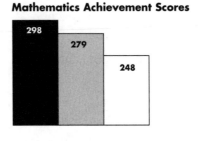

Language Achievement Scores

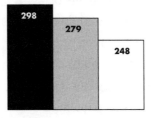

Reading Achievement Scores

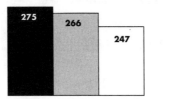

Project Initiative Middle Schools' Implementation Level of Middle Grades Practice

■ High

▨ Partial

□ None

Note: State mean = 250, Standard deviation = 50

schools that administer the Iowa Test of Basic Skills, the California Test of Basic Skills and similar nationally norm referenced assessments. Generally, these additional indicators show strong association with the state-level scores.

We also examined different domains of student outcomes as they related to the level of implementation that schools had obtained. These include teacher ratings of student behaviors as well as student self-reports of behavior, depression (fear, worry), anxiety, and self-esteem. Here the patterns of teacher reports of student behavioral problems, including aggressive, moody/anxious, and learning-related behavior problems, are highly correlated with the patterns noted earlier within achievement data, but in the desired *opposite* direction. In the most fully implemented schools, teachers report far lower levels of student behavior problems than do teachers in less implemented and non-implemented schools. Similarly, teachers in the partially implemented schools still perceive students as showing fewer behavioral problems than those in the least implemented schools. Similar patterns were found for student self-reports of a representative set of the domains of socioemotional function that were measured.

Clearly, across quite different types and sources of data (e.g., achievement tests, teacher reports, student self-reports) there are distinct differences between schools that have attained differing levels of implementation of the recommendations for High Performance middle and other schools. Such patterns are important indicators of the reliability and validity of the joint outcomes.

The above findings notwithstanding, the data reported above are limited by their cross-sectional nature. The focus of the current evaluation is a long-term longitudinal study in which we are following schools as they move *through* different levels of implementation. We will then consider the association of such changes in implementation within schools as they relate to shifts in contextual conditions and, ultimately, student achievement and related outcomes. The focal question here is, does student performance and adjustment improve as the level and quality of implementation increases over time?

As in the cross-sectional analyses, schools in the longitudinal analyses are categorized according to level of implementation. These categorizations, however, have been expanded to consider both the level of implementation obtained, as in the cross-sectional analyses, and the degree of change over the past year. Consequently, a Level 5 school is one that is non-implemented or only marginally so in the previous year and has made no changes during the current one. Level 4 would include those schools that were not or only marginally implemented in the previous year but over the intervening year had initiated planning processes and begun to make some structural changes that, while important, will in the future require further refining to be truly effective. Level 4 schools would also include those that had moved to teams of 130-150 or more students, with teachers having perhaps one to two planning periods, and where the planning did not yet reflect any instructional changes. By contrast, Level 1 schools include those that had attained the highest levels of structural changes, had implemented key changes in instruction and decision-making, and, importantly, were showing continuing refinements in these latter critical areas of teaching and learning processes and practices. These continuing refinements show that even our most fully implemented schools had, and continue to have considerable room to improve, particularly in areas of instructional change and in the extent to which HiPlaces recommendations are embraced by all teachers within the school.

A first set of analyses considered the simple correlations between changes in level of implementation across one and two year periods along with changes in reading and mathematics scores. As schools move up in their level of imple-

mentation of the recommendations of concern from 1991-92 to 1992-93, the one-year correlation of such changes with increases in eighth grade reading scores was .51 ($p < .001$) and with increases in eighth grade mathematics scores was .30 ($p < .001$). Similar patterns were found for two-year changes in implementation level and achievement scores (from 1991-1992 to 1992-1993), with correlations of .53 and .35, respectively (both $p < .001$). It is encouraging to note that longer-term analyses, if anything, tended to yield findings that were as strong and stable or stronger than did shorter-term change analyses.

Patterns similar to those found regarding achievement score gains were also found when we examined indicators of students' experiences of school climate, student adjustment, and health indices. These data complement the cross-sectional data described earlier, showing that whatever the pre-existing levels of student outcomes in these areas, as schools move through levels of implementation of the elements of middle grade reform, there appear to be associated gains in key areas of student behavior and socioemotional adjustment.

We also examined, in a comparison group fashion, the relative magnitude of the gains that were associated with differences in levels of implementation.

For these data we have four years of observations of changes in achievement scores (i.e., from the school year 1990-91 through 1993-1994. These data are available even for schools that joined after 1990-91) and attained changes in LOI from 1991-92 forward. We considered both one and two year changes in achievement scores in mathematics and reading (the most consistently available data for all schools) across LOI change and attainment categories. In all analyses of both one and two year data there were large and meaningful differences between

schools that had reached the highest levels of implementation, or those that had made the most progress toward high levels of implementation, and those schools in which little implementation had occurred and where relatively smaller LOI changes had occurred.

To illustrate the general pattern of these findings, Figure 2 shows the combined average gain in reading and mathematics scores across two sets of changes obtained by schools in each category across two years (i.e., 1990-91 to 1992-93 and 1991-92 to 1993-94).

Figure 2. Average Changes in 6ᵗʰ and 8ᵗʰ Grade Reading/Math Achievement Across Two Years

Amount of Change in Achievement Scores

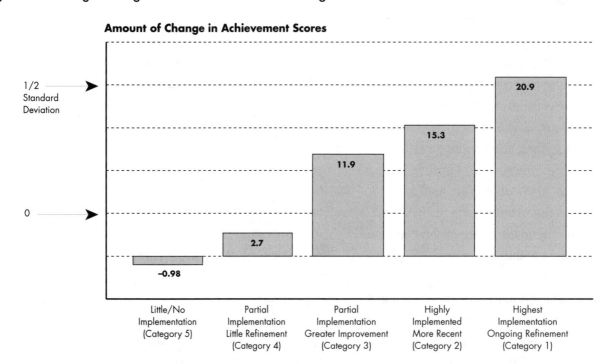

Note: All scores are the combination of the average gains in 6th and 8th grade Math and Reading achievement scores in participating schools across two, 2-year periods.

LOI attainment and change scores are based on 1994 and prior data, as 1994-95 implementation data was not yet fully available for these analyses. As can be seen in Figure 2, the average gain in mathematics/reading achievement scores across two 2-year periods in the most fully implemented schools (Category 1 described above) was nearly 21 points (recall that 25 points is a full half standard deviation on these scales). Schools that had attained high levels of implementation structurally, but had done so most recently and thus had rather moderate levels of change in the core teaching and learning processes (labeled Category 2: "highly implemented, more recent") showed average achievement gains of more than 15 points. Those schools that were not yet highly implemented, but that had shown several categories of LOI gain (labeled "Category 3 - Partial implementation, greater improvement"), had average gain scores of nearly 12 points. By contrast, schools in Category 4: "partial implementation, little refinement" (i.e., where little improvement had recently occurred) showed average gains of less than 3 points, and those schools that had made little or no movement toward implementation showed "negative" average gains scores. In other words, achievement in these schools actually declined.

Taken together, the above findings are extremely encouraging and show the potential impact on the achievement and adjustment of adolescents of the implementation of the elements of high performance middle schools that are consistent with most current recommendations for middle level practice. Yet as teachers and administrators in our Category 1 schools would quickly point out, these highly implemented schools are far from fully transformed, particularly in terms of actual changes in instruction at the classroom level. Hence, if we consider that our most fully implemented schools are only part way there, then the potential positive impact of the comprehensive transformation of a school to reflect the recommendations appears to be well beyond what we have already obtained. This is an issue we will explore further in our ongoing efforts. What will happen if schools fully implement the recommendations? How do we get there and what have we learned about the current process that can help? These are the focus of our ongoing work.

SUMMARY AND CONCLUDING COMMENTS

For the current paper and this Convocation, the results of the above analyses and our continuing work indicate clearly that it is not the recommendations for middle level best practice that have turned the middle grades into a "vast wasteland" in which our young adolescents are underachieving and failing to learn. Instead, it is the failure of schools to actually implement those recommendations and their clinging to practices that do appear to be far less effective (i.e., instruction and structural-procedural conditions that have long been characteristic of the American high school and the junior high school that seeks to emulate it) that appear to constitute the problem. It is important to note that these failed models (i.e., increased emphasis on specific, isolated course work) are in keeping with much of what is now seen as the solution to the problems of middle level achievement. Our results clearly indicate this is the wrong conclusion resulting from a poorly framed understanding of what is actually happening at the middle level.

Panel Discussion on the Organization of Schools at the Middle Grades

The panel, consisting of Stephen Gibson, principal from Patapsco Middle School, Ellicott City, MD; Mary Kay Stein, mathematics education researcher from Learning Research and Development Center, University of Pittsburgh, and Robert Felner, Director, National Center on Public Education, University of Rhode Island, responded to a set of questions prepared in light of the previous day's discussions as well as questions from the floor.

"How do you organizationally foster attention to students and, at the same time, to content, thinking of departmental structure in terms of content and a team structure in terms of students?"

Ms. Stein responded that the heavy demands of content knowledge on the part of teachers make it unreasonable to ask them to teach across all content areas. Consequently, we have to pay attention to the development needs of children within a department structure of learning mathematics. Mr. Gibson agreed and added that compartmentalizing students in a given program does not always meet the diverse needs of a student. Mr. Felner identified the issue as one of trying to serve student needs through special programs instead of understanding that the way instruction is carried out can meet students' needs. He added that the instruction for all students discussed at the Convocation is the same kind of instruction often prescribed for those identified as "gifted."

"How can we ensure that inner city and poor community middle grades children have the same opportunities as suburban and affluent to take challenging mathematics? What structure or system will support this?"

Mr. Felner indicated that there are contexts that can allow all students to do well, but we need to help teachers understand that lowering expectations as an act of kindness is not a good thing. To alibi that "it's not fair to expect this from students" aggravates the problems. Mr. Gibson reinforced the notion of raising expectations and of looking beyond where students come from to increase both teachers' and students' belief in what the students can do. He cited an example of a Saturday school program for inner city students where, when given relevant challenging tasks, the students did the work because they wanted to prove they were smart. He went on to say that we should commend those students for getting where they are without any resources; think of what they can do if they are given resources and support in using them. Ms. Stein agreed but indicated we need to understand what it means to educate children that bring varying kinds of both expertise and problems to the learning situation. She believes that we need to understand how to use assessment to inform teachers about instructional strategies with movable and flexible groups to make up for past deficiencies. We must move away from "pockets of excellence," but to do so we have to level the playing field by ensuring there are teachers of comparable quality in suburban and inner city urban schools.

"How can we structure schools that are attentive to students' differences without short changing their future opportunities?"

Mr. Gibson replied that as middle schools were developed, the initial premise did not include ensuring academic excellence; there was no attempt to make sure that middle schools were content driven. He called for research into what we know works and to avoid changing structures at will (e.g., 42 minute periods, block scheduling) without helping teachers understand how to use the structure to maximize achievement. Ms. Stein responded that the best gift possible for middle grades students is to educate them well in critical areas such as algebra so they can build confidence and move forward whatever their aspirations. Mr. Felner indicated that we have to shift to a mode where there are no acceptable casualties, something that has not ever been the presumption of American education. He used the metaphor of building cars, where in today's world we have special needs kids (Ferraris) that need to be hand built. There is a factor of ten to twelve times more to know today than yesterday. Detroit does not even try to build twice as many cars, half of which are more complex and need to be hand built, in the same number of hours and same ways with the same norms for building. While there is a public sense that schools are not doing well, he feels the contrary is true. We are doing better than ever—the level of the task keeps rising. All students need algebra today whereas in earlier years, it did not matter if some did not have it. We have to re-engineer a system in which the task is different.

The audience raised the issue of teacher turn-over within schools and within grades. Officials in North Carolina project they will need to hire 72,000 new K-12 teachers over the next eight years. How can we set up a reform environment when you do not have a stable staff to create that environment? Ms. Stein's response indicated that involving the classroom level in the organizational structure may increase the chance of keeping some teachers in the same positions. She also mentioned the need for local training institutions for new teachers so that staff development does not have to start at ground zero for every new teacher that is hired. Mr. Gibson received applause when he described his school's staff retention rate of 98% during his nine years as principal. He spoke for instructional leadership and the need to include principals as well as teachers in the conversation, matching principals to teams of teachers, and working with principals to ensure they bring growth to their staff and students.

When pushed by the audience to describe the blend of content area specialists and attention to children, Ms. Stein described the need for a teacher to understand the mathematics she teaches in a profoundly deep way and how this should be put into the foreground in teaching mathematics and in thinking about how mathematics relates to other content areas. Mr. Felner responded that a careful analysis of the NCTM standards reveals that most of the teaching processes and ways to teach students to think about mathematics are taught in all the core subjects. While it is important to have teachers proficient in mathematics on the team, teaching in an integrated unit takes people who know what they are doing and how to work together to make the integration happen. Problem situations such as Marcy's Dots should be seen by all teachers as an expansion problem, not just searching for patterns. Teaching students how to think in terms of a super structure will give them constructs around similarities and issues that can be used in any subject. Mr. Gibson believes that teachers should not look at themselves as a single entity in terms of teaching one subject but must integrate that with recognizing they are teachers in general with a vision that goes beyond their own particular subject.

Closing Remarks

REFLECTIONS ON THE CONVOCATION

Edward Silver, Chair, Program Steering Committee for the Convocation,
Learning Research and Development Center, University of Pittsburgh

Reflections on the Convocation

Adapted from the transcript of remarks by Edward Silver
Chair, Program Steering Committee for the Convocation
Learning Research and Development Center, University of Pittsburgh

Most of us came to this Convocation because we have a serious commitment to enhancing the quality and quantity of mathematics learning in the middle grades, such as the development of important algebra and geometry concepts. Most of us also came here because we have a serious commitment to addressing other needs of young adolescents such as their healthy social and emotional development. The Convocation took as a premise that this dual commitment to both the development of mathematical ideas and the development of children actually could, in many ways, mask differences in perspective regarding these two emphases; that is, individuals and groups might differ with respect to the relative emphasis of these two commitments in their work. For most of us, although both are important, one looms larger in our thinking than the other. This difference in relative emphasis has been evident in the discussions.

A second premise was that the education of young adolescents would be enhanced if we took off the mask, exposed these differences in perspective, seriously examined them in order to identify the convergences and divergences, then tried to crystallize some issues, concerns, and questions that would benefit either from some kind of concerted action or from further serious deliberation. A third premise was that it would be productive in the search for these issues, concerns, and questions, to look for them along three different dimensions—curricular, pedagogical, and contextual—and we organized this conference along these dimensions.

So now the question is: What have we learned? Several different kinds of learning might have occurred. We've identified some things we do agree on and some things we don't agree on. We have gained an enriched understanding of the issues and deeper insights into questions. We now understand some things a little deeper, a little differently than when we walked in. And we have identified some potential areas for concerted action. Finally, we have also identified a set of issues about which we need to think much harder and much longer.

In the remainder of my remarks, I'm going to give you examples of a few areas in which I think we made some progress during the meeting. Let me turn to the first one.

INTEREST AND RELEVANCE

We have broad agreement that the study of mathematics is important for young adolescents. There is also broad agreement that we want mathematics to be interesting to students. The question is, then, how do we make it interesting. We have had a set of examples presented to us that I think challenge a view (which is very prevalent these days) some of us might have held walking into this Convocation—that in order for students to be interested in mathematics, the mathematics has to be relevant. That is, good mathematics for middle grades students has to be tied to some important application or something related in some important way to students' lives.

Glenda Lappan told us on the first night that we need to connect students to things that are generally interesting

to them, and Tom Dickinson described students who were gathering data in experiments about questions that were genuinely of interest to them and then displaying the data. Students were driving the investigations and making decisions about how to display the data in the best way to answer their questions. This is a good example of what it might mean to have interesting mathematics for students.

But then, on the other hand, we saw different examples in the videos. One almost by inference in Linda Foreman's case and the other more directly in the video that Nannette Seago showed of Cindy's teaching, in which students were engaged in the investigation of mathematical ideas in problems that you could hardly call applied. They were problems that didn't come from a meaningful context. They lacked the connection to thematic or application oriented settings that many of us might take to be bound up inextricably with this notion of what's interesting to kids. There is no question that in order for young adolescents to learn mathematics, they're going to have to find it interesting. The question is what is it that makes the mathematics interesting. The videos and the discussion about the videos help to remind us that students can find mathematics inherently interesting. They can find "applied, real-world" tasks interesting, but they can also find tasks that aren't applied in the real world interesting—because these are tasks that arise within a classroom community of students who are investigating mathematical ideas about something that they value.

Yesterday, Deborah Ball talked about the notion that students' interest can be cultivated. That is, students bring their interests to the classroom, but teachers have the capacity to cultivate new areas of interest, as well. In many of the things that I've been involved with in the Quasar Project, and in the work that we're doing related to the new NCTM standards, we've been trying to grapple with this idea of how you cultivate students' interest and thoughtful engagement in classrooms. It is very clear that we have examples, some of which you saw yesterday and many of which you can see in other locations, demonstrating that students can be challenged and supported in engaging with mathematical ideas and find them quite interesting in a variety of ways.

What we should take from this is not that students should never see context nor that everything has to be embedded in context. Rather, our thinking about this issue is enriched when we reflect back on the set of examples that we saw and the way in which they represent mathematical possibilities. They show us that students are engaged when they

have interesting things to think about, and mathematics is filled with interesting things to think about. We need to give students the chance to see mathematics as being interesting and something to think about.

As I reflected on this matter of relevance and engagement, I recalled something from my first year of teaching. I taught seventh grade in the South Bronx in New York City. One of the students in my class was named Jeffrey. I want to tell you about Jeffrey. He was very pleasant, and he had learned that the way you get through school is to smile at the teacher and be polite. Jeffrey was a wonderful little boy, but academic school was not a priority for him. Nevertheless, during the year, Jeffrey, for some reason, became very, very interested in palindromes. For those of you who don't know about palindromes, a number like 1,331 is a palindrome because if you write the number forward or backwards, it's the same number. Jeffrey got very interested in palindromes not because he could apply them to his every day life, but because they struck his curiosity. Jeffrey spent most of the seventh grade in an independent exploration of palindromes. And it turns out that you can learn a lot of algebra by exploring palindromes and looking at the structures of these numbers and what happens if you multiply them by certain numbers, what happens if you combine them in certain ways, how many possibilities there are for certain forms, and so on. Jeffrey had his own independent study course going on because that's really what engaged his interest.

To bring closure about what makes it interesting for kids to grapple with mathematics, the examples we've seen at this Convocation suggest that the "interest" can be in the tasks themselves that we give students, or it can be in challenges raised by the tasks and in the process of grappling. Students can find it very interesting and can learn a lot from struggling with challenging tasks. They can derive a tremendous amount of well-deserved self-esteem from this. Mathematics is not easy. It is not always fun. It is something that's worth struggling with and worth doing well. This struggle can be a very rewarding experience, and it can be meaningful.

Now I want to draw attention to a second area that I heard as a popular topic at this Convocation—algebra.

ALGEBRA

There were many mentions of algebra in the plenary sessions, and from looking at the records from the discussion groups, it is clear that algebra came up quite frequently there. It is quite possible that some of us came to this meeting with a view of algebra in the middle grades as a course very much like the first year course in high school. That is, algebra for middle school students would mean that students in some grade before high school would take this course, whether it's eighth grade or seventh grade or sixth grade. This conception of algebra as the only notion of algebra in the middle grades was called into question by much of the discussion and many of the examples that we saw. That is not to say that one cannot have a one-year course in algebra. But even a one-year course that focuses on algebra can be different than what we might expect. If you think about the video involving Cindy, she was teaching an algebra course, but the way she was teaching that algebra course strikes me as somewhat different than our caricature of the way in which the first year of high school algebra is typically taught.

If we think about the set of ideas that Glenda talked about on the first night, the set of ideas that you might have read about in the first discussion session on algebra in the middle grades section drawn from the *Principles and Standards for School Mathematics: Discussion Draft*, or in other materials for this Convocation, you get a different view. This view suggests it might be possible to think about algebra and the development of algebraic ideas over grades six through eight in some way that doesn't require a separate course for the year we decide to teach algebra. This kind of algebra instruction would be integrated algebra, integrated with the study of numbers, with the study of geometry, and so on. This is, in fact, the approach that is represented in most of the curriculum materials that have been produced and released in recent years. Many of those materials differ in the way that they go about doing this, but they all share a commitment to trying to develop algebraic knowledge or fluency in a more integrated way throughout the middle grades rather than concentrated in a single year. This view of algebra is really quite different than the view that some of us might have had coming into this Convocation. And it is a view that challenges us to think harder about what it would mean to learn algebra in the middle grades.

Now I want to connect that to a last point which I think came through very clearly in the panel session, much more strongly than it had in earlier sessions. Good curriculum and good intentions and good practices and pedagogy may not be enough. There is a range of policy and political matters that need to be considered. As we heard this morning, other kinds of support from parents, administrators, and organizational context matter, and they matter a great deal.

There were a number of people who talked about the politics that surround reform ideas, whether they were middle school reform ideas or mathematics reform ideas. And many kinds of politics have been mentioned in this Convocation—community politics, district politics, school politics, personal politics, professional politics, and so on.

I remember from my first year of teaching when we were trying to create "open classrooms," which was then the avant-garde reform idea. But we didn't have the kind of physical space needed for open classrooms. We had a very old building with lots of walls. In response, we rearranged space and used the hallways. We arranged students in groups rather than having them sitting in straight rows of desks. But we didn't have tables—in fact, we didn't have any of the things that now are standard practice. Instead, we had individual student desks, and so the desks were organized into small groups to allow students to work together. Some students would work in different locations in the room, some out in the hallway, and so on. Every night Tom, the janitor, would come to my room, take all of the desks, whether they were in the hallway or in different corners of the room, wherever they were and arrange them into straight rows. Tom had done this for 22 years in this school. And the fact that a new teacher thought that the furniture was going to be arranged in some other way had no impact whatsoever on Tom.

Every night Tom would come and move the desks. And it quickly became a joke. The first thing the students would do in the morning was rearrange the furniture. No intervention by the principal, no discussion with Tom, nothing would have an impact on this. We did this all year long, and mine wasn't a unique case in the building. There were other teachers doing the same thing. So there is politics even at that level, let alone dealing with communities and parents and so on.

How does this relate to algebra in the middle grades? At this Convocation, we've heard that there is a pretty widespread view of algebra, what it means and how it looks. Essentially, this is the view I described as the one that many of us might have had walking into this Convocation—algebra that looks just like the first year of a high school course, all happening in one year. And if that is, in fact, the common perception of what algebra is, and if you're trying to implement some other way of teaching algebra, there's likely to be a problem because people won't understand it, whether it's Tom the janitor or whether it's Tom's great grandson who is now in your class or his grandson who's a parent in the community. There is a serious set of issues that have to be addressed in terms of unpacking for

ourselves and for the whole community what it means to say that students are learning algebra, and what it would mean for all students to learn algebra.

Can we design programs so that students succeed in learning algebra in the middle grades? Bob Felner's comment about "no acceptable casualties" is a very important one. We don't have a very good conception of what this means. Our programs in mathematics have not always been designed so that everybody could be successful with them. Mathematics education has generally been organized to find the few students who could be successful, so they could get on to the next course. Some folks are working hard to change this way of thinking, and it is now a goal for many that all students should be more successful in mathematics. But we need to recognize that there is a huge education and political job to be done in "unpacking" what it means for "all students" to learn algebra, if we want something that's different from just taking that high school course one or two or three years early. We need to develop a broad understanding of this notion of algebra with others, including administrators and parents and other members of the public. We need to systematically examine different instructional and curricular arrangements that are designed to have all students learn algebra. We have a lot of hunches and a lot of opinions about which way is best or which way will work. Many people believe that if we just did it the old way, it would be fine. But, if we could be more precise about what it is that we're trying to get students to be able to do, what it is that we want them to know, and how it is that we would like them to be able to perform, we could then ask whether or not taking that high school course one or two or three years early really meets these goals. We would also have to ask ourselves whether putting students through a well-taught version of an innovative middle school mathematics program does this. We have to push ourselves to ask this evidence question. What is the evidence that we can, in fact, produce the kinds of competence we want in our students through these different instructional approaches?

So for me, this issue has gotten no less complex. But it strikes me that this is a place where we have an opportunity to begin to work together, because I think the middle school community and the mathematics education community are both very interested in finding ways to increase the competence and confidence of students with respect to mathematics. We want all students to have the opportunities that mathematical competency and mathematical proficiency affords them. Some people call it "mathematical power." Some

people don't like that term, but that's what it's about. It's about having mathematics, owning it, having it be your own and being able to open the doors that mathematics can open. We want this to happen for students, and we want this to happen in ways that are sensitive to their needs. This Convocation has crystallized some of this for us, sharpened some of the issues, and left us with a number of other issues about which we have to continue the conversation. The issue of "mathematics for all students" is one in which we might be ready to begin to act on.

OTHER ISSUES

There are also a few other issues of note that were raised in this morning's conversation and in the discussion groups. The issue of teacher preparation was not discussed explicitly in any of the sessions but was certainly a running theme along with teacher professional development. And those two coalesce around questions about teacher shortages and turnover. Occasionally, there was mention of the special needs of students and teachers in high poverty communities. This is a very important issue that is different in rural communities and in urban communities. This plays out in the middle grades in quite different ways. The organization of schools is often different in those communities, and the ways of thinking about specialist teachers and generalists is quite different also. More conversation is needed about these issues of diversity. Racial and ethnic diversity, linguistic diversity, special needs students, and mainstreaming all need to be considered as we move forward.

Technology was strangely absent in most of the conversations, although it came up in this morning's discussions about the home-school interface in reference to students who have access to technology of a certain kind in the home, but not in school. Technology is very important for students of this age, but technology also has an impact on what's taught, how it's taught, and what the possibilities are for teacher professional development and teacher assistance. Consider, for example, the amount of help that could be provided to teachers to do a better job through the uses of technology. Some people I know in this audience are thinking very hard about that. And we need to be looking at that.

And then lastly, I want to mention the notion of identity because Mary Kay Stein talked a little bit about it this morning, and it came up very strongly in the discussion group sessions. Maybe not everybody would attach the word identity to this notion, but some participants are asking questions about how a teacher should balance attention to competing demands for a group of students. How do you balance your attention to the student with your attention to the discipline or the subject matter? How do we deal with the generalist/specialist notion? How do you balance affiliation with fellow teachers of mathematics versus membership on a cross-disciplinary team of teachers for a group of students? There are ways to frame the question that set up false dichotomies as if it has to be one or the other. Those of you who live in classrooms every day know it isn't that simple. But it is clear that how you think of yourself has an influence on what happens in classrooms. When you think of yourself as a mathematics teacher, you have a particular set of resources and colleagues as well as a set of constraints on what you do. When you think of yourself primarily as a middle school teacher, then you have a different set of resources and colleagues and so on. We have to think about ways of forming a community that has a joint identity and that helps to move the agenda of this Convocation forward.

And I just want to close by reiterating something that Steve Gibson made a point of saying this morning that we need to keep in mind. Engaging in discussions and dialogues such as we have experienced at this Convocation is the way in which we're likely to make progress. Thank you for being part of this very productive first step.

Proceedings of the
Action Conferences

Action Conferences

The National Convocation on Middle Grades Mathematics was followed by three separate Action Conferences, funded by support from the Department of Education and additional support from the American Educational Research Association. The following three papers synthesize the activities and discussion that occurred during the three conferences.

ACTION CONFERENCE ON THE NATURE AND IMPACT OF ALGEBRA AT THE MIDDLE GRADES

Organized by Hyman Bass, Columbia University

This action conference focused on providing school based decision makers with an understanding of the importance of bringing algebra into the middle grades and the issues involved in making this happen.

ACTION CONFERENCE ON RESEARCH IN THE TEACHING AND LEARNING OF MATHEMATICS IN THE MIDDLE GRADES

Organized by Sandra Wilcox, Department of Teacher Education, Michigan State University

The conference was designed around the question: What are the characteristics of research that would be helpful and informative for teaching mathematics in the middle grades?

ACTION CONFERENCE ON THE PROFESSIONAL DEVELOPMENT OF TEACHERS OF MATHEMATICS IN THE MIDDLE GRADES

Organized by Deborah Ball, University of Michigan.

The participants worked through a frame for considering the design and practice of teacher development at the middle grades, examining the ideas that drive professional development in the light of what is known and unknown about teacher learning.

Action Conference on the Nature and Teaching of Algebra in the Middle Grades

Synthesis by Bradford Findell
Program Officer, National Research Council

The Action Conference on the Nature and Teaching of Algebra in the Middle Grades brought together mathematicians, mathematics educators, middle school teachers, mathematics supervisors, curriculum developers, and others to discuss the role of algebra in the middle grades. The conference was provoked in part by recent events and policy decisions that have focused attention on algebra in the middle grades.

Perhaps most prominent among these events was the release in 1997 of results in the Third International Mathematics and Science Study (TIMSS), which indicated, among other things, that the U.S. curriculum at eighth grade is about one year behind many other countries, and that U.S. eighth graders perform, as a group, below the international average in mathematics achievement.

In the policy arena, several states recently mandated that algebra be a required course for high school gradua-tion, and the pressure has expanded into the middle grades as well. In the U.S. Department of Education's White Paper, *Mathematics Equals Opportunity*, Secretary Riley recommends, on the basis of a strong correlation with college attendance, that students take algebra or courses covering algebraic concepts by the end of eighth grade.

Despite the growing public attention to algebra in the middle grades, there has been little discussion (and perhaps little public acknowledgment) of the fact that there are more than a few possibili-ties for what algebra in the middle grades might look like. Thus, the agenda for the Action Conference was designed to bring some of these possi-bilities to light through presentations on various views of algebra and on re-search in the teaching and learning of algebra, together with practical experi-ences of teachers and districts who have been implementing some version of algebra in the middle grades. Discussion was framed by six questions (See Figure 1) that were presented by the Action Conference Organizer, Hyman Bass, a mathematician from Columbia University and Chair of the National Research Council's Mathematical Sciences Education Board.

VIEWS OF ALGEBRA

The first presenter was Jim Fey, a curriculum developer and mathematics education researcher from the University of Maryland. He began the afternoon by reminding the participants that a big factor in the debate about the role of algebra is the social and political context. Algebra serves as a gateway to post-secondary study and to scientific and technical careers. And if algebra is good in ninth grade, then it is better in eighth grade, and some think even better in seventh. But there has been little attention to what the content of algebra is or may be.

In the conventional view, algebra is primarily about calculation with symbols—Bob Davis called it a dance of symbols. And algebra is used to solve word problems. But students are not very good at the word problems that we teach them, never mind problems that they haven't seen before.

The increased availability of calculators and computers provides new demands and opportunities for the teaching and learning of algebra. We may concentrate on the design and use of algorithms, on data modeling and predictions, or on analyzing and projecting trends. Spreadsheets and other computing tools allow us to approach such ideas graphically, numerically, and symbolically.

Fey acknowledged that there is a fair amount of debate about what algebra is, but suggested the question might not be productive. Instead, he suggested that what we want from algebra are some *concepts and techniques for reasoning about quantitative conditions and relationships*. There are four major aspects of such reasoning: representation, calculation, justification, and application. Development of student understanding and skill in these areas can begin in the middle grades. With such an approach, he notes, it will not be sufficient to take high school algebra and move it into the middle grades.

Representation is about expressing complex relationships in efficient, condensed, symbolic form. Traditionally, the typical algebra question has been "What is x?" But representations such as data tables, graphs, symbolic rules, and written expressions may be used to record and describe numerical patterns, formulas, patterns that change over time, and cause and effect relationships.

Figure 1. Framing Questions

SOME IMPORTANT QUESTIONS

Attention to subject matter ↔ attention to students

1. In teaching algebra in the middle grades, what are the tensions between attention to serious and challenging mathematical content, on the one hand, and, on the other hand, sensitivity to developmental, social, and equity issues pertinent to adolescent children?

Algebra as the language of mathematics

2. If one thinks of algebra as the language of mathematics, then does the learning of algebra entail some of the same challenges encountered in the learning of reading, and therefore call for a more deliberate and focused attention to the task of teaching this formalization of mathematical expression and communication?

Real world contexts ↔ generalization and abstraction

3. Many have argued that in order to motivate student learning of mathematics, it should be presented concretely in terms of real life problems and situations. This has been interpreted by some to require that all mathematics learning be embedded in complex empirical investigations and measurements. Is this really warranted, both in terms of the presumptions about student motivation, and as effective pedagogy? Does this shortchange the equally important mathematical processes of generalization and abstraction, i.e., the distillation or decontextualization of mathematical ideas from multiple contexts?

Mathematics curriculum: covering mathematics ↔ uncovering mathematics

4. TIMMS characterizes the U.S. curriculum in mathematics as a mile wide and an inch deep. One manifestation of this is the pressure on teachers to race through an overloaded curriculum—in both standard and accelerated tracks—with little time for student reflection and inquiry with new ideas, a practice that flies in the face of what constructivist ideas tell us about the nature of learning. Is this true? And, if so, what can be done to change this condition?

Situating algebra in the mathematics curriculum?

5. How should algebra be situated in the curriculum? As a traditional focused algebra course, or integrated with other subject areas, such as geometry? As a strand across many grades?

Mathematical curriculum: materials, design, selection criteria, . . .

6. What are the characteristics of currently available curriculum materials in terms of topic coverage, pedagogical approaches, use of technology, support and guidance for teachers, etc. What kinds of tradeoffs must be made in the adoption of one over another of these curricula? How can one measure the impact of curricular choices on issues of equity, teacher preparation, community understanding, program assessment, and articulation with elementary and high school programs?

Traditional approaches to algebra have focused on symbolic calculation, but calculation can be used to construct tables and graphs of relationships, to solve equations, and to describe rates of change and optimal values; major ideas in calculus that are often disregarded by calculus students who rely only on symbolic calculation. Calculation can aid in the construction of equivalent representations for quantitative relationships. The reason the representations are equivalent is that they both make sense for modeling the same situation.

In algebra, justification, reasoning, and proof are often considered in conjunction with the properties of the number system. But the properties of the number system are the way they are because the properties make sense. It is not the case that $2 + 3 = 3 + 2$ because addition is commutative. Rather, addition is commutative because verification that they both equal 5 can be generalized to all numbers.

Finally, applications can be pervasive from start to finish, providing frequent opportunities to move back and forth between abstraction and the real world.

Fey closed by pointing out that these curricular goals should be implemented with consideration of the ways students learn. He suggested that the way students encounter these ideas must be changed from the "demonstrate, imitate, and practice" style that has dominated algebra instruction.

Al Cuoco, Director of the Center for Mathematics Education at EDC, presented a view of algebra that was closer to a traditional view, in that symbol manipulation was more prominent and the problems were more often from the world of mathematics. The emphasis was not on the manipulation, however, but rather on the ways of thinking that emerge from consideration of the historical development of the subject. Many of his points were illustrated by engaging mathematical problems.

Cuoco prefaced his presentation with an acknowledgment that the points made by Fey were important, and then offered a list of possible answers to the question, "What is algebra?"

- Algebra is an area of mathematical research.
- Algebra is the language of mathematics.
- Algebra is a collection of skills.
- Algebra is generalized arithmetic.
- Algebra is about "structure."
- Algebra is about functions.
- Algebra is about graphs.
- Algebra is about modeling.
- Algebra is a tool.

Historically, algebra grew out of a long program of mathematical research that looked for ways to solve equations—ways that didn't depend upon the particulars of the equations. Sometimes the methods for solving these equations worked in situations that had nothing to do with the original situation. People started thinking about properties of operations.

Algebraic thinking involves *reasoning about calculations*. When is the average of two averages the average of the whole lot? What is the sum, $1 + 2 + 4 + 8 + \ldots + 2^8$? Which numbers can be written as sums of a sequence of consecutive whole numbers? In Euclidean division, why do the remainders have to keep getting smaller?

Algebra involves *reasoning about operations*. Consider the following two problems:

1. Mary drives from Boston to Washington, a trip of 500 miles. If she travels at an average of 60 MPH on the way down and 50 MPH on the way back, how many hours does her trip take?

2. Mary drives from Boston to Washington, and she travels at an average of 60 MPH on the way down and 50 MPH on the way back. If the total trip takes 18 1/3 hours, how far is Boston from Washington?

The first problem can be solved by a sequence of direct computations. The second requires reasoning about operations. Students can solve it using a "function machine" computer program that allows reasoning about operations.

Triangular numbers have the recursion formula, $a(n) = a(n-1) + n$. While investigating these numbers, one student saw that $a(n) = n^2 - a(n-1)$. This is surprising enough. Cuoco wants people to see that it is useful: Add the two formulas to get the closed form.

Units digit arithmetic provides some opportunities for reasoning about calculations. What is the units digit of $24 \bullet 348^5 - 75 \bullet 33^2$? Through questions like this, students can very quickly begin to reason about the system of arithmetic modulo ten.

Some have argued that skills in symbol manipulation are less important today, but symbol manipulation is not just a skill.

> Knowledge is not a copy of reality. To know an object, to know an event, is not simply to look at it and make a mental copy or image of it. To know an object is to act on it. To know is to modify, to transform the object, and to understand the process of this transformation, and as a consequence to understand the way an object is constructed. An operation is thus the essence of knowledge; it is an interiorized action, which modifies the object of knowledge.
>
> — *Cognitive development in children: Development and learning.* (Piaget, 1964)

Symbol manipulation can also support mathematical thinking. And many important mathematical ideas, such as geometric series, the binomial theorem, and the number theory behind Pythagorean triples, require rather sophisticated symbol manipulation.

During the question/answer period, both Cuoco and Fey agreed on the importance of algorithmic thinking and reasoning about relationships. Fey elaborated that the contexts provide a series of hooks, but it is important to go beyond the individual contexts to find the commonalities among the representations of various contexts. Hyman Bass suggested that Fey's and Cuoco's approaches are not in opposition, but emphasize two different aspects of the same thing.

RESEARCH ON THE TEACHING AND LEARNING OF ALGEBRA

Orit Zaslavsky, a mathematics education researcher from Israel, began her presentation by noting that in Israel there is no debate about whether to teach algebra. Because complete coverage of the research was not possible, she decided to share an example of her own mathematical learning, which developed into a collaborative study of her graduate student, Hagit Sela, and her colleague, Uri Leron. Through this example she addressed research issues associated with teaching and learning algebra.

She asked participants first to sketch the graph of $f(x) = x$ on axes without scales, and then to sketch the graph of $f(x) = x$ on axes where the scales were different. For each case, she posed the following questions:

1. What is the slope of the line you sketched? How did you determine it?

2. Does the line that you sketched divide the angle between the two axes into two congruent angles? How do you know?

3. Can you calculate $\tan(a)$, for the angle a between the line you sketched and the x-axis? If you were able to, how did you calculate it? If not, why not?

4. Describe your considerations, reactions, dilemmas and other thoughts.

Typical graphs are shown in Figure 2. For the first graph, most participants

---

Figure 2. Typical graphs

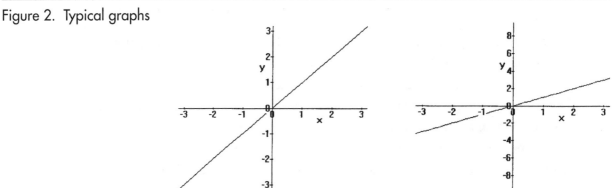

assumed that the scales were the same. Zaslavsky pointed out that most people think of $f(x) = x$ as bisecting the right angle of the coordinate system. None of the four questions were problematic for the first graph.

For the second graph, however, there was disagreement, as some participants focused on the scales of the axes and others focused on the angle visually made by the line in the first quadrant.

Zaslavsky pointed out that with the advent of graphing technologies and the possibilities for scale change, there was a sense that everything was invariant under scale changes. But she thought that there were some things that were varying—the angle in particular.

This example raised many questions: What is the slope of a linear function? What is the relation between the slope and angle? Is the slope a characteristic of a (linear) function that is independent of its representation? Or is it a characteristic of its graphical representation? (Similar questions may be asked about derivative.) Does it make sense to talk about a function without reference to its representation?

As part of a research project, Zaslavsky and her colleagues were investigating approaches to this set of tasks in various populations. Students, mathematics teachers, mathematics educators, and mathematicians all shared a sense of confusion and to some extent, inconsistency or disequilibrium. All felt a need to re-think, re-define, or re-construct meaning for what they had thought of as fundamental and rather elementary concepts: slope, scale, and angle.

In their research (as in the Action Conference) there were several qualitatively different approaches to tackling the problem. Individual people brought their own perspectives. For some, slope is a geometric concept. When the scale is 1:3, the line does not bisect the angle. For others, slope is an analytic concept, and the "fact" that the line bisects the angle is a clear result of the analytic calculation. Still others questioned the meaning of $y = x$ if the units of x are different from the units of y.

What does all this have to do with learning algebra in the middle grades? Learning is about constructing meaning. This meaning can change over time, across learners (even experts) and across contexts. The teacher should provide a rich context for building different perspectives and meanings.

In algebra, even the notion of variable has several meanings: unknown, varying, generalization, etc. Meaningful learning takes place when the learner deals with a "real problem" in the sense that the problem is real to him or her. Research supports a contextual approach in which students engage with problems to which they can relate.

The issue of representations is inherent to the learning of algebra. Students need to build meaning for graphical representations (which although visual are very often symbolic), and the connections between different forms of representation. Students need opportunities for reasoning from within representations and for translating among representations. And instruction should relate to and build on children's own invented representations.

Finally, in mathematical learning, examples play a critical role. In studying functions, for instance, the examples that children see can profoundly influence their concept image of function. Many students believe, for example, that functions are supposed to be continuous, that there can be no jumps, and that there has to be a rule.

There are different levels and ways of knowing. Learning algebra in the middle grades is just the beginning. The hope is that in high school these mathematical concepts and ideas will continue to be revisited and rethought.

IMPLEMENTATION

The morning of the second day was devoted to presentations of various implementations of algebra in the middle grades. Blanche Brownley, Secondary Mathematics Specialist from the District of Columbia Public Schools, served as moderator for presentations about the Connected Mathematics Project (CMP), University of Chicago School Mathematics Project (UCSMP), Mathematics in Context, and Saxon Mathematics. The afternoon begin with a panel discussion of more general issues of implementation and closed with a discussion of the need for research and recommendations on the role of algebra in the middle grades.

CONNECTED MATHEMATICS PROJECT

Yvonne Grant, from Traverse City, Michigan, initially participated in the Connected Mathematics Project as a field tester and received professional development through her involvement. Now she works as a teacher-coach for CMP. Traverse City's move to Connected Mathematics was prompted in part by lack of success with the previous program. The CMP program was designed and developed from the principle that all students should be able to reason and communicate proficiently in mathematics. The materials focus on understanding. The units are built upon big mathematical ideas and are organized as integrated strands of mathematics

Now after completing the CMP

program in grade eight, about half of the Traverse City students go into UCSMP Algebra, and about half go into UCSMP Geometry. The placement decision is made by students and parents because the high school often did not follow the middle school teachers' recommendations.

A central component of Traverse City's implementation effort is professional development for the teachers, which begins with an orientation in the summer. During the academic year, each teacher receives a half-day of professional development before beginning each CMP unit. Grant suggested that professional development has to evolve as teachers evolve, and described four phases in a teacher's implementation of a new program such as CMP:

- How to survive,
- Build a more comprehensive understanding of content,
- Focus on instruction, and
- Widen the view to connect with other units, other grades.

Because there are teachers who are at different places on this continuum, designing school-wide professional development activities is a challenge. The teachers in Traverse City enjoy additional support through the establishment and growth of a professional community, supported through coaching and common preparation times. The teachers also benefit from administrative acceptance and support, and because colleagues and the board of education are well-informed about the program.

Because some parents are concerned about whether students are learning their basic facts, and others are convinced that their children should be separated from the mainstream, the teachers have had to learn about how to talk to parents. It has become easier to talk to parents now that Traverse City Schools have shown some success on the Michigan Educational Assessment Program (MEAP).

UNIVERSITY OF CHICAGO SCHOOL MATHEMATICS PROJECT

Bonnie Buehler discussed the use of the University of Chicago School Mathematics Project materials at Springman Middle School in Glenview, Illinois, a suburb of Chicago. The UCSMP secondary program includes six year-long courses, beginning in grade 6 or 7 with *Transition Mathematics*, which is followed by *Algebra*, and then *Geometry*. The program emphasizes reading, problem-solving, everyday applications, and use of calculators, computers, and other technology. The UCSMP approach is called SPURs: Skills, Processes, Uses, and Representations.

In Glenview, the philosophy is that all students benefit from rigorous mathematics; they shouldn't have to wait until high school. So most students take *Transition Mathematics* in grade 7 and *Algebra* in eighth grade, though the algebra course is broader than the name implies, including a lot of geometry and what is usually called pre-algebra. About 25% of the eighth graders take *Geometry*, with an equal number of girls in this accelerated track. The emphasis on problem solving and cooperative learning seems to have helped gender equity.

Buehler said that her school provides graphing calculators, teacher materials, and a budget for outside resources, and pointed out that there have been huge achievement gains in Chicago schools using UCSMP, even in schools that have more limited resources. She suggested that teacher expectations are more important than resources.

Buehler emphasized that there was extensive staff-development during initial implementation of the UCSMP program. Now, new staff attend UCSMP conferences, and veteran teachers support new faculty. Buehler noted that teachers in Texas recently abandoned UCSMP because they didn't receive the support they needed. Support is the responsibility of the user, not of the curriculum developer, she

thought, although the materials ought to provide guidance on the need for professional development.

For information about the effectiveness of their program, Buehler mentioned that on the Comprehensive Test of Basic Skills (CTBS), the skills scores have stayed the same and the conceptual scores have skyrocketed since the implementation of UCSMP. More recently, the teachers have focused on skills for a few days before the test, and skill scores have gone up as well.

As further evidence of effectiveness, Buehler discussed Glenview schools' participation in the Third International Mathematics and Science Study as part of the First in the World Consortium, a group of school districts in Suburban Chicago. When the Consortium is compared as a country with the other participating countries, only Singapore significantly outperformed the Consortium in mathematics, and no country significantly outperformed the Consortium in science.

MATHEMATICS IN CONTEXT

Susan Hoffmier, from Weimar Hills School, Weimar, California, spoke about Mathematics in Context, a comprehensive middle-school mathematics curriculum for grades 5 through 8, developed with support from the National Science

Foundation. Connections are a key feature of the program: connections among topics, connections to other disciplines, and connections between mathematics and meaningful problems in the real world. Mathematics in Context introduces concepts within realistic contexts that support mathematical abstraction, with tasks and questions designed to stimulate mathematical thinking and to promote discussion among students.

With more than 10 years of experience in efforts to improve their mathematics programs, Hoffmier was already familiar with some of the ideas behind Mathematics in Context and with the idea that all students can achieve higher standards. After removing selection criteria for eighth grade algebra, for example, her district found that the two most important criteria for success were persistence and doing homework. Nonetheless, she was concerned when she first noticed that Mathematics in Context included linear programming and linear regression in the eighth grade curriculum. At first, she didn't believe that students could do it, but she later changed her mind when she saw how the concepts were developed beginning in the fifth grade.

Hoffmier also emphasized the need for support and professional development. Teachers meet once a month from 4 p.m. to 7 p.m. and are paid.

Once a month, teachers get a release day as a team. Teachers need to be provided with good research to support what they are doing. The school's lifeline has been involvement with university mathematics projects that provide professional development, including summer institutes and year-long seminars for teachers who want it.

School boards and parents are also a critical link to what you are doing, Hoffmier suggested. Parents have trouble helping their kids with Mathematics in Context not always because they don't know the mathematics, but because they are not willing to take the time to go back a few pages to understand the concept that is being developed. Right now, the job is complicated by the fact that the California State Mathematics Standards say that all students must have algebra described as a traditional list of skills in eighth grade.

As for resources, the manipulatives required are usually inexpensive items like string or rulers. When the Weimar Hills School was using a popular commercial textbook series, on the other hand, they bought boxes of materials at $400 per set, but the teachers received no training in how to use the materials.

So far, the achievement results have been quite positive, with 68% of the eighth graders and 74% of the seventh graders testing above the norm on the Stanford 9 Achievement Test in 1997-

1998—an improvement over previous years. This improvement was noteworthy especially because some students weren't finishing the test because they were used to using a calculator. Improvements have been more dramatic on an algebra readiness test, which indicates that many more of the eighth graders are ready for algebra.

SAXON MATHEMATICS

Stephen Hake is a teacher and also a co-author on several of the texts in the Saxon Mathematics series, a program based on the principles of incremental development and continual practice. Before discussing the Saxon materials, he responded to the statement that anyone can succeed in algebra in eighth grade through persistence and homework. In particular, Hake cautioned that some concepts and skills are prerequisites for algebra, and urged that some consideration be given to a diagnostic readiness test.

Hake expressed appreciation for the lack of a national curriculum in the United States, because of the many varied approaches and opportunities for experimentation. He argued that decisions in California and Texas are particularly worthy of attention, because those decisions shape the kinds of instructional materials that become available to the rest of the county. The text-book adoption process, for example, is sometimes merely a check-list. Instead, Hake argued, adoption decisions should be supported by efficacy studies, so that publishers will write not for the check-list, but for effectiveness. Hake emphasized that in his writing for Saxon Publishing, he wrote for his own students, working out of his own class. All he cared about was effectiveness in real classrooms.

Skills can be taught, Hake proposed, but concepts are much harder to teach, and so they must be teased out. Saxon materials ask several questions about the same concept, and ask them in different ways. That way, the concept is approached from many different angles. The primary method of instruction is through the questions that we ask students to solve.

TEACHERS AND TEACHING

The afternoon panel discussion was begun by Anne Bartel, Mathematics Project Manager at SciMath MN in Minnesota. She discussed issues that arise during implementation of a new program. Many of the issues, she pointed out, are intimately tied to people's belief systems. For example, ones vision of algebra often depends upon whether ones definition of mathematical understanding is focused on skills or whether it includes something broader like "algebraic thinking." All of today's proponents of algebraic thinking came through a skills-focused curriculum. Why then, she asked, do some teachers move to algebraic thinking while others stay focused on skills?

Bartel pointed out that the goal of "algebra for all" is undermined by peoples' commitment to past practices and varying standards for different groups of students. Some parents say, "algebra for all? Why isn't my kid still special anymore?" Others say, "If this curriculum is good enough for the kids in inner-city Minneapolis, then it is not good enough for us in the suburbs."

To overcome these beliefs, Bartel discussed various ways of marketing the message of "algebra for all" to other audiences: community advisory groups, brochures, parent meetings, posting student work in hallways, teacher to teacher conversation, and even classroom newsletters. Through any of these approaches, the message should be clear, she urged, focusing on why, what, how, and what results should be expected. By using an array of these approaches, one can acknowledge the political nature of the process of change, at the department, school, district, and state levels. At any level, one or a few people can derail change.

Bartel closed her presentation by discussing some characteristics of effective professional development. The algebra must be made explicit, because teachers don't necessarily see the algebra in integrated curricula. Furthermore, instructional strategies must be made explicit, because instructional modeling alone is not sufficient enough for teachers to see and internalize goals that are broader than skills. The professional development must be an ongoing program rather than occasional isolated workshops. Teachers should spend some time as "students" so that they might relearn algebra in new ways and make new connections. The learning environment must be safe so that teachers have opportunities to engage and discuss their learning and their prior misconceptions. The teachers should have opportunities to assess student work so that they might broaden their sense of what students can do. The primary focus should be on mathematics content and instructional strategies that promote higher-order thinking. And finally, the teachers should be given sufficient time—several years—before significant results are expected.

GIFTED AND TALENTED PROGRAMS

Vern Williams spoke from his perspective as Gifted and Talented Coordinator, Longfellow Intermediate School,

Falls Church, Virginia. He called himself a traditional teacher. Through the new mathematics and the back-to-basics movement, he managed to teach the same way.

During his presentation, Williams emphasized that there are children who need more than the norm. Truly gifted students, he said, need an emphasis on theory, structure, and problem solving. In third grade, they hear of this mystical thing called algebra. But when they get there, they realize that they've seen many of the ideas before. And then there is calculus.

Neither algebra nor calculus is a big deal for these students. They live to know why, and so we can stress proof. Students may need to know some things to prepare for the 21st century, but these students couldn't care less whether a skill or concept will help them shop at the supermarket.

These students need an algebra course in order to reach the place where they can make up their own theories. When they can tell good reasoning from faulty reasoning, then they will bring in their ideas and present them to the class.

These students need to learn problem solving; they need a course that gets them fired up about mathematics. If you give them problems that they can't do in five minutes, they will complain at first, but after a few months, they will never go back. Algebra should be offered in 7th grade for gifted and talented students. It is not as possible to get arithmetic problems that provide the same kind of engagement. Algebra opens up the universe.

If you have a successful middle grades algebra program for gifted and talented students, and you want to implement algebra for all, just don't take away the gifted and talented option. These students need to be challenged every day, not just once a week. These kids need to get to a point where they can't do a problem and need to have another student or a teacher help them. Some of the kids in MathCounts, a national mathematics contest for seventh and eighth graders, will tell you that their mathematics classes are a waste. The only challenge they get is after school. Williams believes this should happen in mathematics class.

COMMENTS ABOUT ALGEBRA AND EQUITY

Nancy Doda, Ph.D., is an Assistant Professor of Education at National-Louis University at the Washington, DC Center, who has spent much of the last ten years working in middle school professional development. After acknowledging that many of her positions were contrary to those of Vern Williams, she urged participants to stay true to principles when considering various proposals for implementing algebra in the middle grades. If we believe in the principle of curricular integration, for example, then we must ask whether it is ever appropriate to pull kids out to study algebra.

If we are concerned that gifted kids are bored in class, Doda urged, we should also be concerned about boredom for all students and in all classes. The curriculum is lifeless and dull for too many of our young people, and dull pedagogy is far more dangerous than the absence of a separate algebra class. She agreed with Williams that truly gifted kids need to be accommodated, and asked why that couldn't happen in a regular classroom.

Doda pointed out that the practicalities of scheduling often create equity issues. At many schools, for example, the algebra students are all on one team, and the students who take band are all on that same team. This creates elitist subschools that are clearly distinguishable by social class. With such separation, students are not afforded equal educational opportunities, and yet some of these schools that so schedule claim that they don't track. We lose minds by the year, Doda said, because we are so preoccupied with sorting and labeling kids. We also loose the greatest potential of democratic education which is our charge to address diversity with equity, to build discourse in that context, to create community and harmony where there is otherwise division.

RESPONSES

As Organizer of the action conference, Hyman Bass, professor of mathematics at Columbia University, led the closing discussion by focusing on several dilemmas and questions to be considered regarding the place of algebra in the middle grades. In educational discussion and debate, there is a strong tendency to polarize issues, to contrast competing perspectives. At the Convocation, the contrast was between attention to students and attention to subject matter. The question, Bass proposed, should not be which one to choose, but rather how to make decisions that pay attention to both.

How do we properly attend to the needs of students at both ends of the spectrum? Can we serve a broad range of students in the same classroom? Some participants believed that it is possible by careful task selection, by posing tasks that can be approached at multiple levels and that provide multiple branches. But does such an approach pay a disservice to "algebra for all"? Many schools provide unequal resources in sports and music. Should it be acceptable, then, to provide extra resources for students who show talent in mathematics?

CONCLUSIONS

Although the participants were aware that the action conference was not designed to draft recommendations, many participants expressed a desire for help in making decisions back in their schools and districts. Thus, the remainder of the afternoon was devoted to discussing what kinds of statements would be reasonable and useful for schools and districts who were considering implementing algebra in their middle grades.

There was acknowledgement that the array of approaches is broad and unconnected, so some participants wanted to press for more cohesion in the system. Other participants asked how policy might promote higher understanding for kids—more symbol manipulation and increased enrollment in higher level courses will not be sufficient. The remainder of the discussion fell into three broad areas: mathematics content, curricular design, and use of research.

Mathematics Content. Although the discussion was about algebra, many participants thought about mathematics content broadly, asking first, "What is the quality mathematics that all middle school children should learn?" In considering the subsequent question, "How is algebra part of this?" participants recognized that algebraic thinking has early roots and that algebra at the middle grades will likely be different from algebra at high school or at college. There was broad sentiment that our notions of algebra should expand to include the various views and approaches that were presented.

First, as a mathematical discipline, algebra has a more or less well-defined historical definition, based in the theory of equations, symbolic representation of mathematical quantities and concepts, formal manipulation of symbolic representations, and structural analysis of symbolic systems. Second, in traditional school textbooks, algebra took a form that was influenced by—but different from—the historical definition. Third, in some of the newly developed curricula, algebra has been defined as searching for patterns in data and modeling, and functions. Fourth, algebra may be seen as a tool used extensively in the sciences and more broadly in business and the workplace. These four approaches are distinct, and all are educationally viable. The choice must be based on a mixture of mathematical, historical, pedagogical, and social criteria.

Curricular design. After choosing a view of the mathematics content, there are questions of implementation of that content—i.e., where algebra is situated in the curriculum. As for the organization of the mathematics curriculum in the middle grades, the typical high school courses (Algebra I, geometry) may be transplanted down a grade or two. Alternatively, algebra might be one of several strands that are developed over a number of years in an integrated mathematics curriculum or even in an integrated mathematics/science curriculum. On another dimension, there are decisions to be made about appropriate expectations for symbol manipulation and about the interplay between abstraction and placing ideas in context.

Research. Many participants expressed a need for resources, research, and impartial observers to help in decision making. Some participants expressed the desire that decisions be informed by research, past and ongoing, on assessment and evaluation of various interventions. Other participants urged that one should also consider research on student learning, teaching, implementation, and staff development. Still others expressed a need for research on current practices. There was broad sentiment that decisions be informed by better understandings of what research says, of what can be expected from the research, and of what research needs to be done.

Because teaching and learning are very complex phenomena, much educational discussion, policy, and research employs a typical problem-solving strategy: break the problem into small pieces that we can handle. What often results from this strategy, however, are recommendations and policies that encompass necessary but not sufficient conditions for effective learning. Disaggregation of effects won't help us understand how to improve student learning; sufficiency comes from the combination. In other words, the hardest part is implementation—putting the pieces together effectively, without circumventing the central educational goals.

With so many good new ideas on the table, what kind of evidence and what kinds of conclusions can we draw about the effectiveness of changes in this very complicated educational system? And how do we compare different approaches when their goals are so different? More to the point, participants were looking for guidance on how to scale up these promising programs to realize improved mathematics learning for more students. Perhaps this action conference can provide the beginnings of answers.

Action Conference on Research in the Teaching and Learning of Mathematics in the Middle Grades

Synthesis by Sandra Wilcox
Department of Teacher Education, Michigan State University

INTRODUCTION

Currently, considerable attention is focused on middle grades education and particularly mathematics education. Results from NAEP (Reese, Miller, Mazzeo, & Dossey, 1997) and TIMSS (National Center for Education Statistics, 1996, 1997) provide overwhelming evidence that far too many youngsters in our nation's middle schools are underachieving in most areas of mathematical competence and understanding, especially in using mathematical knowledge and skills to solve relatively complex, multi-step problems. The statistics are particularly alarming for poor students and students of color. At the same time, there is growing evidence that youngsters can achieve at high levels when schools provide quality mathematics programs and teachers prepared to teach students this mathematics (Huntley, Rasmussen, Villarubi, Santong, & Fey, 1999; Hoover, Zawojewski, &

Ridgway, 1997; Hiebert, 1998).

In response to this mounting evidence, states and local school districts are developing standards that set high levels of achievement for all students. The National Science Foundation has funded several curriculum development projects aimed at creating standards-based programs of instruction. Assessment tasks and monitoring instruments are being developed for high-stakes, on-demand and classroom-based assessments that are aligned with standards-based curricula and that provide opportunities for students to show what they know and what they can do. The National Convocation on Middle Grades Mathematics Education (which preceded the Action Conference) drew over 400 educators to Washington to consider the following question: What might a mathematics program look like that is developmentally responsive, academically excellent, and that seeks social equity for all students?

Alongside the considerable activity aimed at improving mathematics curriculum, teaching and learning in the middle grades, there is a concern within the research community that major work is required to better understand and articulate the assumptions that underpin this activity. The Action Conference on Research on Teaching and Learning Mathematics in the Middle Grades was designed around the question: *How can we build a new program of research that integrates theory, research, and practice in meaningful ways for the improvement of mathematics teaching and learning at the middle grades?*

Embedded within this question are several key issues:

- What is the place of theoretical frameworks and practical problems in shaping research activity?
- What major theoretical perspectives underpin research on teaching and learning? Are some theoretical foundations less developed or less understood? To what degree is there consensus?
- What role do problems of practice play in research?
- If research is situated in, grows out of, and informs theory and practice, how can we better articulate the relationship or interface among theory, research, and practice?

The Action Conference brought together approximately 30 professionals including mathematics educators and teachers, mathematics education researchers, curriculum developers, administrators, and representatives from the National Science Foundation and the Department of Education. The group was charged with:

1. making suggestions to those in the field about what further research is needed, and

2. advising the Department of Education and the National Science Foundation who will jointly issue a paper and an RFP for an upcoming funding initiative, on where strategic investments in research might be made.

Several experts were invited to make presentations that would tease out some of the complexity in tackling these issues. The invited talks were organized to move from broad theoretical and practical issues on how to address research to specific research efforts (one on learning using the case of rational number and proportional reasoning, the other on linking research on teaching to research on learning in the context of teachers' use of cognitively challenging problems), to the applications of research knowledge to recent curriculum development projects.

SUMMARY OF INVITED PRESENTATIONS

Useful features of research.

James Hiebert described a tension between solving practical problems and doing good research (Hiebert, 1999; Stigler and Hiebert, 1999; Greenwald, Pratkanis, Lieppe, and Baumgardner, 1986). Hiebert identified three sources of the tensions:

- perceptions of minimal impact of research on solving problems of practice, fueled by inadequate communication to interested audiences, particularly the challenge of talking to the general population about what we know,
- confusion between values, which research cannot settle, and empirical issues; and
- a genuine dilemma that is inherent in the research process, the tension between addressing daunting, complex problems and doing good research.

Hiebert suggested a framework to better understand and resolve tensions by moving research from:

- what works to understanding what works;
- critical experiments to continuing programs of research;
- feature-based to system-based classroom research;
- researcher-driven to a teacher-driven research and development enterprise.

Building a stronger theoretical base for and through research.

Alan Schoenfeld responded to Hiebert's comments by proposing a schema around the space of issues embedded in the question "What are the characteristics of research that would be helpful and informative for teaching mathematics in the middle grades."

Schoenfeld suggested that the current state of theoretical work on understanding schools, students, teachers, and instructional materials and the relationships among them is uneven; so too is the research base and the degree to which underlying assumptions have been articulated or justified. He argued that major work is needed on:

- continuing the study of learning, focusing on key concepts,
- basic and applied studies of teaching in context, which should lead to theories and models of teaching, knowledge trajectories, theories of competence, of change, and of development,
- principled research and development studies of materials development that yields knowledge and principles, and

Figure 1. A Schematic Representation of the Space of Issues

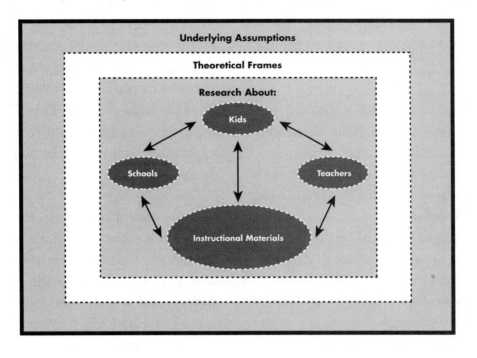

that is tied to research on students and teaching,

- integrating work at the policy level with all of the above.

Problem-driven research. Mary Kay Stein drew on her work in the QUASAR project to highlight how research often grows out of and attempts to solve problems of practice (Stein, Grover, Henningsen, 1996; Henningsen and Stein, 1997; Stein and Lane, 1996). Drawing on her study of teachers' use of cognitively challenging problems as a case of linking research on teaching to research on learning,

Stein argued that classroom-based research can:

- uncover and illuminate patterns of teaching practice that may be problematic in terms of student learning,
- contribute to better understanding and describing these practices, and, in turn,
- be helpful in designing interventions to reshape practices that better support student learning.

Research on a big idea in the middle grades curriculum. Richard Lesh focused his remarks less on the considerable research knowledge produced by colleagues in the Rational Numbers Project and instead commented on how their thinking has been changing. Key points included:

- There is no ladder or stages of development through the middle grades curriculum, but rather many interlinked concepts and representational systems that we need to better understand.
- We need to be more explicit about the big ideas in the middle grades curriculum and figure out how to present those ideas in ways that parents and the community understand.
- Using what students are doing with high-quality tasks in classrooms may be a useful site for the professional development of beginning and experienced teachers.

Using research to shape curriculum design. James Fey and Koeno Gravemeijer, developers on the Connected Mathematics Project and the Mathematics in Context Project, respectively, described the ways and the extent to which research on rational number and proportional reasoning shaped design decisions in their projects.

Fey noted that many theoretical ideas (e.g., constructivism, conceptual and procedural knowledge, multiple representations, research on coopera- tive learning, teacher change and school change) guided the development of the grade 6–8 Connected Mathematics curriculum. In the area of proportional reasoning, the design- ers drew on research and theory in the literature where it seemed useful, as well as their own earlier curriculum experiences in this area (Lambdin and Lappan, 1997).

Gravemeijer described the influence of the developmental research con- ducted at the Freudenthal Institute on the design of Mathematics in Context. Specifically, the curriculum is undergirded by a theory that children learn mathematics by mathematizing their own activity. The theory of instruction embodies a cyclic process of spiraling through thought experi- ments (about student thinking) and teaching experiments, where teachers develop their own theories of learning for their classrooms. The developers drew heavily on the work of Streefland in the area of rational number (Gravemeijer, 1998).

Fey emphasized that as curriculum developers, they needed to know how well their materials worked for purposes of improving the product. He argued that the classrooms in which new curriculum materials are used provide opportunities for research and for testing the robustness of our theories. He suggested two kinds of activity:

- Studies of implementation—e.g, how do teachers interpret the intent of the materials and how does this shape their use of the materials; what is the relation between teachers' knowledge and their practice; what role does context play and what features are particularly salient.
- Studies of student learning—what do these materials contribute to deepening students' understanding of big ideas.

Echoing earlier comments, Fey noted that conducting research on either is messy.

Deepening teachers' knowledge of mathematics

It is well known that a serious impediment to improving the learning opportunities for youngsters is teachers' own lack of mathematical knowledge. Judith Sowder presented findings from a two-year project aimed at having teachers explore some of the complex mathematical ideas that are typically a part of the middle grades curriculum (Sowder, Philipp, Armstrong & Schappelle, 1998; Sowder & Philipp, in press; Fennema, Sowder, & Carpenter, in press; Thompson, 1995). While the outcomes of this study were very encouraging (e.g., teachers began to see questioning as a teaching approach and started to listen to their students more closely), the number of participants (5 teachers and a team of

researchers) raised issues about the costs of taking this level of work to scale.

RECOMMENDATIONS FROM THE PARTICIPANTS

The participants made recommendations in three areas: teaching and teacher learning; student learning; and communicating with a variety of interested constituencies.

Teaching and teacher learning

1. Especially in the light of international comparisons, it is essential to rethink both theoretical and pragmatic assumptions about the nature of professional competency and growth, beginning with pre-service experience and continuing through the development of true competency.

2. We need models of teaching that help us better understand how teaching works, and what kinds of knowledge, beliefs, and goals lead or enable teachers to do or not do certain things.

3. We need to better understand the bases of "good teaching," including the bodies of knowledge that are central to "good teaching" (e.g., teachers' knowledge of mathematics, of students, and of students' understanding of mathematics; learning how to listen to students).

4. We need models of how to improve teaching that include descriptions

of trajectories for teachers' professional growth (what is appropriate to learn at different points in a teacher's career), how to support communities of inquiry for continuing professional growth.

5. We need to better understand what the system needs to be like, in order to take the best prepared novice and support her/him.

6. We need to better understand what makes rich teaming environments for teachers (including standards-based curriculum materials), what they learn in these environments, and how to scale up this activity. This includes understanding productive connections between research and professional development.

7. We need to develop research tools and methodologies for examining and describing complex settings like classrooms.

8. We need to enlist teachers as colleagues in developing knowledge about these issues.

Student learning

1. We know a lot about student thinking in some domains of the middle grades curriculum. We need to expand this knowledge to other content areas as well as across content domains

2. Much of what we know about student thinking has unstated premises (e.g., social and instructional conditions are assumed) and we need to be ready to question what we know.

3. We need to broaden the "we" in the research community. We may learn that there is more shared knowledge than there is shared theoretical commitment.

4. We need to combine model building with model testing.

5. We need to better understand whether and in what ways reform curricula support the development of mathematical power for all students, particularly poor students, students of color, and students with special needs.

6. We need to look at good teaching as a context for student learning.

7. We need to learn more about distributed learning communities, and about the relation of individual thinking to shared social practice.

Communicating with various constituencies

Here we raised a number of issues.

1. Who are we doing research for?

2. What does it mean to do systematic research? What is the role of collaboration between teachers and researchers?

3. Does our research address problems that are widely recognized as significant? Do we know the concerns that parents have and how concerns change?

4. How do we package what we believe is useful and compelling for others (e.g., school boards, parents, community)? How do we present data that is credible and acceptable to the public?

REFERENCES

Fennema, E., Sowder, J., & Carpenter, T. (in press). Creating classrooms that promote understanding. In T. Romberg and E. Fennema, (Eds.), *Teaching and learning mathematics with understanding.* Hillsdale, NJ: Erlbaum.

Huntley, M.A., Rasmussen, C.L., Villarubi, R.S., Sangtong, J., & Fey, J.T. (in press). Effects of *Standards*-based mathematics education: A study of the Core-Plus Mathematics Project Algebra/Functions strand. *Journal for Research in Mathematics Education.*

Gravemeijer, K. (1998). Developmental research as a research method. In A. Sierpinska and J. Kilpatrick (Eds.), *Mathematics education as a research domain: A search for identity* (An ICMI Study Publication, Book 2 (pp. 277-295). Dordrecht, The Netherlands: Kluwer Academic Publishers.

Greenwald, A., Pratkanis, A., Lieppe, M., & Baumgardner, M. (1986). Under what conditions does theory obstruct research progress? *Psychological Review*, 93, 216-229.

Henningsen, M., & Stein, M.K. (1997). Mathematical tasks and student cognition: Classroom-based factors that support and inhibit high-level mathematical thinking and reasoning. *Journal for Research in Mathematics Education*, 28(5), 524-549.

Hiebert, J. (1998). Aiming research toward understanding: lessons we can learn from children. In A. Sierpinska & J. Kilpatrick (Eds.), *Mathematics education as a research domain: A search for identity.* Dordrecht, The Netherlands: Kluwer Academic Publishers.

Hiebert, J. (1999). Relationships between research and the NCTM *Standards. Journal for Research in Mathematics Education.*

Hoover, M., Zawojewski, J., & Ridgway, J. (1997). Effects of the Connected Mathematics Project on student attainment. www.mth.msu.edu/cmp/effect.html.

Lambdin, D., & Lappan, G. (1997, April). Dilemmas and issues in curriculum reform: Reflections from the Connected Mathematics project. Paper presented at the Annual Meeting of the American Educational Research Association in Chicago, IL.

National Center for Educational Statistics. (1996). *Pursuing excellence: A study of U.S. eighth-grade mathematics and science achievement in international context.* Washington, DC: Author.

National Center for Educational Statistics. (1997). *Pursuing excellence: A Study of U.S. fourth-grade mathematics and science achievement in international context.* Washington, DC: Author.

Reese, C.M., Miller, K.E., Mazzeo, J., & Dossey, J.A. (1997) *NAEP 1996 mathematics report card for the nation and the states: Findings from the National Assessment of Educational Progress.* Washington, DC: National Center for Education Statistics.

Sowder, J.T., Philipp, R.A., Armstrong, B.E., & Schappelle, B. (1998). *Middle grades teachers' mathematical knowledge and its relationship to instruction.* Albany, NY: SUNY Press.

Sowder, J.T., & Philipp, R. (in press) The role of the teacher in promoting learning in middle school mathematics. In T. Romberg & E. Fennema (Eds.), *Teaching and learning mathematics with understanding.* Hillsdale, NJ: Erlbaum.

Stein, M.K., Grover, B.W., & Henningsen, M. (1996). Building student capacity for mathematical thinking and reasoning: An analysis of mathematical tasks used in reform classrooms. *American Educational Research Journal, 33*(2), 455-488.

Stein, M.K., & Lane, S. (1996). Instructional tasks and the development of student capacity to think and reason: An analysis of the relationship between teaching and learning in a reform mathematics project. *Educational Research and Evaluation, 2*(1), 50-80.

Stigler, J.W., & Hiebert, J. (1999). *The teaching gap.* New York: Free Press.

Thompson, P. W. (1995). Notation, convention, and quantity in elementary mathematics. In Sowder, J.T., & Schappelle, B.P. (Eds.). *Providing a foundation for teaching mathematics in the middle grades* (pp. 199-219). Albany, NY: SUNY Press.

Action Conference on the Professional Development of Teachers of Mathematics in the Middle Grades

Synthesis by Megan Loef Franke, University of California, Los Angeles and Deborah Ball, University of Michigan

National attention to teaching, higher student achievement, and the need for more and better-qualified teachers is on the rise. Professional development and teacher education are of increasing interest and concern.

All the concern for professional development is occurring at a time when views on teacher learning continue to evolve. The change that teachers are being asked to make in order to enact standards-based reforms are ambitious and complex (Little, 1993; Cohen and Hill, 1998). Little points out that the current reforms require teachers "to discover and develop practices that embody central values and principles." Here teachers are seen as learners, "teaching and learning are interdependent, not separate functions... [teachers] are problem posers and problem-solvers; they are researchers, and they are intellectuals engaged in

unraveling the process both for themselves and for [their students]" (Lieberman & Miller, 1990).

The Action Conference on Professional Development was designed to afford an opportunity to examine promising approaches to professional development.

The premise was that extant knowledge about professional development is underdeveloped. Ideology and belief all too often dominate practice and policy. The Conference was intended to create an analytic and practical conversation about the sorts of opportunities in professional development most likely to lead to teachers' learning and improvements in their practice. With a focus on mathematics at the middle grades, the structure of the Action Conference was grounded in analysis of the practice of teaching middle grades mathematics, considering the major tasks teachers face and what knowledge and skill it takes to perform those tasks. This analysis of teaching practice was used to take a fresh look at the kinds of opportunities for learning that teachers need.

What does teaching demand of teachers and what does this imply for teacher learning?

Deborah Ball, as conference leader, framed the workshop discussion with the diagram (Figure 1). Ball pointed out that the focus of the discussion throughout the workshop would be from the vantage point of teacher educators, and would consider sites through which teachers might most profitably learn mathematics content needed in teaching, based on tasks which teachers regularly do as part of their teaching. Participants observed that the diagram helps make clear that the content to learn becomes more complex at each level. Schoolchildren are learning mathematics. Teachers are learning about mathematics, but also about children's learning of that mathematics, and about the teaching of that mathematics. The diagram does not incorporate all elements of what would be needed in a national infrastructure for systemic change. It depicts relations among learning mathematics, learning to teach mathematics, learning to teach about the teaching of mathematics.

Ball indicated that mathematicians,

mathematics education researchers and teacher educators have all created lists specifying knowledge for teachers. Although these lists enable professionals in the field to discuss content in professional development, these lists are not grounded in an analysis of the work of teaching. Such lists tend not to consider questions about the mathematical content knowledge that is necessary in the context of teaching or the knowledge of mathematics required when teaching extends beyond how to add fractions or identify geometric patterns. It includes being able to frame a mathematically strategic question, come up with the right example, construct an equivalent problem, or understand a child's non-standard solution. The kind of mathematical knowledge it

Figure 1. Teaching, Learning, and Learning to Teach Mathematics

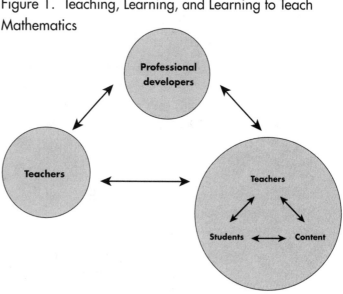

takes to teach a problem goes beyond knowing the content that the students are learning, and includes the capacity to know and use mathematics in the course of teaching.

Participants considered the implications of this perspective on mathematical knowledge. In the practice of teaching, the teacher's mathematical knowledge is called upon in many different ways in figuring out what a student means, in listening to what students say, in choosing and adapting mathematical tasks, and in knowing whether the students are understanding. How do teachers use their knowledge of the content, their knowledge of pedagogy and other knowledge in an interaction with their students? How do they decide which students' ideas to pursue? How do they decide which paths will further the particular content in which they are engaged? How do teachers decide what a student means by a question or an answer, or judge whether students actually understand the concept in question? It is in these interactions that knowledge of the content is critical.

Ball, together with Joan Ferrini-Mundy, Center for Science, Mathematics and Engineering Education at the National Research Council, led an activity designed to engage participants in considering mathematics knowledge as it is used in one task of teaching. Ball presented a mathematics problem and asked participants to solve the problem and to describe the mathematical territories into which it might head.

> I have some pennies, nickels, and dimes in my pocket. I put three of the coins in my hand. How much money could I have?
>
> — (NCTM, 1989)

Having analyzed the mathematical territory of the problem, participants were then asked to make a "downsized or upsized version" that was mathematically similar in structure. The participants considered what students might say or do. Was making the problem more complicated numerically a means of "upsizing"? What did it mean to make a "similar" problem, and what sorts of mathematical knowledge and reasoning did it take to do this? Participants discussed different versions of the problem and considered the mathematics they used to create and evaluate them.

What do we know about professional development, teacher learning, and the improvement of practice?

Although there is a lot of professional development in the U.S., much of it is ineffective. Approaches to professional development in the U.S. are often fragmented and incoherent, with little basis in the curriculum teachers will have to teach. Much professional development centers around features such as manipulatives or cooperative groups rather than on the substance of improving students' mathematics learning. Generally, evidence about the effects of professional development on student achievement is scattered and thin. Too often, professional development is defined by belief and propagated by enthusiasm. Some professional development works, but there is a large gap even between effective professional development and changes in practice.

Often teachers view the focus of mathematics professional development as engaging in process: learning how to be a mathematics teacher or figuring out what the process of teaching should look like. Yet as teachers identify process goals, the substance of the process is left unchallenged. Teachers need opportunities to think about how the processes in which they engage serve the students' learning as well as their own, how the processes relate to the mathematical ideas, student thinking, and mathematical discourse.

As one example, Ball cited the Cohen and Hill (1998) study in California that found that professional development that was grounded in the curriculum that teachers had to teach—that is, provided teachers with opportunities to learn about the content, to learn how children think about that same content, and to learn ways to represent that content in teaching—made a significant difference in student scores. Their findings indicated that professional development that made a difference provided opportunities to learn that

- grounded content in the student curriculum;
- were about students' thinking about that content;
- were about ways to connect students and content;
- and were situated in context, materials, and sites of practice.

OPPORTUNITY TO LEARN SITUATED IN SITES OF PRACTICE

The Action Conference explored the promise and potential problems of situating opportunities for teachers' learning in practice. Much teacher professional development offers teachers the opportunity to learn a new idea or activity and transfer that idea to their classroom. Professional development focused on helping teachers develop expertise within the context of their practice emphasizes the interrelationship of ideas and practice. Some professional developers engage teachers with cases of teachers engaged in teaching mathematics and discuss what the teacher did and why. Some professional developers engage teachers in the curriculum that they are going to teach and use that as the practice context, while others engage teachers with video examples of classroom mathematics practice, or some with student work. Each of these situates opportunities for teacher learning in practice. In each case the teacher is pushed to consider how the mathematical ideas play out in the context of teaching mathematics, and they are compelled to consider the details related to the students' thinking, the nature of the mathematics and its relation to their instruction. Each of these approaches affords opportunities for learning. Each holds pitfalls that might impede such learning. Critical questions then are: How might the potential affordances be exploited? How might the potential pitfalls be managed? To learn more about what people are trying and how it is working, and to sharpen the ability to examine their own designs and practices as professional developers, participants engaged in several examples of professional development projects.

WRITTEN CASES

Margaret Smith, Pennsylvania State University, engaged the participants in a case study of student work (The Case of Ed Taylor; Smith, Henningsen, Silver, & Stein, 1998) and worked through the S Pattern Task (Figure 2). Analyzing student responses led the participants to discuss the importance of the mathematical knowledge of the teacher in analyzing the mathematics students do. The participants offered the following potential affordances for professional developers using cases as a medium for learning. Cases offer the possibilities of metacognition about the mathematics, provide an in-depth look at the mathematics because the student thinking in the case is visible; provide the opportunity to study the particular mathematics involved in the case in context, provide an opportunity to read mathematics, can be used in many ways with different groups including administrators, and create opportunities to learn mathematics in teaching. Potential pitfalls included the challenge of asking questions that focus on the mathematics, focusing more on pedagogy than the mathematics, making the best use of time, hard to read mathematics, and the fact the teachers may not know the mathematics.

CURRICULUM-MATERIALS

Karen Economopoulos, TERC, engaged participants in an experience designed to show how curriculum materials might serve as a site of practice where teachers might learn mathematics in their work. Economopoulos posed two

Figure 2. The S Pattern Task

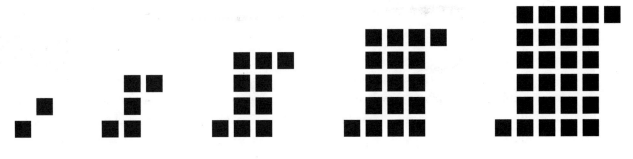

a. Sketch the next two figures in the S Pattern.
b. Make observations about the pattern that help describe larger figure numbers in the pattern.
c. Sketch and describe two figure numbers in the pattern that were larger than 20.
d. Describe a method for finding the total number of tiles in the larger figure numbers.
e. Write a generalized description/formula to find the total number of tiles in any figure in the pattern.

questions for reflection and discussion: How might curriculum materials such as these offer professional development opportunities for teachers? How might these materials influence or support a teacher's daily decisions? Potential affordances to exploit suggested by the participants included: The material speaks directly to the teacher; the mathematics is very near the surface, new materials generate thinking and learning. It is possible for administrators to see more depth in the mathematics. Materials can provide the opportunity to see a broader view of mathematics. Materials can move the mathematics preferred by the teacher forward. Continuity is built into the lessons; the common material promotes communication among the teachers. The pitfalls to be managed included the following: It is easy to turn the search for the mathematics into a make-and-take situation devoid of thinking. If teachers do not understand the content, using the materials to focus on the mathematics might increase frustration levels. Re-learning familiar materials might result in resistance. In some tasks, it might be easy to avoid the mathematics.

VIDEOTAPES OF TEACHING AND LEARNING

Nanette Seago, Mathematics Renaissance Project, engaged participants in examining a videotape of a professional development workshop, "Facilitating the Cindy Lesson Tape." The teachers had previously viewed a videotape of an eighth grade math lesson. The tape provided an opportunity to consider the challenges of using videotape as an instructional medium in professional development. Watching this video focused on the task of "facilitation" of a teacher group discussion and raised explicit issues about the challenges of keeping the professional development work centered on specific learning goals—teachers' learning of mathematics, for example. There was considerable interest expressed in the potential of videotape as a medium and discussion about its role in helping teachers think about their practice. Seago encouraged the viewers to think back to the framing diagram of the conference and the use of video in the context of teachers as learners. Affordances cited included the opportunity to look at a shared instance of teaching, to see mathematics in use by teachers and students. Some of the pitfalls included the problem of keeping teachers focused on particular content, questions about the quality of the teaching portrayed, and the difficulty of concentrating on the mathematics in the midst of the many other things to watch.

REFLECTIONS ON THE IMPROVEMENT OF PROFESSIONAL DEVELOPMENT

A panel, moderated by Mark Saul, from Bronxville Public Schools, consisting of Iris Weiss, Horizon Research; Stephanie Williamson, Louisiana Systemic Initiative; and John Moyer, from Marquette University, reacted to the issues raised at the Conference through the lens of their experiences. Weiss, from the perspective of large scale research about implementation, argued for the need to help teachers develop some way to filter and make decisions. She also raised a concern about the issue of scale; how to move from a teacher and a classroom to the system, and in the process, the need for a central vision and coordination and for some form of quality control. Weiss indicated her belief that the issue is a design problem. Professional development models designed for a best case or for small numbers do not work when scaled up. Moyer, reflecting on professional development done with urban, large city middle grades teachers, indicated that scaling up had to be done creatively and in small steps. Leaders who had been developed from earlier small projects became facilitators in the larger one but also remained as part of the cadre of learners. He observed that one of the most successful efforts was to observe teachers as they taught, with the observer writing down what the teacher said. When the observer later asked why the teacher had used those words, the teachers began the process of reflection on their practice that led to some lasting changes. Williamson described the work done in the state of Louisiana through the National Science Foundation funded LASIP systemic initiative and the focus on teacher content knowledge. Williamson noted that the guidelines for the program require collaboration among school systems and universities and stimulated partnerships among K-12 and higher education. An outgrowth of the programs has been the development of a "Core of Essential Mathematics for Grades K-8" that focuses on growth of important ideas across grade levels and is now guiding decisions for both professional development and preservice programs about what teachers need to know and be able to do to teach these concepts in depth.

At the close of the panel, Nora Sabelli from the National Science Foundation discussed the new opportunities for research on middle grades mathematics in the Department of Education/ National Science Foundation Research Initiative. She indicated that the focus of the initiative will be on long-term agendas, strategic plans for implementation, and ensuring that there is the human, methodological and institutional capacity for converting schools into learning communities.

SUMMARY

Participants discussed the lack of opportunities for professional development leaders to engage in the study of professional development. As a consequence, professional developers must use their work with teachers as sites for ongoing learning and research as they create opportunities for teachers to learn working to ensure that those opportunities impact teachers' knowledge and practice as well as student achievement. Professional developers are expected to work with large numbers of teachers and do so quickly. Under these conditions, professional developers have the opportunities to see themselves as learners. The Action Conference did, however, take seriously professional development as a field and attempted to create a frame for thinking about theoretical, research, and practice-based learning.

Most professional development providers are convinced that the approaches they take enable teachers to learn and students to benefit; otherwise, they would not pursue the approaches. However, little is known about what various approaches afford or do not afford, especially in relation to classroom practice and student achievement. Little is known about the details of the various approaches to professional development. The message as the field considers the issues raised at the Conference is to reflect on the circle of learners and on their relation to middle grades mathematics and to each other, to design research studies around professional development approaches, and to think deeply about the mathematics middle grades teachers need to know to teach well and how they can come to know that mathematics for themselves.

REFERENCES

Cohen, D.K., & Hill, H. (1998, January). State policy and classroom performance: Mathematics reform in California. *CPRE Policy Briefs*. Philadelphia, PA: University of Pennsylvania.

Lieberman, A., & Miller, L. (1990). Teacher development in professional practice schools. *Teachers College Record, 92*(1), 105-122.

Little, J.W. (1993). Teachers' professional development in a climate of educational reform. *Educational Evaluation and Policy Analysis, 15(2)*, 129-151.

National Council of Teachers of Mathematics. (1989). *Curriculum and evaluation standards for school mathematics*. Reston, VA: Author.

Smith, M., Henningsen, M., Silver, E.A., & Stein, M.K. (1998) The case of Ed Taylor. Unpublished document, University of Pittsburgh.

PARTICIPANT BACKGROUND MATERIAL

Ball, D.L. (1997). Developing mathematics reform: What don't we know about teacher learning—but would make good working hypotheses. In Friel, S., & Bright, G. (Eds.), *Reflecting on our work. NSF Teacher Enhancement in K-6 Mathematics* (pp. 79-111). Lanham, MD: University Press of America.

Good Teaching Matters (1998). *Thinking K-16*. Vol 3, Issue 2. Education Trust.

Rhine, S. (1998, June-July). The role of research and teachers' knowledge base in professional development. *Research News and Comment* (pp. 27-31).

Appendices

Appendix 1

Convocation and Action Conference Agendas
National Convocation on Mathematics Education
in the Middle Grades

National Academy of Sciences/National Research Council
2101 Constitution Avenue, NW, Washington, DC
25-27 September 1998

AGENDA

Friday, 25 September 1998

4:00 p.m. - 7:00 p.m.	Registration	**2100 C Street**
6:00 p.m. - 7:00 p.m.	Cocktail Reception and Light Dinner	**Great Hall**
7:00 p.m. - 7:30 p.m.	Opening Session	**Auditorium**

Introductions
Edward Silver, Professor of Instruction and Learning, University of Pittsburgh, and Chair, Program Steering Committee

Welcome
Bruce Alberts, President, National Academy of Sciences
The Honorable C. Kent McGuire, Assistant Secretary for Educational Research and Improvement, U.S. Department of Education

7:30 p.m. - 8:30 p.m.   Teaching and Learning Mathematics at the Middle Grades: Setting the Stage
Glenda Lappan, President, National Council of Teachers of Mathematics
Tom Dickinson, Indiana State University

8:30 p.m.   Adjourn for the day

Saturday, 26 September 1998

7:30 a.m. - 8:30 a.m.	Registration (continued)	**2100 C Street**
7:30 a.m. - 8:30 a.m.	Continental Breakfast	**Great Hall**
8:30 a.m. - 9:00 a.m.	Morning Session	**Auditorium**

Welcome
Edward Silver
Remarks, Luther Williams, Assistant Director, Education and
Human Resources Directorate, National Science Foundation

9:00 a.m. - 10:30 a.m. Content and Learning Issues in the Middle Grades
Presider: Catherine Brown, Associate Professor of Curriculum and
Instruction, Indiana University
Nancy Doda, Professor of Education, National-Louis University
Katherine Hart, Professor, School of Education, University of
Nottingham, England

- What developmental considerations are important in thinking about middle school students as learners? as learners of mathematics?
- What do we know about middle school students' capacity for learning? for learning mathematics?
- What are important ideas in mathematics for the middle grades and how are these related to developmental learning considerations?

10:30 a.m. - 11:00 a.m.	Break	
11:00 a.m. - 12:30 p.m.	Discussion Sessions	**Assigned Rooms**
12:30 p.m. - 1:30 p.m.	Lunch	**Great Hall**

(TIMSS video will be available for viewing in the Auditorium)

1:30 p.m. - 3:45 p.m. Teaching Issues in the Middle Grades: Auditorium
Classroom Practice
Presider: Katherine Rasch, Dean and Professor of Education,
Maryville University
Nanette Seago, Project Director, Video Cases for Mathematics
Professional Development Project
Linda Foreman, Middle School Classroom Teacher and
Curriculum Specialist, Mathematics Learning Center, Portland
State University

Panel:

Hyman Bass, Professor of Mathematics, Columbia University

Deborah Loewenberg Ball, Professor, School of Education,
  University of Michigan

Sam Chattin, Science Teacher, William H. English Middle School,
  Scottsberg, Indiana

- What are the important characteristics of effective teaching in the middle grades? of effective teaching of mathematics in the middle grades?
- How can instruction in middle grades classrooms be organized to maximize learning? How can we tell when learning is happening?
- What tools and strategies will make a difference in how middle grades students learn mathematics?

3:45 p.m. - 4:00 p.m.	Break	
4:00 p.m. - 5:30 p.m.	Discussion Sessions	**Assigned Rooms**
5:30 p.m. - 6:00 p.m.	Teams meet	**Assigned Rooms**
6:00 p.m.	Adjourn for the day, dinner on own	

Sunday, 27 September 1998

8:00 a.m. - 8:30 a.m.	Continental Breakfast	**Great Hall**
8:30 a.m. - 10:00 a.m.	Panel Presentation	**Auditorium**

The Organization and Structure of Schools at the Middle Grades: What is the Impact on the Teaching and Learning of Mathematics?

Moderator: Susan Wood, Professor of Mathematics, J. Sargeant
  Reynolds Community College

Panel:

Stephen O. Gibson, Principal, Patapsco Middle School, Ellicott
  City, Maryland

Mary Kay Stein, Research Scientist, Learning Research and
  Development Center, University of Pittsburgh

Robert Felner, Professor and Department Chair, Education; and
  Director, National Center on Public Education, University of
  Rhode Island

- What are the important characteristics of school organization and mathematics programs that support teaching and learning meaningful mathematics in the middle grades?
- How can the schedules of teachers and students be organized to implement what we know about effective teaching and learning in the middle grades?
- What are the issues surrounding specialists vs. generalists? What kind of teaching assignments maximize program effectiveness in mathematics?

10:00 a.m. - 10:30 a.m.	Break	
10:30 a.m. - 11:30 a.m.	Discussion Sessions	**Assigned Rooms**
11:30 a.m. - 12:00 p.m.	Convocation Summary *Edward Silver*	**Auditorium**
12:00 p.m.	Convocation adjourns	

Action Conference on the Nature and Teaching of Algebra in the Middle Grades

National Academy of Sciences/National Research Council
2101 Constitution Avenue, NW, Washington, DC
27–28 September 1998

AGENDA

Sunday, 27 September 1998

12:00 p.m. - 1:00 p.m.	Lunch	**Lecture Room**
1:00 p.m. - 1:15 p.m.	Welcome and Introductions *Hyman Bass*	
1:15 p.m. - 2:45 p.m.	Views on the Nature of Algebra *Jim Fey* *Al Cuoco*	
2:45 p.m. - 3:00 p.m.	Question and Answer Period	
3:00 p.m. - 3:15 p.m.	Break	
3:15 p.m. - 4:00 p.m.	Views on the Learning of Algebra *Orit Zaslavsky*	
4:00 p.m. - 5:00 p.m.	Discussion *Moderator: Hyman Bass*	
5:00 p.m. - 6:00 p.m.	Reception and Light Dinner	**Great Hall**

Monday, 28 September 1998

	Teaching Algebra: Case Studies of Implementation *Blanche Brownley, Moderator*	**Lecture Room**
8:30 a.m. - 9:15 a.m.	Case Study 1: Connected Mathematics, Traverse City *Yvonne Grant*	

9:15 a.m. - 10:00 a.m.	Case Study 2: University of Chicago School Mathematics Project
Bonnie Buehler
10:00 a.m. -10:15 a.m.	Break
10:15 a.m. - 11:00 a.m.	Case Study 3: Change from Within, Mathematics in Context
Susan Hoffmier
11:00 a.m. - 11:45 a.m.	Case Study 4: Saxon Mathematics
Stephen Hake
11:45 a.m. - 12:15 p.m.	Framing the Issues
12:15 p.m. - 1:15 p.m.	Lunch
1:15 p.m. - 2:15 p.m.	Panel

General Observations on Implementation
Ann Bartel

Algebra in Gifted/Talented Programs
Vernon Williams

Implementation in Middle Schools
Nancy Doda |
| 2:15 p.m. - 4:00 p.m. | Break-out Discussions |
| 4:00 p.m. - 5:00 p.m. | Reports from Break-out Discussions

Recommendations |
| 5:00 p.m. | Conference Adjourns |

Action Conference on Research in the Teaching and Learning of Mathematics in the Middle Grades

National Academy of Sciences/National Research Council
2101 Constitution Avenue, NW, Washington, DC
27–28 September 1998

AGENDA

Sunday, 27 September 1998

1:00 p.m. - 1:15 p.m.	Welcome *Edward Silver*	**Board Room**

What Should Result from this Conference?
Sandra Wilcox

1:15 p.m. - 2:00 p.m. Features of Research that Might be Useful for Mathematics Education: The Place of Theoretical Frameworks and Practical Problems
James Hiebert
Reactor: Alan Schoenfeld

2:00 p.m. - 2:30 p.m. Questions from Participants
Facilitator: Sandra Wilcox

2:30 p.m. - 2:45 p.m. Break

2:45 p.m. - 4:00 p.m. What does Research Say About Topics Difficult to Learn and Teach in the Middle Grades?

The Case of Proportional Reasoning
Richard Lesh

Linking Research and Practice: The Case of Teachers' Use of Cognitively Challenging Problems
Mary Kay Stein

4:00 p.m. - 5:00 p.m. Discussion: Defining the Major Issues

5:00 p.m. - 6:00 p.m. Reception and Light Dinner **Great Hall**

Monday, 28 September 1998

8:30 a.m. - 9:30 a.m.   Applications of Research to Practice   **Board Room**
and Implications of Practice for Research:
The Case of Innovative Curriculum for Students
James Fey
Kueno Gravemeijer

9:30 a.m. - 10:00 a.m.   Thinking about the Research/Practice Interface
Judy Sowder
Reactor: Edward Silver

10:00 a.m. - 11:30 a.m.   Discussion Groups: Defining the Major Issues (continued)

11:30 a.m. - 12:15 p.m.   Reports from Discussion Groups

12:15 p.m. - 1:15 p.m.   Lunch

1:15 p.m. - 1:30 p.m.   New Opportunities for Research on Middle Grades
Mathematics: The DOEd/NSF Research Initiative
Nora Sabelli

1:30 p.m. - 3:15 p.m.   Defining an Agenda of Research: Recommendations

3:15 p.m. - - 3:30 p.m.   Break

3:30 p.m. - 5:00 p.m.   Summary and Refining of Recommendations

5:00 p.m.   Conference Adjourns

Action Conference on the Professional Development of Teachers of Mathematics in the Middle Grades

National Academy of Sciences/National Research Council
2101 Constitution Avenue, NW, Washington, DC
27–28 September 1998

AGENDA

Sunday, 27 September 1998

12:30 p.m. – 1:00 p.m.	Lunch	**Board Room**

1:00 p.m. - 1:45 p.m.   Professional Development: Part I   **Members Room**
What Is Entailed in Trying to Teach Mathematics for
Understanding?
- View video of eighth grade class and discuss what teaching
  demands of teachers and what that implies for teacher learning

1:45 p.m. - 3:00 p.m.   Part II: What Do We Know about Professional
Development, Teacher Learning, and the Improvement of
Practice?
- Consider what we think we know about professional develop-
  ment and teacher learning and what the evidence is for our
  "knowledge"
Deborah Loewenberg Ball, University of Michigan-Ann Arbor

3:00 p.m. - 3:15 p.m.   Break

3:15 p.m. - 4:00 p.m.   Part III: Reflections on a Framework
- Given what we know about teaching and learning and what we
  know about professional development, where are the gaps?
  How can we work to develop and improve professional devel-
  opment in itself? What are the areas of need? What are
  promising directions?
Deborah Loewenberg Ball
Joan Ferrini-Mundy, National Research Council

4:00 p.m. - 5:00 p.m.   Discussion of Part III and Preparation for Monday Session

5:00 p.m. - 6:00 p.m.   Reception and Light Dinner   **Great Hall**

Monday, 28 September 1998

8:00 a.m. – 8:30 a.m.	Continental Breakfast	**Members Room**

8:30 a.m. – 10:00 a.m. Case Studies as Site and Medium for Teachers' Learning
Margaret Smith, Pennsylvania State University

10:00 a.m. – 10:15 a.m. Break

10:15 a.m. – 11:45 a.m. Curriculum Materials as Site and Medium for Teachers' Learning
Karen Economopoulos, TERC, Boston, MA

11:45 a.m. – 12:00 p.m. Observations for Framework
Deborah Loewenberg Ball

12:00 p.m. – 1:00 p.m. Lunch

1:00 p.m. – 2:30 p.m. Videotapes as Site and Medium for Teachers' Learning
Nanette Seago, Video Cases for Mathematics Professional Development, Riverside, CA

2:30 p.m. – 2:45 p.m. Break

2:45 p.m. – 3:45 p.m. Panel: Reflections on the Improvement of Professional Development
Moderator: Mark Saul, Bronxville Public Schools
Iris Weiss, Horizon Research
Stephanie Williamson, Louisiana Systemic Initiative
John Moyer, Marquette University

3:45 p.m. – 5:00 p.m. Part V: Conclusions—Group Work and Discussion

5:00 p.m. Conference Adjourns

Biographical Information on Convocation and Action Conference Speakers

Bruce Alberts, president of the National Academy of Sciences in Washington, D.C., is a respected biochemist recognized for his work both in biochemistry and molecular biology. He is noted particularly for his extensive study of the protein complexes that allow chromosomes to be replicated, as required for a living cell to divide.

He has spent his career making significant contributions to the field of life sciences, serving in different capacities on a number of prestigious advisory and editorial boards, including as chair of the Commission on Life Sciences, National Research Council. Until his election as President of the Academy, he was President-Elect of the American Society of Biochemistry and Molecular Biology.

Born in 1938 in Chicago, Illinois, Alberts graduated from Harvard College in Cambridge, Massachusetts, with a degree in biochemical sciences. He earned a doctorate from Harvard University in 1965. He joined the faculty of Princeton University in 1966 and after ten years was appointed professor and vice chair of the Department of Biochemistry and Biophysics at the University of California, San Francisco (UCSF). In 1980, he was awarded the honor of an American Cancer Society Lifetime Research Professorship. In 1985, he was named chair of the UCSF Department of Biochemistry and Biophysics.

Alberts has long been committed to the improvement of science education, dedicating much of his time to educational projects such as City Science, a program seeking to improve science teaching in San Francisco elementary schools. He has served on the advisory board of the National Science Resources Center—a joint project of the National Academy of Sciences and the Smithsonian Institution working with teachers, scientists, and school systems to improve teaching of science—as well as on the National Academy of Sciences' National Committee on Science Education Standards and Assessment.

He is a principal author of *The Mo-*

lecular Biology of the Cell, considered the leading textbook of its kind and used widely in U.S. colleges and universities. His most recent text, *Essential Cell Biology* (1997), is intended to approach this subject matter for a wider audience.

Deborah Loewenberg Ball is professor of educational studies at the University of Michigan. Her work as a researcher and teacher educator draws directly and indirectly on her long experience as an elementary classroom teacher. With mathematics as the main context for the work, Ball studies the practice of teaching and the processes of learning to teach. Her work also examines efforts to improve teaching through policy, reform initiatives, and teacher education. Ball's publications include articles on teacher learning and teacher education; the role of subject matter knowledge in teaching and learning to teach; endemic challenges of teaching; and the relations of policy and practice in instructional reform.

Hyman Bass is the Adrian Professor of Mathematics at Columbia University, where he has taught since 1959. He holds a Ph.D. from the University of Chicago, and a B.A. from Princeton. His research is mainly in algebra—group theory, K-theory, number theory, and algebraic geometry. Dr. Bass received the Van Amringe Prize for his book, *Algebraic K-theory*, the Cole Prize in algebra from the American Mathematical Society, and was a Phi Beta Kappa National Visiting Scholar. He is a member of the National Academy of Sciences and of the American Academy of Arts and Sciences. He currently chairs the Mathematical Sciences Education Board at the National Research Council. Bass is a member of the Program Steering Committee for this Convocation.

Catherine Brown is an Associate Professor in the Department of Curriculum and Instruction at Indiana University. She has an extensive background in teacher professional development, elementary and secondary mathematics pedagogy, and instruction in mathematics education at the middle school, high school, and university levels. She is a member of the National Council of Teachers of Mathematics, Mathematical Association of America, and the American Educational Research Association. Brown received her doctor of education in mathematics education from the University of Georgia in 1985 and has been a reviewer and author for numerous mathematics education journals. Brown is a member of the Program Steering Committee for this Convocation.

Sam Chattin is a science teacher at William H. English Middle School in Scottsberg, Indiana. He has expertise in middle level teaching and learning, having taught at the middle school level for more than twenty years. He is a member of the National Middle School Association, the National Association of Biology Teachers , and served on the Board of the National Science Teachers Association. Chattin has received several awards for his work—the Presidential Award for Excellence in Science Teaching, the Kohl International Teaching Award, the Walt Disney Salute to the American Teacher, the Lifetime Cable Award, along with several others. Chattin is a member of the Program Steering Committee for this Convocation.

Tom Dickinson attended Wake Forest University where he received his B.A. in history in 1969. He taught social studies to both middle school and high school students for seven years and he earned his M.Ed. in social studies education from the University of Virginia in Charlottesville. In 1978, Dickinson worked on his doctoral degree full time, graduating in 1980 with a Ed.D. in social studies education and a minor in supervision of instruction.

Dickinson worked at the college level for the majority of the last nineteen years at North Carolina Wesleyan College, Eastern Illinois University, Georgia Southern College (later University), and is currently a professor of curriculum and instruction at Indiana State University in Terre Haute, Indiana. His primary teaching, writing and research concerns deal with middle school education, specifically middle school teacher education.

He served as editor of the *Middle School Journal* for the National Middle School Association and authored or edited a number of books on middle school education. In addition he wrote, with C. Kenneth McEwin in 1996, a background paper for the Middle Grade School State Policy Initiative (MGSSPI) of the Carnegie Corporation titled *Forgotten youth, forgotten teachers: Transformation of the professional preparation of teachers of young adolescents.*

Dickinson is a member of the Professional Preparation and Certification Committee of the National Middle School Association, a standing committee that is charged with oversight of the NCATE review process for middle school teacher education. He has also served as a Board of Examiner for NCATE and a member of the Steering Committee of the 1994 National Assessment of Education Progress (NAEP) U.S. History Consensus Project.

Dickinson has written a number of grants in the last five years that were aimed at the development of middle school and high school performance-based teacher education programs and K-12 teacher creativity staff development workshops. His research interests include middle school teacher education and the origins of the middle school movement.

Nancy Doda is a President and founder of Teacher to Teacher, a consulting firm for middle level education. She began her career as a middle school teacher and since then has continued to act as a teacher advocate and helper in both her writings and presentations. Doda has a Ph.D. from University of Florida, in Middle School Curriculum and Instruction. She has been a Team Leader on an Interdisciplinary Team; Teacher-Advisor in Advisor-Advisee Program, has authored a regular column for teachers for four years called "Teacher to Teacher" in the *Middle School Journal*; now a monograph called *Teacher to Teacher*. Since 1976, when she began consulting work during the summers, to a full-time job as a teacher helper today, she has worked with middle level teachers, administrators, and parents in over forty states, Canada, Europe, and the Far East. She was a featured guest on the NBC Today Show in 1988. Doda has co-authored *Team Organization: Promise—Practices and Possibilities* with Dr. Tom Erb for NEA,

authored many articles, and recently wrote for *Instructor* on the subject of homebase called, "Who's Afraid of Homebase"? Middle Years, 1991. Doda was the first teacher to keynote the National Middle School Association's annual conference in 1977 and has keynoted that conference on two additional occasions. She has served on the Board of Directors of the National Middle School Association for five years.

Robert Felner is currently Chair of the Department of Education and Director of the National Center on Public Education and Social Policy at the University of Rhode Island. The Center's central focus is on developing and implementing more effective models through which universities can partner with K-12 public education to ensure academic success and positive developmental outcomes for all students. In this work, the Center partners with schools and local communities, local and state agencies, and other branches of government to enhance their joint capacity to address pressing educational, social, health and economic issues and to improve the lives of all children, youth, and families through collaborative efforts.

Previously, at the University of Illinois, he was Professor of Public Policy, Education, and Social Welfare, and the Professor of Psychology and Director of the Graduate Programs in Clinical and Community Psychology. While at Illinois he served as founding Director of the Center for Prevention Research and Development where the Center worked to develop more systematic applications of land-grant university traditions to the lives of the residents of Illinois and the nation. In 1990 he was appointed by the University of Illinois to the "Irving B. Harris Professorship"—a faculty position for interdisciplinary scholarship in social policy and education. He was the founding president of the Board of Directors of the Martin Luther King Community Services of Illinois Foundation, an organization that focuses on the needs of economically disadvantaged children and families. Felner has also served as Director of the Graduate Programs in Clinical and Community Psychology at Auburn University, and before that as Assistant Professor of Clinical/Community Psychology at Yale University. He earned his Ph.D. in Clinical/Community Psychology at the University of Rochester.

He serves or has served on the editorial boards of nearly a dozen scientific journals and as a member of more than two dozen federal and foundation research and demonstration advisory and grant review panels. He is a fellow of the American Psychological Association, the American Psychological Society, and the American Orthopsychiatric Association. In recognition of his work in the prevention field he received the Administrator's Award from the U.S. Alcohol, Drug Abuse, and Mental Health Administration and, in 1988 his work on educational reform as prevention was selected by the American Psychological Association as one of fourteen "Exemplary" Prevention Programs in the United States. He is the author of over 150 papers, articles, chapters, and volumes. A primary focus of his work is on understanding and guiding local, statewide, and national policy and reform efforts to transform elementary, middle level, and secondary education. Of particular concern are the needs of students and families from economically and socially disadvantaged backgrounds, and the preparation of youth and families to participate in the workforce and democracy of the 21st Century. This work has involved over 1,000 schools and partnerships across more than 22 states and has been funded by the Carnegie Corporation, the Lilly Endowment, the Kellogg Foundation, and the Kauffman and Danforth Foundations, several states and large school districts.

A second major focus of his work has been on the reform and evaluation of social and health policy and programs that address welfare dependence, mental health, substance abuse, and improving the developmental, educational, and vocational outcomes of children, youth, and families.

Linda Cooper Foreman has been a high school and middle school classroom teacher for twenty-three years. For the past eleven years, she has also worked as Curriculum Specialist for The Mathematics Learning Center (MLC) at Portland State University, Portland, Oregon. At MLC, she works extensively with teachers and teacher leaders from across the nation, supporting the implementation of mathematics reform. She is currently co-authoring an NSF supported comprehensive mathematics curriculum for grades 5-8, *Mathematics Alive! Courses I-IV* (the first 2 courses were originally published as *Visual Mathematics*). Foreman is a recipient of the Presidential Award for Excellence in Mathematics Teaching.

Stephen O. Gibson is the Principal at Patapsco Middle School in Ellicott City, Maryland. He has been the principal at this middle school for the past nine years.

Katherine Hart has recently retired from the Chair of Mathematics Education at the University of Nottingham. She was director of the Shell Centre. Hart started her career as a mathemat-

ics teacher in England, the U.S., and Bermuda. She was then a teacher-trainer for ten years with a year as a UNESCO field officer in Bangkok, Thailand. After obtaining an Ed.D. at the University of Indiana she did research at London University for ten years, producing books for teachers on the research projects: Concepts in Secondary Mathematics and Science (CSMS), Strategies and Errors in Secondary Mathematics (SESM), and Children's Mathematical Frameworks (CMF).

She was an inspector of schools (HMI) for two years and then became director of a curriculum development project before directing the Shell Centre for the last five years.

Hart was president of the British Society for Research in Learning Mathematics, Psychology of Mathematics Education Workshop and the International Group Psychology of Mathematics Education. She has worked in many third-world countries and is currently committed to working in Kwazulu, Natal in South Africa and Sri Lanka.

Glenda Lappan is a University Distinguished Professor at the Department of Mathematics at Michigan State University. She received her Ed.D. in Mathematics and Education, with distinction, from the University of Georgia in 1965. She has been a member of the Department of Mathematics faculty at MSU since she received her degree. From 1989-91 she was on leave to serve as the Program Director for Teacher Preparation at the National Science Foundation. Her research and development interests are in the connected areas of students' learning of mathematics and mathematics teacher change at the middle and secondary levels. She is the Co-Director of the Connected Mathematics Project, which is funded by the National Science Foundation to develop a complete middle school curriculum for teachers and for students. She served as the Chair of the middle school writing group for the National Council of Teachers of Mathematics' (NCTM) *Curriculum and Evaluation Standards for School Mathematics*, and as Chair of the Commission that developed the NCTM *Professional Standards for Teaching Mathematics*. She served on the NCTM Board of Directors from 1989 to 1992 and is currently serving on the Board through 2001.

Lappan was a member of the National Advisory Boards of the following: Glenn T. Seaborg Center for Teaching and Learning Science and Mathematics, the Ford Foundation/University of Pittsburgh QUASAR project, the NSF/University of Maryland Teacher Preparation Collaborative, the NSF/San Diego State University Mathematics for Elementary Teacher Preparation Materials Development Project, the University of Chicago School Mathematics Project, the NSF/University of Wisconsin Cognitively Guided Instruction Project and many others. In 1993 she received a Distinguished Faculty Award from Michigan State University and the Michigan Council of Teachers of Mathematics Service Award for 1993. She served as Vice-Chair of the Mathematical Sciences Education Board for five years and continues as a member of MSEB. In 1995 she was appointed by the Secretary of Education to the National Education Research Policy and Priorities Board. In 1996 she received the Association of Women in Mathematics Louise Hay Award for outstanding contributions to Mathematics Education. In 1997 she received a Meritorious Faculty Award for the College of Natural Science Alumni. In 1998 she was named University Distinguished Professor at MSU. She is currently the President of the National Council of Teachers of Mathematics.

Cyril Kent McGuire is the assistant secretary for the Office of Educational Research and Improvement at the U.S. Department of Education. He was nominated by President Clinton in October 1997 and confirmed by the Senate in May 1998. This office funds research and demonstration projects to improve education, and collects and disseminates statistical information on the condition of education.

McGuire, of Moorestown, NJ, joined the department after serving as program officer of the education portfolio for the Pew Charitable Trusts in Philadelphia, where he was responsible for the Trusts and national initiatives in education reform. From 1991 to 1995, he was program director of education for the Lilly Endowment, where he directed all grant making related to education reform in Indiana, as well as national education policy initiatives.

From 1980 to 1989, he served as policy analyst and then as director of the School Finance Collaborative at the Education Commission of the States. There, he directed national projects related to at-risk youth, education technology and education choice; participated in the design and implementation of the organization's core initiatives in K-12/higher education reform; and led efforts to provide technical assistance to states in school finance and governance.

McGuire received a B.A. in economics from the University of Michigan, an M.A. in education administration and policy from Columbia University, and a Ph.D. in public administration from the University of Colorado.

Katherine Rasch is Dean and Professor of Education in the School of Education at Maryville University in St. Louis, Missouri. She has expertise in teacher and mathematics education and coursework design. She is a member of the National Middle School Association, National Council of Supervisors of Mathematics, National Council of Teachers of Mathematics, American Association of Colleges for Teacher Education. Rasch received her Ph.D. in education from Saint Louis University in 1983. She has taught at the graduate and undergraduate levels and worked in collaborative design of coursework with teachers in partner schools. Rasch currently serves as the president of the Missouri Association for Colleges of Teacher Education. She has published and presented on teacher education and preparation. Rasch is a member of the Program Steering Committee for this Convocation.

Nanette Seago is currently the Project Director for the Video Cases for Mathematics Professional Development Project, funded by the National Science Foundation. This past year she directed the Mathematics Renaissance K-12 Video Pilot Study. For six years (1991-1997) she was a Regional Director for the Middle Grades Mathematics Renaissance. She has taught in kindergarten and upper elementary grades as well as mathematics at the middle school level. She authored the *TIMSS Video Moderator's Guide* for the U.S. Department of Education.

Edward Silver is a Professor in the Department of Instruction and Learning at the University of Pittsburgh's School of Education, and senior scientist with the Learning Research and Development Center. He has an extensive background in mathematics education at the secondary and post-secondary levels, having taught at the secondary level for six years and at the university level for nearly twenty years. He currently serves on the Mathematical Sciences Education Board (MSEB). During 1984-1985 he worked in the private sector as Project Director for secondary school algebra and geometry courseware. Silver is a member of the National Council of Teachers of Mathematics (NCTM) and is leader of the NCTM Standards 2000 Project, Grade 6-8 Writing Group. Other activities include being a member of the editorial panel for *Cognition and Instruction*, 1995-1999; member of the editorial panel for *Journal for Research in Mathematics Education*, 1995-1998; member, Mathematical Sciences Academic Advisory Committee of the College Board, 1994-1997; and member, National Board for Professional Teaching Standards (NBPTS) Middle Childhood and Early Adolescence Mathematics Standards Committee, 1992-1996. He has authored many professional articles and has been the recipient of major grants in the mathematics education field. Silver is the Chair of the Program Steering Committee for this Convocation.

Mary Kay Stein is a Research Scientist at the Learning Research and Development Center at the University of Pittsburgh. She has conducted numerous studies of classroom-based teaching and learning in a variety of educational reform contexts. She was the director of the documentation component of the QUASAR Project, a multi-year middle school mathematics instructional reform project. The QUASAR research provided measures of program implementation at each of the project's six middle schools with a focus on the setup and implementation of mathematics instructional tasks. Based on this work, Stein has published a series of studies on mathematics reform and teacher professional development in high-poverty urban middle schools.

Stein's current work attempts to integrate the teaching and learning of subject matter with the study of social and organizational arrangements of schools as institutions. Currently, Stein is Director of Research for the High Performance Learning Communities Project, a multi-year OERI-funded contract to study the district-wide, content-driven improvement strategy of New York City's Community School District 2.

Stein has also been active in building bridges between research and practice. Along with Margaret Smith, Marjorie Henningsen, and Edward Silver, she has authored a casebook on middle school mathematics instruction (Teachers College Press, forthcoming) which builds on the research findings of the QUASAR Project. Stein is also a Co-Principal Investigator of an NSF-funded project to develop mathematics instructional cases for professional development of middle school mathematics teachers.

Luther Williams is the Assistant Director of Education and Human Resources at the National Science Foundation. The Directorate includes programs addressing pre-college, undergraduate, graduate and postdoctoral science, mathematics, engineering and technology education; human resource development activities; and a program to stimulate S&T infrastructure development in states.

Williams has a distinguished record as a scientist, educator, and administrator. He held faculty and administrative positions at Purdue University, Washington University in St. Louis, the University of Colorado, and Atlanta University. He served as the NIH Deputy Director for the National Institute of General Medical Sciences.

Williams earned a B.A. in biology from Miles College, an M.S. from Atlanta University, a Ph.D. from Purdue University, and was a postdoctoral biochemistry fellow at the State University of New York at Stony Brook. The author of over 50 scientific publications, he is a member and/or fellow of several professional organizations, the recipient of four honorary doctorate degrees and the Presidential Meritorious Rank Award in 1993.

Susan S. Wood is a Professor of Mathematics at the J. Sargeant Reynolds Community College in Richmond, Virginia. She has been actively involved in national mathematics education issues and has an extensive background in mathematics education at the community college level, having taught mathematics at the community college level for twenty-five years. She received her Ed.D. from the University of Virginia in 1979. Awards include the first J. Sargeant Reynolds Community College Sabbatical, 1996; Distinguished Service in Mathematics Education Award, 1995; William C. Lowry Outstanding Mathematics Teacher Award, Virginia Council of Teachers of Mathematics, 1995; Faculty Development Grant, 1995; Chancellors Commonwealth Professor, 1994; Employee Recognition, 1990 and 1994; State Council of Higher Education for Virginia Outstanding Faculty Award,

1992; Outstanding Work in Developmental Studies, 1989; and Education Professions Development Act Fellowship, 1971-1973. Wood has strong ties to several mathematics professional organizations, significant national involvement, and has made about seventy conference presentations to students and teachers since 1990. She is a member of the National Research Council's Mathematical Sciences Education Board, President-Elect of the American Mathematical Association of Two-Year Colleges, and a member of the National Council of Teachers of Mathematics, and the Mathematical Association of America. Wood is a member of the Program Steering Committee for this Convocation.

Biographical Statements for Speakers at the Action Conference on the Nature and Learning of Algebra in the Middle Grades

Anne Bartel is currently on loan from the Minneapolis Public Schools to SciMathMN, Minnesota's state-funded State Systemic Initiative. She serves as the mathematics Project Manager, with primary responsibility for the development and dissemination of the MN K-12 Mathematics Curriculum Framework and professional development programs in mathematics education. In this last capacity, Ann serves as the co-project director of an NSF Teacher Enhancement Grant involving the implementation of the Connected Mathematics Project in Minneapolis middle schools. She has also trained members of the Minnesota K-12 Best Practice Network and supported the implementation of NSF reform curriculum projects statewide.

Ms. Bartel has teaching and professional development experience at all levels K-12. She received her B.S. degree in Mathematics Education from the University of Minnesota and her M.A. in Special Education at the University of St. Thomas in St. Paul. She has done additional coursework in mathematics education and elementary education. She holds both a 7-12 mathematics and a K-12 special education teaching license from the state of Minnesota.

Ms. Bartel has served in many capacities in both state and national professional organizations. She currently serves as President of the Minnesota Council of Teachers of Mathematics. Bartel served on the Editorial panel of NCTM's *The Arithmetic Teacher* and the co-editor of the "Tech Time" column in *Teaching Children Mathematics*. She has served on conference committees for the NCTM 1997 Annual Meeting, as well as the 1992, 1987 and 1981 NCTM Regional Conferences, and was responsible for initiating and establishing the MCTM annual spring conference in Minnesota. In addition, Ms. Bartel has made numerous presentations at district, state, and national meetings.

Ms. Bartel has been a co-author of the *MN K-12 Mathematics Framework* published by SciMathMN, *New Curriculum Maths for Schools* published by Longman in England, the *Basic Skills in Mathematics* series published by Allyn & Bacon, Inc., *Algebra I* blackline problem-solving masters published by

D.C. Health, Inc., and assorted supplementary materials published by The Mathematics Group, Inc.

Hyman Bass is the Adrian Professor of Mathematics at Columbia University, where he has taught since 1959. He holds a Ph.D. from the University of Chicago, and a B.A. from Princeton. His research is mainly in algebra—group theory, K-theory, number theory, and algebraic geometry. Dr. Bass received the Van Amringe Prize for his book, Algebraic K-theory, the Cole Prize in algebra from the American Mathematical Society, and was a Phi Beta Kappa National Visiting Scholar. He is a member of the National Academy of Sciences and of the American Academy of Arts and Sciences. He currently chairs the Mathematical Sciences Education Board at the National Research Council. Bass was the organizer for this Action Conference.

Blanche Brownley graduated from the District of Columbia public schools and received undergraduate and graduate degrees from Howard University and the University of the District of Columbia. She has been an employee of the District of Columbia school system for the past 26 years, serving as junior high school mathematics teacher, curriculum writer, mentor teacher, and staff developer. She is currently the secondary mathematics

content specialist. She has received many honors and awards including a Presidential Teaching Award, a GTE Gift Award, and a NASA NEWMAST Honor Teacher Award. Active in her professional organizations, she is the Past President of the D.C. Council of Teachers of Mathematics, and has served on the committee and as chair of the Regional Services Committee of the National Council of Teachers of Mathematics (NCTM), and most recently as the Local Arrangements Chair for the annual meeting of NCTM that was held in D.C. in spring, 1998.

Bonnie Buehler has taught high school and middle school mathematics for the last 21 years. Currently, she teaches 8th grade algebra and geometry at the Springman School in Glenview, Illinois. She served for six years as department chair during the school's transition to the University of Chicago Mathematics Project curriculum. Ms. Buehler participates in the First in the World Consortium, a group of school districts from Chicago's North Shore that came together in 1995 to provide a "world-class education" for their students. She serves as a Teacher Facilitator in the First in the World Consortium Teacher Learning Network

Al Cuoco is Senior scientist and Director of the Center for Mathematics Education at Education Development

Center. A student of Ralph Greenberg, he received his Ph.D. in mathematics from Brandeis in 1980, specializing in algebraic number theory. Cuoco taught high school mathematics to a wide range of students in the Woburn, Massachusetts, public schools from 1969 until 1993, chairing the department for the last decade of this term.

At EDC, he has worked in curriculum development, professional development, and education policy. He currently codirects two high school curriculum development projects, an undergraduate research project, and a project that attempts to involve more mathematicians in K-12 education. His favorite publication is his 1991 article in the American Mathematical Monthly, described by his wife as "an attempt to explain a number system no one understands with a picture no one can see."

Nancy Doda is a President and founder of Teacher to Teacher, a consulting firm for middle level education. She began her career as a middle school teacher and since then has continued to act as a teacher advocate and helper in both her writings and presentations. Doda has a Ph.D. from University of Florida, in Middle School Curriculum and Instruction. She has been a Team Leader on an Interdisciplinary Team; Teacher-Advisor in Advisor-Advisee Program, has authored a regular column

for teachers for four years called 'Teacher to Teacher' in the Middle School Journal; now a monograph called Teacher to Teacher. Since 1976, when she began consulting work during the summers, to a full-time job as a teacher helper today, she has worked with middle level teachers, administrators, and parents in over forty states, Canada, Europe, and the Far East. She was a featured guest on the NBC Today Show in 1988. Doda has co-authored *Team Organization: Promise—Practices and Possibilities* with Dr. Tom Erb for NEA, authored many articles, and recently wrote for *Instructor* on the subject of homebase called, "Who's Afraid of homebase"? Middle Years, 1991. Doda was the first teacher to keynote the National Middle School Association's annual conference in 1977 and has keynoted that conference on two additional occasions. She served on the Board of Directors of the National Middle School Association for five years.

James Fey is Professor of Curriculum and Instruction and Mathematics at the University of Maryland. His special interest is development of innovative secondary school mathematics curriculum materials and research on their effects. He has been author of algebra materials in the Connected Mathematics Project, the Core-Plus Mathematics Project, and the Computer-Intensive Algebra project.

Yvonne Grant is currently a teacher consultant and peer coach for teachers of the Connected Mathematics Project in Traverse City Public Schools in Traverse City, Michigan. This position began in January of 1997 as a result of a grant through Michigan State University. Prior to this, she taught 7th and 8th grade mathematics at Portland Middle School, Portland, Michigan for nine and a half years. In 1992, her mathematics department received the "A+ for Breaking the Mold" Award from the U.S. Department of Education.

Her involvement with the Connected Mathematics Project has taken on varied roles. Ms. Grant began in 1992 as a field development teacher piloting the materials and giving feedback to the developers. She worked as a part of the teacher assessment writing team for 4 years developing assessment pieces, editing and contributing to teachers editions.

Ms. Grant has helped create professional development plans for school districts, statewide initiatives, and leadership conferences. Her presentations have included staff development involving reform mathematics, implementation issues, instruction and assessment.

Stephen Hake is an educator from Southern California. Hake completed his undergraduate work at USIU in San Diego. After serving in the Air Force, he earned a Masters in Curriculum and Instruction from Chapman College and began teaching in El Monte, California, in 1973. He has eighteen years of mathematics teaching experience in grades five through twelve, with most of those years at the middle school level. While teaching in El Monte, he established district-wide mathematics competitions for fifth through eighth grade students and coached junior high mathematics teams to frequent victories in district and regional competitions.

In 1983, Hake began writing a mathematics curriculum that was later published by Saxon Publishers. His four books range from fourth through seventh grade levels. He has been a school board member in his community for ten years.

Susan Hoffmier has been teaching mathematics in the same school district for the past 23 years. Currently, she is teaching eighth grade mathematics and algebra. Since 1987, she has been committed to mathematics reform for all children.

Ms. Hoffmier is the mathematics mentor for her school; a fellow for the Northern California Mathematics Project; a past cluster leader for Mathematics Renaissance; and is on the leadership team for the Golden State Exam. She is also a teacher consultant for Mathematics in Context as well as a teacher leader for College Preparatory Mathematics, Changes from Within.

Vernon Williams specializes in teaching mathematics to gifted and talented students at the Longfellow Intermediate School in Fairfax County and has been teaching mathematics to middle school students for twenty six years in Fairfax County, Virginia. Williams attended the University of Maryland where Jim Fey was his student teaching supervisor. He has won various teaching awards, including the 1990 Fairfax County Teacher of the Year. He has coached Longfellow's MathCounts Team for sixteen years and has won the State Championship thirteen times. He decided to become a Junior High School mathematics teacher as a student in middle school because he considered his teachers such great role models and wanted to emulate them.

Orit Zaslavsky is a senior lecturer at the Department of Education in Technology and Science, Technion–Israel Institute of Technology, Haifa, Israel. She received her Ph.D. in Mathematics Education from the Technion in 1987 and spent the two following years as a post doctoral fellow at the Learning Research and Development Center, University of Pittsburgh, where she co-authored a highly cited review paper on Functions, Graphs, and Graphing. Her Ph.D. dissertation and some of her current research are connected to learning algebra in grades 7-12. Her research interests include: Students' and teachers' mathematical thinking; the role of examples and counter-examples in learning mathematics; analysis and enhancement classroom mathematical interactions and discourse; and characteristics and underlying processes fostering the professional development of mathematics teachers and teacher educators.

Zaslavsky taught secondary mathematics for 12 years, and has been involved in teaching pre-service and in-service mathematics teachers for the past 15 years. For the past nine years she has been director of large professional development projects for middle and secondary mathematics teachers. She is now a member of the International Committee of the International Group for the Psychology of Mathematics Education (PME), and a member of the editorial board of the *Journal of Mathematics Teacher Education*.

Biographical Statements for Speakers at the Action Conference on Research in the Teaching and Learning of Mathematics in the Middle Grades

James Fey is Professor of Curriculum and Instruction and Mathematics at the University of Maryland. His special interest is development of innovative secondary school mathematics curriculum materials and research on their effects. He has been author of algebra materials in the Connected Mathematics Project, the Core-Plus Mathematics Project, and the Computer-Intensive Algebra project.

Kueno Gravemeijer is on the faculty of the Freudenthal Institute research group on mathematics education. The Freudenthal Institute (FI) is part of Utrecht University, the department of Mathematics and Computer Science and the Center for Education in the Exact (beta) Sciences. The FI is the National Expertise Center for Mathematics Education in primary and secondary education.

James Hiebert is the H. Rodney Sharp Professor of Educational Development at the University of Delaware. Hiebert worked closely with, and has co-authored with, James Stigler on the

mathematics video in TIMSS. He testified before the Committee on Science at the U.S. Congress regarding TIMSS. One focus of his work is to research and understand the effects of conceptually based instruction in mathematics. He has expertise in the whole of the TIMSS study and its following analyses, questions, concerns, and impact on current U.S. mathematics and science reform.

Richard Lesh is the R.B. Kane Distinguished Professor of Education, Associate Dean for Research and Development, and Director of the School Mathematics and Science Center at Purdue University. He is also the Director for the Princeton Research Institute on Science and Mathematics Learning, and Associate Editor for *Mathematical Thinking & Learning: An International Journal*. Areas of specialization include research and assessment on problem solving, learning; instruction in mathematics and science education, teacher education; computer-based and text-based curriculum development for children and adults; and research design in mathematics and science education. He has been a Research Director of the SIMCALC project, in collaboration with Jeremy Roschelle and Jim Kaput, and is the director at the Purdue satellite of the University of Wisconsin's National Center for Improving Student Learning and Achievement in Mathematics and the Sciences. From 1994 to 1999, Dr. Lesh was the Director for Mathematics and Science Instruction at the World Institute for Computer Assisted Teaching (WICAT), and, from 1989 to 1995, he was a Principal Scientist at the Educational Testing Service in Princeton, where he was also the Director of the Center on Technology and Assessment. He also has served as Chief Program Designer for the Education Testing Service's PACKETS Performance Assessment System for Grades 3-5. Dr. Lesh received a B.A. in Mathematics and Physics from Hanover College, and M.A. and Ph.D. degrees from Indiana University. Dr. Lesh was a Professor of Mathematics and Education at Northwestern University, and, from 1984 to 1989, he was Northwestern's Associate Dean for Research and Program Development in the School of Education.

Nora Sabelli is a senior program director in the Directorate for Education and Human Resources (EHR) at the National Science Foundation (NSF).

During part of 1998, Sabelli was on assignment to the National Science and Technology Council, working at the Office of Science and Technology Policy. Now, following a career as a research scientist and faculty member, she is focusing on helping understand how to provide quality science, mathematics, and technology education reflective of current scientific advances and technology trends. Her directorship included coordination of the NSF-wide program of research in Learning and Intelligent Systems; the Research on Education, Policy and Practice Program; and membership in the NSF-wide Knowledge and Distributed Intelligence implementation group and in the EHR-wide Technology Integration into Education working group. Dr. Sabelli received a Ph.D. in Chemistry (Theoretical Organic) from the University of Buenos Aires, Argentina for research performed at the University of Chicago while a recipient of one of the first CONICET external fellowships. Her former positions include Senior Research Scientist, National Center for Supercomputing Applications, University of Illinois at Urbana-Champaign; Assistant Director for Education, National Center for Supercomputing Applications, University of Illinois at Urbana-Champaign; Associate Professor of Chemistry, Department of Chemistry; Large Scale Computing Coordinator, Academic Computer Center, University of Illinois at Chicago. She authored 11 research publications in her research field between 1980 and 1991, and has co-directed three research theses.

Alan Schoenfeld is a member of the National Academy of Education. His research deals with thinking, teaching, and learning, with an emphasis on mathematics. One focus of his work has been on problem solving, and his book, *Mathematical Problem Solving* (1985), characterizes what it means to "think mathematically" and describes a research-based undergraduate course in mathematical problem solving. A second line of his work focuses on understanding and teaching the concepts of functions and graphs. A third deals with assessment, and Schoenfeld heads the Balanced Assessment Project, which is developing alternative assessments for K-12 mathematics curricula. He chaired the National Science Foundation's Working Group on Assessment in Calculus, and serves on the National Research Council's Board on Testing and Assessment. He is associate editor of *Cognition and Instruction* and an editor of *Research in Collegiate Mathematics Education*. His efforts to bring together teachers, mathematicians, educators, and cognitive researchers to collaborate on issues in mathematics education have produced the two volumes: *Mathematical Thinking and Problem Solving* (editor, 1994) and *Cognitive Science and Mathematics Education* (editor, 1987).

Edward Silver is a Professor in the Department of Instruction and Learning at the University of Pittsburgh's School of Education, and senior scientist with the Learning Research and Development Center. He has an extensive background in mathematics education at the secondary and post-secondary levels, having taught at the secondary level for six years and at the university level for nearly twenty years. He currently serves on the Mathematical Sciences Education Board (MSEB). During 1984-1985 he worked in the private sector as Project Director for secondary school algebra and geometry courseware. Silver is a member of the National Council of Teachers of Mathematics (NCTM) and is leader of the NCTM Standards 2000 Project, Grade 6-8 Writing Group. Other activities include being a member of the editorial panel for *Cognition and Instruction*, 1995-1999; member of the editorial panel for *Journal for Research in Mathematics Education*, 1995-1998; member, Mathematical Sciences Academic Advisory Committee of the College Board, 1994-1997; and member, National Board for Professional Teaching Standards (NBPTS) Middle Childhood and Early

Adolescence Mathematics Standards Committee, 1992-1996. He has authored many professional articles and has been the recipient of major grants in the mathematics education field. Silver is the Chair of the Program Steering Committee for the Convocation.

Judy Sowder is a Professor of Mathematical Sciences and Director of the Center for Research in Mathematics and Science Education at San Diego State University. Before returning to study for her Ph.D., she taught elementary and middle school, then secondary and college mathematics. Since receiving a doctorate in mathematics education in 1976 she has focused her teaching on the preparation of teachers and graduate students in mathematics education. She has published over forty papers, nineteen book chapters, and three books, all on topics of mathematics learning and teaching. Two of the books focus on research on preparing middle school teachers of mathematics. She is currently the Editor of the *Journal for Research in Mathematics Education* and is the director of a curriculum development project aimed at producing course materials in mathematics for elementary and middle school teachers, both preservice and inservice. She has served on many national and international committees and advisory boards, including secretary and program com-

mittee member for the International Group for Psychology in Mathematics Education, steering committee member of Leading Mathematics Education into the 21st Century Project, chair of the NCTM Standards Coordinating Committee, and chair of the NCTM Research Advisory Committee. She has directed numerous projects funded by NSF and OERI and has received awards for teaching and research.

Mary Kay Stein is a Research Scientist at the Learning Research and Development Center at the University of Pittsburgh. She has conducted numerous studies of classroom-based teaching and learning in a variety of educational reform contexts. She was the director of the documentation component of the QUASAR Project, a multi-year middle school mathematics instructional reform project. The QUASAR research provided measures of program implementation at each of the project's six middle schools with a focus on the setup and implementation of mathematics instructional tasks. Based on this work, Stein has published a series of studies on mathematics reform and teacher professional development in high-poverty urban middle schools.

Stein's current work attempts to integrate the teaching and learning of subject matter with the study of social and organizational arrangements of schools as institutions. Currently, Stein is Director of Research for the High Performance Learning Communities Project, a multi-year OERI-funded contract to study the district-wide, content-driven improvement strategy of New York City's Community School District 2.

Stein has also been active in building bridges between research and practice. Along with Margaret Smith, Marjorie Henningsen, and Edward Silver, she has authored a casebook on middle school mathematics instruction (Teachers College Press, forthcoming) which builds on the research findings of the QUASAR Project. Stein is also a Co-Principal Investigator of an NSF-funded project to develop mathematics instructional cases for professional development of middle school mathematics teachers.

Sandra Wilcox is an Associate Professor in the Department of Teacher Education at Michigan State University (MSU) and Director of the Mathematics Assessment Resource Service (MARS). She has expertise in mathematics education and assessment, having taught education classes at the university level for twelve years and participated in several projects examining assessment in mathematics. She is a member of the American Educational Research Association (AERA), the National Council of Teachers of Mathematics (NTCM), and National Council of Supervisors of Mathematics (NCSM). Wilcox received her Ph.D. in 1989. Prior to her work at MSU, she taught secondary mathematics in the Detroit Public Schools. She received the Outstanding Dissertation Award at MSU's College of Education in 1990. Wilcox is interested in the initial and continuing professional development of elementary and middle school teachers and the role of new forms of curriculum and assessment in fostering teacher learning and teacher change. She is also interested in qualitative methods instruction and in collaborative studies of mathematics education reform with regard to issues of equity and access and the multiple context within which reform exists.

Biographical Statements for Speakers at the Action Conference on the Professional Development of Teachers of Mathematics in the Middle Grades

Deborah Loewenberg Ball is professor of educational studies at the University of Michigan. Her work as a researcher and teacher educator draws directly and indirectly on her long experience as an elementary classroom teacher. With mathematics as the main context for the work, Ball studies the practice of teaching and the processes of learning to teach. Her work also examines efforts to improve teaching through policy, reform initiatives, and teacher education. Ball's publications include articles on teacher learning and teacher education; the role of subject matter knowledge in teaching and learning to teach; endemic challenges of teaching; and the relations of policy and practice in instructional reform.

Karen Economopoulos is a developer of *Investigations in Number, Data and Space,* a K-5 mathematics curriculum funded by the National Science Foundation. In addition to curriculum development, she works extensively with classroom teachers, administrators, and school districts in the area of curriculum reform. She is a co-author

of *Beyond Arithmetic: Changing Mathematics in the Elementary Classroom* and a former classroom teacher.

Joan Ferrini-Mundy is Director of the Mathematical Sciences Education Board and Associate Executive Director of the Center for Science, Mathematics, and Engineering Education at the National Research Council. She is on leave from her position as a professor of mathematics at the University of New Hampshire, where she joined the faculty in 1983. She holds a Ph.D. in mathematics education from the University of New Hampshire. Ferrini-Mundy taught mathematics at Mount Holyoke College in 1982-83, where she co-founded the SummerMath for Teachers program. She was the Principal Investigator for the National Council of Teachers of Mathematics' (NCTM) Recognizing and Recording Reform in Mathematics Education (R3M) project. She served as a visiting scientist at the National Science Foundation from 1989-91. She chaired the NCTM's Research Advisory Committee, was a member of the NCTM Board of Directors, and served on the Mathematical Sciences Education Board. Ferrini-Mundy has chaired the American Educational Research Association Special Interest Group for Research in Mathematics Education. Her research interests are in calculus learning and reform in mathematics education, K-14. Currently she chairs the Writing Group for Standards 2000, the revision of the NCTM Standards.

John Moyer is currently a member of the Department of Mathematics Statistics and Computer science at Marquette University in Milwaukee, Wisconsin. He received a B.S. in Mathematics and Physics from Christian Brothers College in 1967, an M.S. in Mathematics from Northwestern University in 1974. He taught mathematics and physics in Chicago area high schools from 1967-1972. He joined the faculty at Marquette University in 1974, where he has taught mathematics, computer science, and mathematics education courses.

Since he has been at Marquette University, he has received funding for many mathematics education projects, most aimed at improving the professional development of middle school mathematics teachers. Recent projects include the Middle School Teachers' Mathematics Project (MSTMP), 1986-98; the Metropolitan Milwaukee Mathematics Collaborative (M³C), 1989-present; the Mathematics and Science Teachers' Business and Industry Awareness Project, 1989-present; the QUASAR project, 1990-97; the Project for the Improvement of Mathematics Education (PRIME), 1991-96; Preparing for Algebra Through Community Engagement, 1995-96; Rethinking Professional Development Goals 2000, 1996-8; Leadership for Urban Mathematics Reform, 1996-98; Linked Learning in Mathematics Project, 1997-present.

Mark Saul is a teacher at Bronxville High School, New York. He has taught for twenty-eight years and has been a Mathematics Adjunct Associate Professor at City College of New York for nine years. He is also Director of the American Regions Mathematics League Russian Exchange Program. He received his Ph.D. in mathematics education from New York University in 1987. He was awarded the Sigma Xi Recognition for Outstanding High School Science Teacher, Lehman College Chapter in 1981, and received a Westinghouse Science Talent Search Certificate of Honor, 1980-1983. He was recognized with the Presidential Award for Excellence in the Teaching of Mathematics, NSF in 1984. Saul is a member of the NRC's Mathematical Sciences Education Board. He has been continuously active in professional workshops, activities, presentations, and has authored over twenty publications.

Nanette Seago is currently the Project Director for the Video Cases for Mathematics Professional Development Project, funded by the National Science Foundation. This past year she directed the Mathematics Renaissance K-12 Video Pilot Study. For six years (1991-1997) she was a Regional Director for the Middle Grades Mathematics Renaissance. She has taught in kindergarten and upper elementary grades as well as mathematics at the middle school level. She authored the *TIMSS Video Moderator's Guide* for the U.S. Department of Education.

Margaret Smith is an assistant professor in the department of curriculum and instruction at the Pennsylvania State University. She has an Ed.D. in mathematics education from the University of Pittsburgh and has taught mathematics at the junior high, high school, and college levels. She was the coordinator of the QUASAR project between 1990 and 1997 where she focused primarily on supporting and studying the professional development of project teachers. She is currently working in preservice teacher education and is co-principal investigator of COMET (Cases of Mathematics Instruction to Enhance Teaching), a project aimed at developing case materials for teacher professional development in mathematics.

Iris Weiss is President of Horizon Research, Inc. in Chapel Hill, North Carolina. Weiss has a B.S. in biology from Cornell University, a Master's in Science Education from Harvard University, and a Ph.D. in Curriculum and Instruction from the University of North Carolina at Chapel Hill. Prior to establishing HRI in 1987, Weiss was Senior Research Scientist at the Research Triangle Institute. Her activities have included directing several national surveys of science and mathematics teachers; evaluating a number of science and mathematics education projects and systemic reform efforts; and providing technical assistance to agencies and professional organizations such as the National Science Foundation, the American Association for the Advancement of Science, the Council of Chief State School Officers, the National Council of Teachers of Mathematics, the National Science Teachers Association, and the Office of Technology Assessment. She is currently directing the design and implementation of a 50-project cross-site evaluation of NSF's Local Systemic Change Initiative.

Stephanie Williamson is the Assistant Director for Mathematics of the Louisiana Systemic Initiatives Program (LaSIP), has been a mathematics educator for twenty-five years, as an elementary, middle, and high school mathematics teacher. She has held leadership positions in several of the professional organizations of which she is a member: National Council of Teachers of Mathematics (NCTM), National Council of Supervisors of Mathematics (NCSM), Louisiana Association of Teachers of Mathematics (LATM), and Louisiana Council of Supervisors of Mathematics (LCSM). Williamson's primary responsibilities at LaSIP involve coordinating statewide mathematics professional development programs. She is currently a member of NCTM's Professional Development and Status Advisory Committee.

Appendix 3

CONVOCATION AND ACTION CONFERENCE PARTICIPANT LISTS

National Convocation on Mathematics Education in the Middle Grades Participant List

Elaine Abbas
Mathematics Teacher
Alice Deal Junior High School
Washington, DC

George Abshire
7th Grade Mathematics
 Instructor
Jenks 7th/8th Grade Center
Tulsa, OK

Lillie Albert
Assistant Professor
Boston College
Chestnut Hill, MA

Gordon Ambach
Executive Director
Council of Chief State School
 Officers
Washington, DC

Scott Anderson
School Site Coordinator
New Orleans Public Schools
New Orleans, LA

Ann Bacon
Coordinator of Mathematics
 K-12
Abington School District
Oreland, PA

Deborah Loewenberg Ball
University of Michigan
Ann Arbor, MI

Wyomie Barlow
Shaw Junior High School
Washington, DC

Ann Bartosh
Mathematics Consultant
Kentucky Department of
 Education
Lexington, KY

Hyman Bass
Professor of Mathematics
Columbia University
New York, NY

DeAnna Banks Beane
Youth ALIVE! Project Director
Association of Science-
 Technology Centers
Washington, DC

Charlene Beckmann
Professor
Grand Valley State University
Allendale, MI

George Bennett
Duval County Public Schools
Jacksonville, FL

Sarah Berenson
Professor and Director, Center
 for Research in Mathematics
 and Science Education
North Carolina State
 University
Raleigh, NC

Sandra Berger
Program Specialist
Eisenhower Consortium for
 Mathematics and Science
 Education
Tallahassee, FL

Donna Berlin
Associate Professor
Ohio State University
Columbus,OH

Catherine Bernhard
District Mathematics Specialist
Beaverton School District
Portland, OR

Fran Berry
Principal Investigator
Colorado State Systemic
 Initiative
Denver, CO

Betsy Berry
Middle/Secondary
  Mathematics Coordinator
Maine Mathematics and
  Science Alliance
Augusta, ME

Richard Bisk
Professor of Mathematics
Fitchburg State College
Princeton, MA

Benjamin Blackhawk
Mathematics Teacher
St. Paul Academy and Summit
  School
Crystal, MN

James Bohan
K-12 Mathematics Program
  Coordinator
Manheim Township School
  District
Lancaster, PA

L. Carey Bolster
Director, PBS Mathline
Public Broadcasting Service
Laurel, MD

Margaret Bondorew
Associate Director,
  Mathematics
CESAME at Northeastern
  University
Boston, MA

Melissa Booker
Manager, Publications and
  Special Projects
Association for Women in
  Science
Washington, DC

Frances Bouknight
Director of Instruction
Lexington County School
  District Three
Batesburg-Leesville, SC

Laura Brader-Araje
Doctoral Student
University of North Carolina,
  Chapel Hill
Durham, NC

John Bradley
Acting Deputy Division
  Director
National Science Foundation
Arlington, VA

Sadie Bragg
AMATYC, President
Vice President, Borough of
  Manhattan Community
  College
New York, NY

Teresa Bray
Teacher, Mathematics and
  Science
Evergreen School District
Vancouver, WA

Lisa Breidenbach
Mathematics Teacher
Fairfax County Public Schools
Ashburn, VA

Eileen Brett
Principal, Holy Angels School
  and Chair, Young Adolescent
  Committee for the Diocese
  of Trenton
Holy Angels School
Bordentown, NJ

Gregory Bridges
Mathematics Instructor
Jenks Public Schools
Jenks, OK

George Bright
Professor
University of North Carolina-
  Greensboro
Greensboro, NC

Cynthia Broadus
P.R. Harris Educational Center
Washington, DC

Catherine Brown
Associate Professor
Indiana University
Bloomington, IN

Elaine Brown
School Site Coordinator
New Orleans Public Schools
New Orleans, LA

Linda Brown
Elliot Junior High School
Washington, DC

Blanche Brownley
Secondary Mathematics
  Specialist
District of Columbia Public
  Schools
Camp Springs, MD

Naida Brueland
Mathematics Teacher
Irving Middle School
San Antonio, TX

Suzanne Buckwalter
Teacher and Mathematics
  Chair
University of Chicago
  Laboratory Schools
Chesterton, IN

Ella Burnett
Associate Professor of
  Education
California State University,
  Long Beach
Long Beach, CA

Valerie Butler
Mathematics Teacher
Houston Independent School
  District
Houston, TX

Sally Caldwell
Education Associate,
    Mathematics
Delaware Department of
    Education
Dover, DE

Andrew Callard
Mathematics Teacher
Sidwell Friends School
Washington, DC

Carol Cameron
Lead Mathematics Teacher
Heatherwood Middle School,
Everett School District
Seattle, WA

Gerald Capone
Mathematics Teacher
Wallenpaupack Area Middle
    School
Hawley, PA

Iris Carl
Past President
National Council of Teachers of
    Mathematics
Houston, TX

**Shereese Williamson
Carlisle**
Program Director
Philadelphia Education Fund
Philadelphia, PA

Wendell Cave
Eisenhower Project Director
Kentucky Council on
    Postsecondary Education
Frankfort, KY

Ruth Chamberlin
Curriculum Specialist,
    Mathematics
Everett School District
Everett, WA

Gregory Chamblee
Assistant Professor
Georgia Southern University
Statesboro, GA

Carolyn Chandler
Director of Studies
Girls Preparatory School
Chattanooga, TN

Kathleen Chapman
Journal Editor
National Council of Teachers of
    Mathematics
Reston, VA

Michaele Chappell
Associate Professor of
    Mathematics Education
University of South Florida
Tampa, FL

Sam Chattin
Teacher
Lexington, IN

Kathryn Chval
Co-Director, All Learn
    Mathematics
University of Illinois at Chicago
Chicago, IL

Armando Cisneros
Mathematics Specialist
Austin Independent School
    District
Austin, TX

Laura Clay
Mathematics Teacher
Solebury School
Lambertville, NJ

Wanda Clay
Instructional Coordinator
St. Louis Public Schools
St. Louis, MO

Christopher Clewis
Mathematics Teacher, Ryan
    Middle School
Houston Independent School
    District
Houston, TX

Georgia Cobbs
Assistant Professor
University of Montana
Missoula, MT

Gayle Coleman
Mathematics Supervisor
St. Louis Public Schools
St. Louis, MO

William Collins
Adjunct Professor
Syracuse University
Syracuse, NY

Kathleen Conway
Assistant Professor,
    Department of Elementary,
    Early & Special Education
Southeast Missouri State
    University
Cape Girardeau, MO

Duane A. Cooper
Assistant Professor of
    Mathematics Education and
    Mathematics
University of Maryland
College Park, MD

Cherie Cornick
Director
Alliance for Mathematics &
    Science
Redford, MI

Linda Coutts
K-7 Mathematics Coordinator
Columbia Public Schools
Department of Elementary and
    Secondary Education
Columbia, MO

Deborah Cox
6th Grade Teacher
Oklahoma State Department of
Education
Oklahoma City, OK

Joan Cox
Mathematics Facilitator
Memphis City Schools
Memphis, TN

Gilberto Cuevas
Professor of Mathematics
Education
University of Miami
Coral Gables, FL

Margaret Cunningham
Project Scimatch Teacher
Leader
Ohio Valley Educational
Cooperative
Shelbyville, KY

Frances Curcio
Professor of Mathematics
Education
New York University
Staten Island, NY

Edward D'Souza
Mathematics Coordinator
Riverside County Office of
Education
Rialto, CA

Kerry Davidson
MSEA Project Director
Louisiana Board of Regents
Baton Rouge, LA

Anselm Davis, Jr.
Principal Investigator
Navajo Nation Rural Systemic
Initiative
Window Rock, AZ

Linda DeGuire
Professor of Mathematics
Education
California State University-
Long Beach
Long Beach, CA

Thomas Dickinson
Professor, Curriculum,
Instruction, and Media
Technology
Indiana State University
Terre Haute, IN

Barbara Diliegghio
Teacher (Mathematics,
Science)
Waterford Schools
Waterford, MI

Kathryn Dillard
Principal
Wright Middle School
Nashville, TN

Nancy Doda
Assistant Professor
National-Louis University
Burke, VA

Lawrence J. Dolan
Technical Services
Coordinator
The College Board, Equity
2000
Washington, DC

Merrylle Doughty
Lincoln Middle School
Washington, DC

Mimi Downey
Teacher, Ranch View Middle
School
Douglas County Schools
Highlands Ranch, CO

Gayle Dudley
School Site Coordinator
New Orleans Public Schools
New Orleans, LA

James Earle
Mathematics Department
Chair
Ammons Middle School
Miami, FL

Janice Earle
Senior Program Director
National Science Foundation
Arlington, VA

Joyce Eaton
Mathematics Supervisor
St. Louis Public Schools
St. Louis, MO

Barbara Edwards
Assistant Professor
Oregon State University
Corvallis, OR

Jill Edwards
Program Officer
U.S. Department of Education
Washington, DC

Marjorie Enneking
Professor of Mathematics/
OCEPT Project Director
Portland State University
Portland, OR

Susan Enyart
Assistant Professor of
Mathematics
Otterbein College
Westerville, OH

David Erickson
Associate Professor
University of Montana
Missoula, MT

Sheldon Erickson
Middle School Teacher
Fresno Unified School District
Fresno, CA

Edward Esty
Consultant
U.S. Department of Education
Chevy Chase, MD

Joyce Evans
Program Director, Teacher
    Enhancement
National Science Foundation
Arlington, VA

Richard Evans
Professor of Mathematics
Plymouth State College
Plymouth, NH

Annette Fante
West Region Board of Trustees
    Member, National Middle
    School Assocation, and
    Director of Middle Schools,
    Douglas County School
    District
Castle Rock, CO

Marvana Farney
Mathematics Teacher
Rachel Carson Middle School
Centreville, VA

Susan Jane Feeley
Doctoral Candidate/Graduate
    Researcher
Pennsylvania State University
State College, PA

Robert Felner
Professor and Department
    Chair, Education; and
Director, National Center on
    Public Education
University of Rhode Island
Providence, RI

Francis Fennell
Program Director
National Science Foundation
Arlington, VA

James Fey
Professor, Mathematics
University of Maryland,
    College Park
College Park, MD

Gwen Fholer
Master Teacher in Residence
Oklahoma Teacher Education
    Collaborative
Edmond, OK

Hyman Field
Acting Division Director
    Elementary, Secondary, and
    Informal Education
National Science Foundation
Arlington, VA

Liana Finn
Teacher, Parker Vista Middle
    School
Douglas County Schools
Parker, CO

Linda Fisher
Program Specialist,
    Mathematics
Florida Department of
    Education
Tallahassee, FL

Charlotte Foreman
Collaborating Teacher
    Mathematics
School District of Philadelphia
Langhorne, PA

Linda Foreman
Middle School Classroom
    Teacher and Curriculum
    Specialist
Portland State University
West Linn, OR

Roy Foutz
Teacher
Middletown/Monroe School
    District
Middletown, OH

Stephen Francis
Principal, Ryan Middle School
Houston Independent School
    District
Houston, TX

Megan Franke
University of California, Los
    Angeles
Los Angeles, CA

Judd Freeman
Mathematics Consultant
Iowa Department of Education
Clive, IA

Susan Friel
Associate Professor
UNC-Chapel Hill
Chapel Hill, NC

Frank Gardella
Associate Professor-
    Mathematics Education
Hunter College - CUNY
East Brunswick, NJ

Lois Gardner
Teacher, 6th Grade
    Mathematics
Broadview Middle School
Newtown, CT

Joseph Gargiulo
Principal
Allen Middle School
Camp Hill, PA

William Gasper
Product Manager for
    Mathematics in Context
Encyclopaedia Britannica, Inc.
Chicago, IL

June Gaston
Professor of Mathematics
Borough of Manhattan
    Community College
Cambria Heights, NY

Kim Gattis
Mathematics Consultant
Kansas Department of
    Education
Lawrence, KS

William Geeslin
Associate Professor of
    Mathematics & Mathematics
    Education
University of New Hampshire
Durham, NH

William Geppert
Senior Mathematics Associate
Mid-Atlantic Eisenhower
    Consortium for Mathematics
    & Science Education
Philadelphia, PA

Randy Gilliam
Secondary Curriculum
    Coordinator
Middletown/Monroe City
    School District
Middletown, OH

Linda Gojak
Board of Directors
National Council of Teachers of
    Mathematics
Euclid, OH

John Golden
Assistant Professor
Grand Valley State University
Allendale, MI

Wendy Goldstein
U.S. Department of Education
Washington, DC

Janeane Golliher
Mathematics Coordinator
St. Vrain School District
Longmont, CO

Roxanne Gorman
Director
UCAN - Navajo Nation
    Coalition
Window Rock, AZ

Diane Gorski
Mathematics Teacher
Greenhills School
Ann Arbor, MI

Anna Graeber
Associate Professor,
    Department of Curriculum
    and Instruction
University of Maryland
College Park, MD

Karen Graham
Professor
University of New Hampshire
Durham, NH

Yvonne Grant
Classroom Coach
Traverse City Schools
Traverse City, MI

Koeno Gravemeijer
Professor, Freudenthal
    Institute
Utrecht University
The Netherlands

Susan Green
7-12 Mathematics Resource
    Teacher
San Juan Unified School
    District
Carmichael, CA

Jodeen Grunow
Mathematics Consultant
Wisconsin Department of
    Public Instruction
Dodgeville, WI

Judy Guess
Mathematics Coach
Long Beach Unified School
    District
Long Beach, CA

Norman T. Guffy
Principal Investigator, Texas
    RSI
West Texas A&M University
Canyon, TX

Linda Hall
Educator
Tulsa Public Schools
Tulsa, OK

Benjamin Halperin
University of Illinois
Urbana, IL

Robert Hamada
Mathematics Coordinator
Los Angeles Unified School
    District
Los Angeles, CA

James Hamling
7-8 Mathematics Teacher
Lewistown School District # 1
Lewistown, MT

Peirce Hammond
Director, Office of Reform
    Assistance and
    Dissemination
U.S. Department of Education
Washington, DC

Terri Hammond
Title I Coordinator:
    Mathematics
West Virginia Department of
    Education
Charleston, WV

Joseph Hansen
Executive Director, Planning,
    Research & Evaluation
Colorado Springs School
    District #11
Colorado Springs, CO

Philip Harding
Teacher Trustee, North/West
    Regions
National Middle School
    Association
Vancouver, WA

Ellen Hardwick
Aerospace Education Specialist
NASA
Laurel, MD

Marieta Harris
Project Director
Memphis City Schools
Memphis, TN

Merle Harris
Mathematics Educator
New Orleans Algebra Project
New Orleans, LA

Kathleen Hart
Professor
School of Education
University of Nottingham
England

Christopher Hartmann
Project Assistant
University of Wisconsin,
    Madison
Madison, WI

Gary Heath
Chief, Science and
    Mathematics Section
Maryland State Department of
    Education
Baltimore, MD

Norma G. Hernandez
Professor, Mathematics
    Education
University of Texas at El Paso
El Paso, TX

Terese Herrera
Mathematics Resource
    Specialist
Eisenhower National
    Clearinghouse
Columbus, OH

Timothy Hicks
Teacher
International School of
    Dusseldorf
Dusseldorf, 40489

Barbara Hicks
Research Libarian
Region III Comprehensive
    Center
Arlington, VA

James Hiebert
Professor, College of Education
University of Delaware
Newark, DE

Marcine Hill
Instructional Coordinator
St. Louis Public Schools
St. Louis, MO

Margie Hill
District Coordinating Teacher
    for Mathematics K-12
Blue Valley School District
Overland Park, KS

Larry Hines
Interim Director of Center of
    Excellence
Black Hills State University
Spearfish, SD

Arlene Hirsch
Vice Principal
Whitford Middle School
Beaverton, OR

Susan Hoffmier
Weimar Hills School
Auburn, CA

Betty Jo Horton
Girls Preparatory School
Chattanooga, TN

Mary Jo Howland
Research Associate
Tennessee State Board of
    Education
Nashville, TN

Deborah Hughes-Hallett
Professor of Mathematics
University of Arizona
Tucson, AZ

Jane Braddock Hunt
Vice President for Middle
    Grades
Kentucky Council of Teachers
    of Mathematics
Elizabethtown, KY

Nancy Hurd
7th Grade Mathematics
    Teacher
Mt. Ararat Middle School
West Bath, ME

Tanya Ivey
Mathematics Specialist
Salem-Keizer School District
Salem, OR

Judith Jacobs
Director
Center for Education and
    Equity in Mathematics,
    Science, and Technology
Pomona, CA

Idorenyin Jamar
Assistant Professor
University of Pittsburgh
Pittsburgh, PA

Angela Jasper
Roper Middle School
Washington, DC

Fredryn Jenkins
Garnet-Patterson Middle
    School
Washington, DC

Shirley Conner Jenkins
Program Officer, Professional
    Development
Southern Initiative of Algebra
    Project
Hollandale, MS

Martin Johnson
Professor and Chair,
    Department of Curriculum
    & Instruction
University of Maryland,
    College Park
College Park, MD

Keith Jones
Coordinator, Elementary
    Mathematics (K-8)
Montgomery County (MD)
    Public Schools
Rockville, MD

Mary Jones
Teacher
Iroquois Middle School
Allendale, MI

Tameica Jones
Teacher
Prince George's County Public
    Schools
Burke, VA

James Kaput
Chancellor Professor of
    Mathematics
University of Massachusetts
    Dartmouth
North Dartmouth, MA

Judy Kasabian
Professor of Mathematics
El Camino College
Rolling Hills Estates, CA

Julie Keener
Association Professor of
    Mathematics
Central Oregon Community
    College
Bend, OR

Marilyn Kilgore
Mathematics Instructor
Jenks Public Schools
Jenks, OK

Joellen Killion
Project Director, Results-Based
    Staff Development for the
    Middle Grades
National Staff Development
    Council
Arvada, CO

Jennifer King
Steven Vail Middle School
Middletown, OH

Walter Mae King
School Site Coordinator
New Orleans Public Schools
New Orleans, LA

Vicky Kirschner
Independent Consultant and
    Professor, Ohio Wesleyan
    University
Columbus, OH

Noël Klimenko
Mathematics Department
    Chairperson
Fairfax County Public Schools
Herndon, VA

Genevieve Knight
Visiting Fellow
The Council of Scientific
    Society Presidents
Columbia, MD

Judith Knight
Middle School Mathematics
    Teacher and Department
    Head
Georgetown Day School
Chevy Chase, MD

Debra Kohuth
Mathematics Teacher
Wallenpaupack Area Middle
    School
Hawley, PA

Nina Koltnow
Mathematics Department
    Chair
Sidwell Friends School
Washington, DC

Jane Konrad
Executive Director
Pittsburgh Regional Center for
    Science Teachers
Sewickley, PA

Angela Krebs
Assistant Professor of
    Mathematics
University of Michigan-
    Dearborn
Brighton, MI

Gerald Kulm
Program Director
Project 2061/AAAS
Washington, DC

Ken Labuskes
Demonstration Teacher
Pittsburgh Public Schools
Pittsburgh, PA

Carole LaCampagne
Senior Research Associate,
   Office of Educational
   Research and Improvement
U.S. Department of Education
Washington, DC

Stan Lake
Mathematics Teacher/
   Department Chair
Oakland Unified School
   District
Oakland, CA

Donna Landin
Coordinator, WVDE/IBM
   Reinventing Education
West Virginia Department of
   Education
Hurricane, WV

Glenda Lappan
Professor of Mathematics
Connected Mathematics
   Project
East Lansing, MI

Elizabeth Lashley
Mathematics Specialist
Anderson Oconee Pickens
   HUB
Clemson, SC

Mona Lasley
Mathematics Consultant for
   the Northern California
   Mathematics Project
Natomas Unified School
   District
Woodland, CA

Granville Lee
Teacher
Francis Junior High School
Washington, DC

Bonnie Lehet
Senior Mathematics/
   Technology Specialist
New Jersey Statewide Systemic
   Initiative
Highland Park, NJ

Charles Leighton
Jefferson Junior High School
Washington, DC

Cathy Liebars
Assistant Professor
The College of New Jersey
Ewing, NJ

Mary Lindquist
Professor
Columbus State University
Columbus, GA

JoAnn Lingel
Middle School Mathematics
   Teacher
Riverdale School
Muscoda, WI

Madeleine J. Long
Vice President
The Implementation Group
Washington, DC

Karen Longhart
Mathematics Teacher
Flathead High School
Kalispell, MT

Johnny Lott
Professor of Mathematics
University of Montana
Missoula, MT

Cheryl Lubinski
Associate Professor of
   Mathematics
Illinois State University
Normal, IL

John Luczak
U.S. Department of Education
Washington, DC

John Luedeman
Program Director
National Science Foundation
Arlington, VA

Michele Luke
7th Grade Mathematics
   Teacher
Jackson Middle School
Maple Grove, MN

Linda Lytle
District Mathematics Mentor
El Centro School District
Calexico, CA

Sandi Machit
Middle School Mathematics
   Teachers' Coach
Long Beach Unified School
   District
Cypress, CA

Adele Macula
District Supervisor, Programs
   that Maximize Potential
Jersey City Public Schools
Nutley, NJ

Mark Maldet
Assistant Principal
Cedar Cliff High School
Camp Hill, PA

Syndee Sue Malek
Teacher
South Redford Schools
Livonia, MI

Amy Maley
Mathematics Department
    Coordinator
Keith Valley Middle School,
    Hatboro-Horsham School
    District, PA
Lower Gwynedd, PA

Charlene Marchese
Mathematics Teacher
Millburn Middle School,
    Millburn, NJ
Livingston, NJ

Dona Marler
Director
Commonwealth Partnership
Philadelphia, PA

Amy Martin
Mathematics Teacher
Los Angeles Unified School
    District
Los Angeles, CA

Juanita Martinez
Mathematics Teacher
Lowell Middle School
San Antonio, TX

Raine Martinez
Mathematics Specialist
Fresno, CA

Marguerite Mason
Assistant Professor of
    Mathematics Education
College of William and Mary
Williamsburg, VA

Joan Mast
Mathematics Supervisor
Millburn Township Public
    Schools
Millburn, NJ

Tami Matsumoto
Teacher
Carmichael Middle School
Richland, WA

Marilyn McArthur
Teacher, Department Chair,
    Middle School Mathematics
Page Middle School, Page
    Unified School District # 8
Page, AZ

Delores McClain
Hine Junior High School
Washington, DC

Jacqueline McDonald
Assistant Professor
Adelphi University
Garden City, NY

Mike McGehee
Mathematics Instructor
Jenks Public Schools
Jenks, OK

Mercedes McGowen
Chair, Education
    Subcommittee on Teacher
    Preparation
AMATYC
Palatine, IL

C. Kent McGuire
Assistant Secretary for the
    Educational Research and
    Improvement
U.S. Department of Education
Washington, DC

Alexina Hazzard McIver
Middle School Mathematics
    Resource Teacher
Los Angeles Unified School
    District
Los Angeles, CA

Denise Meany
Teacher, 6th Grade
    Mathematics
Broadview Middle School
Newtown, CT

Nancy Metz
Coordinator, Secondary
    Mathematics
Montgomery County Public
    Schools
Rockville, MD

Margaret Meyer
Director, Mathematics in
    Context
University of Wisconsin,
    Madison
Madison, WI

Alice Mikovch
Special Assistant to the Dean's
    Ofice
Western Kentucky University
Bowling Green, KY

Ann Miller
Teacher, Castle Rock Middle
    School
Douglas County Schools
Castle Rock, CO

Joan Miller
Mathematics Curriculum
    Specialist
Portland Public Schools
Portland, OR

Nedra Miller
Standards Coach - Teacher
Long Beach Unified School
    District
Carson, CA

Donna Mirabelli
Mathematics Supervisor
West New York Board of
    Education
North Bergen, NJ

Arlene Mitchell
Senior Associate in
    Mathematics
Eisenhower High Plains
    Consortium
Aurora, CO

Greg Miyata
Secondary Mathematics/
    Technology Resource
    Teacher
Los Angeles Unified School
    District
Rosemead, CA

Concepcion Molina
Program Specialist in
    Mathematics
Southwest Educational
    Development Laboratories
Austin, TX

Barbara Montalto
Assistant Director of
    Mathematics
Texas Education Agency
Austin, TX

Ralph Montgomery
Principal, Parker Vista Middle
    School
Douglas County Schools
Parker, CO

Frances Moore
Mathematics Teacher
Miami-Dade County Public
    Schools
Hialeah, FL

Kathleen Morris
Senior Program Associate
Project 2061/AAAS
Washington, DC

Ronald Morris
Shaw Junior High School
Washington, DC

Judy Mumme
Director, Mathematics
    Renaissance K-12
San Diego State University
Camarillo, CA

Masaya Mura
Teacher
Los Angeles Unified School
    District
Los Angeles, CA

Mari Muri
Mathematics Consultant
CSDE
Hartford, CT

Cynthia Nahrgang
Mathematics Teacher/
    Computer Coordinator
    Grades 6-8
The Blake Middle School
Wayzata, MN

Dierdie L. Neal
Sixth Grade Teacher
Stuart-Hobson Middle School
Washington, DC

Ted Nelson
Professor of Mathematics
Portland State University
Portland, OR

Edward Nolan
Mathematics Department
    Chair
Montgomery County Public
    Schools
Rockville, MD

Marianne O'Connor
Demonstration Teacher
Pittsburgh Public Schools
Pittsburgh, PA

Susan Ohanian
Writer/Teacher
Heinemann
Charlotte, VT

Dale Oliver
Associate Professor of
    Mathematics
Humboldt State University
Arcata, CA

Judith Olson
Professor of Mathematics
Western Illinois University
Macomb, IL

Melfried Olson
Professor of Mathematics
Western Illinois University
Macomb, IL

Albert Otto
Professor of Mathematics
Illinois State University
Normal, IL

Christine Palmer
Middle School Mathematics
    Teacher
Perkiomen Valley School
    District
Audubon, PA

Linda Patch
Mathematics Consultant
North Carolina Department of
    Public Instruction
Raleigh, NC

Weyman Patterson
Mathematics Coordinator
Atlanta Public Schools
Atlanta, GA

Debra Paulson
8th Grade Mathematics
    Teacher
El Paso Independent School
    District, Hornedo Middle
    School
El Paso, TX

Julie Peck
Mathematics Coordinator
Spokane Public Schools
Spokane, WA

Sauzette Pelton
Teacher
Berrien Springs Public Schools
Berrien Springs, MI

Marcia Perry
Eisenhower Program Specialist
Virginia Department of
  Education
Richmond, VA

Jeanine Pickering
Mathematics Teacher, CY
  Junior High
Natrona County School
  District, WY
Evansville, WY

Jacqueline Pisauro
Mathematics Educator -
  Grade 8
Southmoor Middle School,
  Columbus Public Schools
Columbus, OH

John Polking
Professor
Rice University
Houston, TX

Mattye Pollard-Cole
Mathematics Senior
  Consultant
Colorado Department of
  Education
Denver, CO

Lydia Polonsky
Mathematics Teacher
University of Chicago
  Laboratory Schools
Chicago, IL

Barbara Pond
Teacher, Cresthill Middle
  School
Douglas County Schools
Highlands Ranch, CO

Judith Poppell
Director, Academic Programs
Duval County Public Schools
Jacksonville, FL

Neil Portnoy
Assistant Professor
University of Tennessee
Knoxville, TN

Susan Powell
Middle School Mathematics
  Teacher
Oklahoma State Department of
  Education
Ames, OK

Pharyll Pretlow
MacFarland Middle School
Washington, DC

Joan Prival
Science Education Analyst
National Science Foundation
Arlington, VA

Susan Pruet
Director, South Alabama
  Systemic Initiative in
  Mathematics
University of South Alabama
Fairhope, AL

Dorothy Purvis
Teacher, Parker Vista–West
Douglas County Schools
Parker, CO

Curtis Pyke
Assistant Professor of
  Mathematics Education
The George Washington
  University
Washington, DC

Sid Rachlin
Director, Middle Mathematics
  Project
East Carolina University
Washington, NC

Mary Lynn Raith
Mathematics Curriculum
  Specialist
Pittsburgh Public Schools
Pittsburgh, PA

Reynaldo Ramirez
Project Director
Center for Education Research
  in Teaching and Learning
Brownsville, TX

Katherine Rasch
Dean and Professor of
  Education
School of Education
Chesterfield, MO

Karen Rasmussen
Writer
Association for Supervision
  and Curriculum
  Development
Alexandria, VA

Joyce Reagon
Elliot Junior High School
Washington, DC

Sara Reed
Resource Teacher, Middle
  School Mathematics
Montgomery County Public
  Schools
Silver Spring, MD

Sue Reehm
Associate Professor
  Mathematics Education
Eastern Kentucky University
Richmond, KY

Caran Resciniti
Secondary Mathematics
  Specialist
Fresno Unified School District
Fresno, CA

Laura Resendez
Director of Mathematics and
    School Initiatives
San Antonio Independent
    School District
San Antonio, TX

Barbara Reys
Professor & Director of the
    NSF Show-Me Center
University of Missouri
Columbia, MO

Carol Rezba
Principal Mathematics
    Specialist
Virginia Department of
    Education
Richmond, VA

Sherri Roberti
Mathematics Teacher
Beaverton Schools
Portland, OR

Patricia Robertson
Mathematics Supervisor
Arlington Public Schools
Arlington, VA

Jan Robinson
Curriculum Coordinator
Community Consolidated
    School District 21
Palatine, IL

Ellen Rose
Middle School Teacher
Montana Council of Teachers
    of Mathematics
Bozeman, MT

Linda P. Rosen
Expert Consultant
United States Department of
    Education
Washington, DC

Pat O'Connell Ross
U.S. Department of Education
Washington, DC

Susan Ross
Interim Director of the Center
    for Science and Mathematics
    Education
University of Southern
    Mississippi
Hattiesburg, MS

Wimberly Royster
Principal Investigator,
    Appalachian Rural Systemic
    Initiative
Kentucky Science and
    Technology Council, Inc.
Lexington, KY

John Russell
Computer Specialist Teacher
Natrona County School District
Casper, WY

Don Ryoti
Professor
Eastern Kentucky University
Richmond, KY

Shirley Sagawa
Executive Director
Learning First Alliance
Washington, DC

Emiliano Sanchez
Bilingual Mathematics Teacher
Oakland Unified School
    District
Oakland, CA

James Sandefur
Professor of Mathematics
Georgetown University
Washington, DC

Diane Schaefer
Mathematics Specialist
Rhode Island Department of
    Education
Cranston, RI

Donald Scheuer
President
Pennsylvania Council of
    Teachers of Mathematics
Fort Washington, PA

Debbie Schmidt
Head of Mathematics
    Department
Central Lutheran School
New Haven, IN

Sandra Schoff
Mathematics Coordinator
Anchorage School District
Anchorage, AK

Peggy Schroeder
Principal, Castle Rock Middle
    School
Douglas County Schools
Castle Rock, CO

William Scott
Mathematics Supervisor
Colorado Springs School
    District # 11
Colorado Springs, CO

Nanette Seago
Project Director
Video Cases for Mathematics
    Professional Development
    Project
Riverside, CA

Mary Shafer
Director, Longitudinal/Cross-
    Sectional Study of
    Mathematics in Context
University of Wisconsin-
    Madison
Madison, WI

Robert Sheedy
Deputy Superintendent
New York City Board of
   Education - School Program
   and Support Services
Parlin, NJ

Lorrie Shepard
President-Elect, AERA
Professor
University of Colorado at
   Boulder
Boulder, CO

Dennis Sherard
Principal
Ahwahnee Middle School
Fresno, CA

Clementine Sherman
Director, USI Mathematics and
   Science
Miami Dade County Public
   Schools
Miami, FL

Karen Sherman
6th Grade Teacher
Greenhills School
Ann Arbor, MI

Jeff Sherrill
Program Manager
National Association of
   Secondary School Principals
Reston, VA

Edward Silver
Professor and Senior Scientist,
   Learning Research
   Development Center
University of Pittsburgh
Pittsburgh, PA

Beth Skipper
Mathematics Coordinator
Louisiana Systemic Initiatives
   Program (LaSIP)
Baton Rouge, LA

Julie Sliva
Professor
Lesley College
Durham, NC

Margaret Smith
Assistant Professor of
   Mathematics Education
Penn State University
University Park, PA

Shirley Smith
NCTM Representative to the
   DC Council of Teachers of
   Mathematics, and
   Mathematics Teacher,
   Springbrook High School
Silver Spring, MD

Pearl Solomon
Professor of Education
St. Thomas Aquinas College
Sparkill, NY

Sheryl Spalding
Board of Education Member
Blue Valley School District
Overland Park, KS

Bill Sparks
Professor of Mathematics
University of Wisconsin, Eau
   Claire
Eau Claire, WI

Kristin Speakman
Mathematics Instructor
Jenks Public Schools
Jenks, OK

Marsha Spees
Middle School Principal
Riverdale School
Muscoda, WI

Craig Spilman
Principal
Canton Middle School
Baltimore, MD

Diane Spresser
Program Director, Teacher
   Enhancement
National Science Foundation
Arlington, VA

Frances Stage
Professor
Indiana University
Bloomington, IN

Gale Hansen Starich
Faculty Associate & K-16
   Coordinator
University and Community
   College System of Nevada
Reno, NV

Mary Kay Stein
Research Scientist
Learning Research and
   Development Center
Pittsburgh, PA

Frances Stern
Instructor in Mathematics
   Education
New York University
New York, NY

Stephanie Stokloza
Seventh Grade Teacher
Laconia Memorial Middle
   School
Plymouth, NH

Arsena Strange
Teacher
Model Secondary School for
   the Deaf at Gallaudet
   University
Washington, DC

Harold Stratigos
Mathematics Education
   Adviser
Pennsylvania Department of
   Education
Harrisburg, PA

Annette Sulzman
Principal, Ranch View Middle
School
Douglas County Schools
Highlands Ranch, CO

Wei Sun
Assistant Professor of
Mathematics Education
Towson University
Towson, MD

Judy Sunley
Assistant to the Director for
Science Policy & Planning
National Science Foundation
Arlington, VA

Jane Swafford
Professor
Illinois State University
Normal, IL

Elizabeth Swierzawski
Mathematics Teacher
Keith Valley Middle School,
Hatboro-Horsham School
District, PA
Hatfield, PA

Nancy Taylor
School Improvement Program
Assistant
Salem-Keizer School District
Salem, OR

James Telese
Assistant Professor of
Secondary Education &
Mathematics Education
University of Texas,
Brownsville
Rancho Viego, TX

Larry Tendis
Mathematics Teacher/
Mathematics Standards
Coach
Long Beach Unified School
District
Huntington Beach, CA

Jennifer Thayer
Mathematics Consultant
Wisconsin Department of
Public Instruction
Madison, WI

Roselyne Thomas
Instructional Coordinator
Batesburg-Leesville Middle
School
Batesburg-Leesville, SC

Mary Thomas
School Site Coordinator
New Orleans Public Schools
New Orleans, LA

Andrea Thompson
Thurgood Marshall Middle
School
Washington, DC

Mary Thompson
Mathematics Specialist
New Orleans Public Schools
New Orleans, LA

John A. Thorpe
Executive Director
National Council of Teachers of
Mathematics
Reston, VA

Cynthia Tocci
Program Administrator
Educational Testing Service
Princeton, NJ

Clara Tolbert
Director, Urban Systemic
Initiative
School District of Philadelphia
Philadelphia, PA

William Tomhave
Professor of Mathematics
Concordia College
Moorhead, MN

Maria Torres
Program Associate
Southwest Educational
Development Laboratories
Austin, TX

Debbie Turner
Mathematics Instructor
Jenks Public Schools
Jenks, OK

Kathleen Ulrich
Mathematics/Technology
Consultant
Ohio Department of Education
Columbus, OH

Josephine Urso
Educational Administrator:
Mathematics
New York City Board of
Education
Brooklyn, NY

Lisa Usher
Resource Teacher
Los Angeles Unified School
District
Long Beach, CA

Judy Vail
Middle Mathematics
Consultant
Calcasieu Parish Schools
Lake Charles, LA

Roger VanderPloeg
Mathematics Teacher Leader
Madison School District #38
Phoenix, AZ

Jean Vanski
Senior Staff Associate for
    Budget and Program
    Analysis
National Science Foundation
Arlington, VA

Virginia Vargas
Mathematics Teacher
Mann Middle School
San Antonio, TX

Nancy Varner
Acting Director, Office of
    Mathematics
Detroit Public Schools
Detroit, MI

Roger Verhey
Professor of Mathematics and
    Education
University of Michigan-
    Dearborn
Dearborn, MI

Germaine Wagner
6th Grade Teacher, Paradise
    Valley Elementary School
Natrona County School
    District, WY
Casper, WY

Barbara Waite-Jaques
Instructional Specialist,
    Secondary Mathematics
Montgomery County Public
    Schools
Rockville, MD

Patsy Wang-Iverson
Senior Assocaite
Research for Better Schools
Philadelphia, PA

Janet Warfield
Assistant Professor of
    Mathematics Education
Purdue University
West Lafayette, IN

Ava Warren
Mathematics Coordinator
Hamilton County Department
    of Education
Lookout Mountain, GA

Jesse Warren
Curriculum Facilitator
South Bend Community
    School Corporation
South Bend, IN

Don Watson
Teacher, Whiteaker Middle
    School
Salem-Keizer School District
Salem, OR

Brenda Watson
Teacher
Wallenpaupack Area Middle
    School
Hawley, PA

Stephanie Weaver
Assistant Director
INSIGHT
Columbia, MD

Richard Weir
Director, Mathematics
    Education
Oklahoma State Department of
    Education
Yukon, OK

Rosamond Welchman
Professor
Brooklyn College-CUNY
Brooklyn, NY

Tracey Weller
Teacher
Naperville School District #203
Downers Grove, IL

Jo Wenzler
Middle School Mathematics
    Teacher
Riverdale School
Muscoda, WI

Carol West
Acting Director for Technical
    Services
The College Board, Equity
    2000
Washington, DC

Linda Barton White
Manager, Academic Programs
    Unit
California Postsecondary
    Education Commission
Sacramento, CA

Carmen Whitman
Mathematics Specialist
Charles A. Dana Center and
    Austin Collaborative for
    Mathematics Education
Pflugerville, TX

Dawayne Whittington
Horizon Research, Inc.
Chapel Hill, NC

Sandra Wilcox
Associate Professor
Michigan State University
East Lansing, MI

Cash Williams
Teacher
District of Columbia Public
    Schools
Washington, DC

Claudette Williams
Director of Elementary and
    Middle Grades Education
Tennessee Department of
    Education
Nashville, TN

Luther Williams
Assistant Director, Education
    and Human Resources
National Science Foundation
Arlington, VA

Sheila Williams
Executive Director
St. Louis Public Schools
St. Louis, MO

Vernon Williams
Gifted and Talented
    Coordinator
Longfellow Intermediate
    School
Falls Church, VA

Stephanie Williamson
Assistant Director for
    Mathematics
Louisiana Systemic Initiatives
    Program (LaSIP)
Baton Rouge, LA

Wanda Wilson
School Site Coordinator
New Orleans Public Schools
New Orleans, LA

Kay Wohlhuter
Assistant Professor of
    Mathematics Education
Western Illinois University
Macomb, IL

Susan Wood
Professor of Mathematics
J. Sargeant Reynolds
    Community College
Richmond, VA

Terry Woodin
Program Director
National Science Foundation
Arlington, VA

Judy Wurtzel
U.S. Department of Education
Washington, DC

Dennis Yemma
President, European Council of
    Teachers of Mathematics
Middle School Mathematics
    Teacher, Department of
    Defense Dependents
    Schools
APO, AE

M. Hope Yursa
Facilitator, Teaching and
    Learning Network
School District of Philadelphia
Philadelphia, PA

Orit Zaslavsky
Professor
Department of Education in
    Science and Technology
Haifa 32000, Israel

Janie Zimmer
Coordinator of Mathematics,
    K-12
Howard County Public Schools
Ellicott City, MD

Deborah Zopf
Coordinator: Pre-Education
    Programs
Henry Ford Community
    College
Plymouth, MI

Action Conference on the Nature and Teaching of Algebra in the Middle Grades Participant List

Ann Bacon
Coordinator of Mathematics
  K-12
Abington School District
Oreland, PA

Anne Bartel
Mathematics Project Manager
Sci Mathematics MN
Minneapolis, MN

L. Carey Bolster
Director, PBS Mathline
Public Broadcasting Service
Laurel, MD

Elaine Brown
School Site Coordinator
New Orleans Public Schools
New Orleans, LA

Blanche Brownley
Secondary Mathematics
  Specialist
District of Columbia Public
  Schools
Camp Springs, MD

Bonnie Buehler
Springman Middle School
Glenview, IL

Al Cuoco
Director, Center for
  Mathematics Education
Education Development
  Center, Inc.
Newton, MA

Kathryn Dillard
Principal
Wright Middle School
Nashville, TN

Nancy Doda
Assistant Professor
National-Louis University
Washington, DC

Lawrence J. Dolan
Technical Services
  Coordinator
The College Board, Equity
  2000
Washington, DC

Gayle Dudley
School Site Coordinator
New Orleans Public Schools
New Orleans, LA

James Fey
Professor, Mathematics
University of Maryland,
  College Park, MD

Wendy Goldstein
U.S. Department of Education
Washington, DC

Yvonne Grant
Classroom Coach
Traverse City Schools
Traverse City, MI

Laura Grier
Project Coordinator
  (Mathematics Curriculum)
Project 2061
American Association for the
  Advancement of Science
Washington, DC

Jodeen Grunow
Mathematics Consultant
Wisconsin Department of
  Public Instruction
Dodgeville, WI

Stephen Hake
Author
Saxon Publishers
Temple City, CA

Robert Hamada
Mathematics Coordinator
Los Angeles Unified School
  District
Los Angeles, CA

Susan Hoffmier
Weimar Hills School
Auburn, CA

Idorenyin Jamar
Assistant Professor
University of Pittsburgh
Department of Instruction &
  Learning
Pittsburgh, PA

Shirley Conner Jenkins
Program Officer, Professional
  Development
Southern Initiative of Project
Hollandale, MS

Cathy Kelso
Co-Director, TIMS Project
University of Illinois at Chicago
Institute for Mathematics and
  Science Education
Chicago, IL

Judith Knight
Middle School Mathematics
  Teacher and Department
  Head
Georgetown Day School
Chevy Chase, MD

Madeleine J. Long
Vice President
The Implementation Group
Washington, DC

Nancy Metz
Coordinator, Secondary
    Mathematics
Montgomery County Public
    Schools
Rockville, MD

Susan Ohanian
Writer/Teacher
Heinemann
Charlotte, VT

Linda Patch
Mathematics Consultant
North Carolina Department of
    Public Instruction
Raleigh, NC

Weyman Patterson
Mathematics Coordinator
Atlanta Public Schools
Atlanta, GA

Debra Paulson
8th Grade Mathematics
    Teacher
El Paso Independent School
    District, Hornedo Middle
    School
El Paso, TX

Mattye Pollard-Cole
Mathematics Senior
    Consultant
Colorado Department of
    Education
Denver, CO

Judith Poppell
Director, Academic Programs
Duval County Public Schools
Jacksonville, FL

Curtis Pyke
Assistant Professor of
    Mathematics Education
The George Washington
    University
Washington, DC

Donald Scheuer
President
Pennsylvania Council of
    Teachers of Mathematics
Fort Washington, PA

Sandra Schoff
Mathematics Coordinator
Anchorage School District
Anchorage, AK

Robert Sheedy
Deputy Superintendent
New York City Board of
    Education - School Program
    and Support Services
Parlin, NJ

Clementine Sherman
Director, USI Mathematics and
    Science
Miami Dade County Public
    Schools
Miami, FL

Bill Sparks
Professor of Mathematics
University of Wisconsin, Eau
    Claire
Eau Claire, WI

Nancy Varner
Acting Director, Office of
    Mathematics
Detroit Public Schools
Detroit, MI

Patsy Wang-Iverson
Senior Associate
Research for Better Schools
Philadelphia, PA

Rosamond Welchman
Professor
Brooklyn College-CUNY
Brooklyn, NY

Cash Williams
Teacher
District of Columbia Public
    Schools
Washington, DC

Vernon Williams
Gifted and Talented
    Coordinator
Longfellow Intermediate
    School
Falls Church, VA

Terry Woodin
Program Director
National Science Foundation
Arlington, VA

Orit Zaslavsky
Professor
Department of Education in
    Science and Technology
Technion–Israel Institute of
    Technology
Israel

Action Conference on Research in the Teaching and Learning of Mathematics in the Middle Grades Participant List

Daniel B. Berch
Scientific Review Administrator
National Institutes of Health
Center for Scientific Review
Bethesda, MD

George Bright
Professor
University of North Carolina-
    Greensboro
Greensboro, NC

Jinfa Cai
Assistant Professor and
    Director of Mathematics
    Education Program
University of Delaware
Newark, DE

Michaele Chappell
Associate Professor of
    Mathematics Education
University of South Florida
Tampa, FL

Janice Earle
Senior Program Director
National Science Foundation
Arlington, VA

Edward Esty
Consultant
U.S. Department of Education
Washington, DC

Joyce Evans
Program Director, Teacher
    Enhancement
National Science Foundation
Arlington, VA

James Fey
Professor, Mathematics
University of Maryland,
    College Park
College Park, MD

Anna Graeber
Associate Professor,
    Department of Curriculum
    and Instruction
University of Maryland
College Park, MD

Koeno Gravemeijer
Professor, Freudenthal
    Institute
Utrecht University
The Netherlands

Joseph Hansen
Executive Director, Planning,
    Research & Evaluation
Colorado Springs School
    District #11
Colorado Springs, CO

Kathleen Hart
Professor
School of Education
University of Nottingham
England

James Hiebert
Professor, College of Education
University of Delaware
Newark, DE

Carole LaCampagne
Senior Research Associate,
    Office of Educational
    Research and Improvement
U.S. Department of Education
Washington, DC

Glenda Lappan
Professor of Mathematics
Connected Mathematics
    Project
Michigan State University
East Lansing, MI

Karen Longhart
Mathematics Teacher
Flathead High School
Kalispell, MT

Carolyn Maher
Professor of Mathematics
    Education
Rutgers University
New Brunswick, NJ

Kay McClain
Lecturer
Vanderbilt University
Nashville, TN

James Middleton
Associate Professor
Arizona State University
Tempe, AZ

Kathleen Morris
Senior Program Associate
AAAS/Project 2061
Washington, DC

Meera Pradhan
Intern
Department of Education
Deputy Secretary's Office
Washington, DC

James Sandefur
Professor of Mathematics
Georgetown University
Washington, DC

Deborah Schifter
Senior Scientist
Education Development
    Center
Northampton, MA

Alan Schoenfeld
Elizabeth and Edward Connor
    Professor of Education
University of California,
    Berkeley
Berkeley, CA

Mary Shafer
Director, Longitudinal/Cross-
    Sectional Study of
    Mathematics in Context
University of Wisconsin-
    Madison
Madison, WI

Jack Smith
Assistant Professor
Michigan State University
East Lansing, MI

Judith Sowder
Professor of Mathematical
    Sciences
San Diego State University
San Diego, CA

Diane Spresser
Program Director, Teacher
    Enhancement
National Science Foundation
Division of Elementary,
    Secondary, and Informal
    Education
Arlington, VA

Frances Stage
Professor
Indiana University
Bloomington, IN

Mary Kay Stein
Research Scientist
Learning Research and
    Development Center
University of Pittsburgh
Pittsburgh, PA

Jane Swafford
Professor
Illinois State University
Normal, IL

Mary Thomas
School Site Coordinator
New Orleans Public Schools
New Orleans, LA

Mary Thompson
Mathematics Specialist
New Orleans Public Schools
New Orleans, LA

Jean Vanski
Senior Staff Associate for
    Budget and Program
    Analysis
National Science Foundation
Directorate for Education and
    Human Resources
Arlington, VA

Sandra Wilcox
Associate Professor
Michigan State University
East Lansing, MI

Linda Dager Wilson
Assistant Professor
University of Delaware
Newark, DE

Wanda Wilson
School Site Coordinator
New Orleans Public Schools
New Orleans, LA

Action Conference on the Professional Development of Teachers of Mathematics in the Middle Grades Participant List

Scott Anderson
New Orleans Public Schools
New Orleans, LA 70114

Deborah Loewenberg Ball
University of Michigan
Ann Arbor, MI

Ann Bartosh
Mathematics Consultant
Kentucky Department of
    Education
Lexington, KY

Fran Berry
Principal Investigator
Colorado State Systemic
    Initiative
CONNECT
Denver, CO

Iris Carl
Past President
National Council of Teachers of
    Mathematics
Houston, TX

Duane A. Cooper
Assistant Professor of
    Mathematics Education and
    Mathematics
University of Maryland
College Park, MD

Linda DeGuire
Mathematics Department
California State University-
    Long Beach
Long Beach, CA

Lloyd Douglas
Program Director
National Science Foundation
Arlington, VA

Karen Economopoulos
TERC
Cambridge, MA

Marjorie Enneking
Professor of Mathematics/
    OCEPT Project Director
Portland State University
Portland, OR

David Erickson
University of Montana
Department of Curriculum and
    Instruction
Missoula, MT

Ms. Linda Foreman
President
Teachers Development Group
West Linn, OR

Dr. Megan Franke
University of California, Los
    Angeles
Los Angeles, CA

Alice Gill
Associate Director
American Federation of
    Teachers
Washington, DC

Linda Hall
Tulsa Public Schools
Tulsa, OK

Peirce Hammond
Director, Office of Reform
    Assistance and
    Dissemination
U.S. Department of Education
Washington, DC

Merle Harris
New Orleans Algebra Project
New Orleans, LA

Christopher Hartmann
University of Wisconsin,
    Madison
Madison, WI

Joellen Killion
National Staff Development
    Council
Arvada, CO

Walter Mae King
New Orleans Public Schools
New Orleans, LA

Genevieve Knight
Visiting Fellow
The Council of Scientific
    Society Presidents
Washington, DC

Gerald Kulm
Program Director
Project 2061/AAAS
Washington, DC

Mary Lindquist
Professor
Columbus State University
Columbus, GA

Madeleine J. Long
The Implementation Group
Washington, DC

Johnny Lott
Professor of Mathematics
University of Montana
Missoula, MT

Alexina Hazzard McIver
Middle School Mathematics
    Resource Teacher
Los Angeles Unified School
    District/Los Angeles
    Systemic Initiative
Los Angeles, CA

Greg Miyata
Secondary Mathematics/
    Technology Resource
    Teacher
Los Angeles Unified School
    District/Los Angeles
    Systemic Initiative
Los Angeles, CA

John (Jack) Moyer
Professor, Department of
    Mathematics, Statistics, and
    Computer Science
Marquette University
Milwaukee, WI

Judy Mumme
Director, Mathematics
    Renaissance K-12
San Diego State University
San Diego, CA

Judith Olson
Professor of Mathematics
Western Illinois University
Macomb, IL

Melfried Olson
Professor of Mathematics
Western Illinois University
Macomb, IL

Bruce Palka
Program Director, Division of
    Mathematical Sciences
National Science Foundation
Arlington, VA

Elizabeth Phillips
Senior Academic Specialist
Michigan State University
Mathematics Department
East Lansing, MI

Joan Prival
National Science Foundation
Division of Undergraduate
    Education
Arlington, VA

Susan Pruet
Director, South Alabama
    Systemic Initiative in
    Mathematics
University of South Alabama
Fairhope, AL

Sid Rachlin
Director, Middle Mathematics
    Project
East Carolina University
Washington, NC

Karen Rasmussen
Writer
Association for Supervision
    and Curriculum
    Development
Alexandria, VA

Linda P. Rosen
Expert Consultant
United States Department of
    Education
Washington, DC

Shirley Sagawa
Executive Director
Learning First Alliance
Washington, DC

James Sandefur
Professor of Mathematics
Georgetown University
Washington, DC

Mark Saul
Teacher
Bronxville Public Schools
New York, NY

Ms. Nanette Seago
Project Director
Video Cases for Mathematics
    Professional Development
    Project
Riverside, CA

Beth Skipper
Mathematics Coordinator
Louisiana Systemic Initiatives
    Program (LaSIP)
Baton Rouge, LA

Margaret Smith
Assistant Professor of
    Mathematics Education
Penn State University
University Park, PA

Cynthia Tocci
Program Administrator
Educational Testing Service
Princeton, NJ

Lisa Usher
Secondary Mathematics
    Resource Teacher
Los Angeles Unified School
    District/Los Angeles
    Systemic Initiative
Los Angeles, CA

Judy Vail
Middle Mathematics
    Consultant
Calcasieu Parish Schools
Lake Charles, LA

Iris Weiss
President
Horizon Research, Inc.
Chapel Hill, NC

Carol West
Acting Director for Technical
    Services
The College Board, Equity
    2000
Washington, DC

Dawayne Whittington
Horizon Research, Inc.
Chapel Hill, NC

Stephanie Williamson
Assistant Director for
    Mathematics
Louisiana Systemic Initiatives
    Program (LaSIP)
Baton Rouge, LA

Judy Wurtzel
Director, Mathematics
    Initiative
Office of the Deputy Secretary
U.S. Department of Education
Washington, DC

Appendix 4

MARCY'S DOTS

Participant Handout

A pattern of dots is shown below. At each step, more dots are added to the pattern. The number of dots added at each step is more than the number added in the previous step. The pattern continues infinitely.

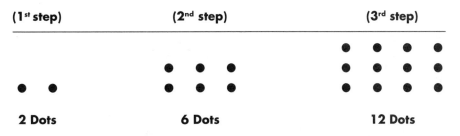

(1ˢᵗ step)	(2ⁿᵈ step)	(3ʳᵈ step)
2 Dots	6 Dots	12 Dots

Marcy has to determine the number of dots in the 20th step, but she does not want to draw all 20 pictures and then count them. Explain or show how she could do this *and* give the answer that Marcy should get for the number of dots.

Did you use the calculator on this question?

☐ Yes   ☐ No

SOURCE: National Assessment of Educational Progress (NAEP), 1992 Mathematics Assessment

Sample student responses

1

Explain or show how she could do this and give the answer that Marcy ~~9 to dots~~
should get for the number of dots.

answer

~~9 to dots~~

pattern
+4, +6

step 2 (4) = 6 + 6 = 12

[columns of handwritten step calculations for steps 4 through 20]

2

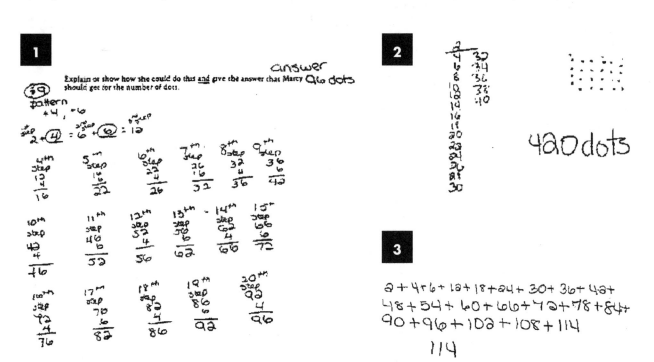

420 dots

3

2+4+6+12+18+24+ 30+ 36+ 42+
48+54+ 60+66+72+78+84+
90+96+ 102+ 108+ 114

114

4

For every step you add one dot on the bottom
row. Then you go up as many dots as
the number of the step. For example, if it
is step #7 you would have seven dots up and
down.

Example ⇒ step #5

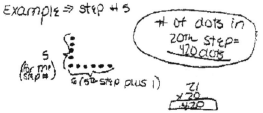

# of dots in
20th step=
420 dots

6(5th step plus 1)

21
×20
420

5

Multiply ×3 and then 2 over and over again

12 ÷ 6 = 2 and when you go on say
6×12=72 so 72÷12=6.

6

420 Dots

20 Dots   6
         7—— and so on
42 Dots
20 Dots
5420   21——

21
×20
420

7

```
4   12
5   36    (×3)
6   72    (×2)
7   216   (×3)
    432   (×2)
    1296  (×3)
    2592  (×2)
10  ...   (×4?)
```

MULTIPLY BY 3 THEN BY 2 BECAUSE: DERIVING THIS INFO FROM THE 3 STEPS SHOWN... DO THIS UNTIL THE 19TH STEP HAS BEEN REACHED, WHAT EVER NUMBER IS REACHED IS THE ANSWER.

8

In each consecutive step, the number of dots to add goes up by 2.
Then the formula would be 2 + 4 + 6 + 8...

this is a formula for adding patterns →
$(40+2)\ 70 \div 2$
$(42)\ 70 \div 2$
$= 840 \div 2$
$= 420$

answer: 420

9

Marcy doesn't have to draw 20 pictures to get 20 dots. She would just draw 3 pictures of dots divided the 20 dots by 6 and then draw 2 more dots to get the 20 dots. (1st step) (2nd step) (3rd step)(4th step)

10

The 1st step is a figure that is 1×2. The second figure is a 2×3. The third figure is a 3×4. This is a pattern. The next step would be a 4×5 figure.

1. 1×2	7. 7×8	12. 12×13	18. 18×19
2. 2×3	8. 8×9	13. 13×14	19. 19×20
3. 3×4	9. 9×10	14. 14×15	20. 20×21
4. 4×5	10. 10×11	15. 15×16	
5. 5×6	11. 11×12	16. 16×17	
6. 6×7		17. 17×18	

The 20th figure would be 20 dots × 21 dots. 420 dots.

Did you use the calculator on this question?

$$\begin{array}{r} 21 \\ \times\ 20 \\ \hline 420 \end{array}$$

11

Step #20 has 420 dots.

12

2, 6, 12, 24, 48, 96, 192, 384, 768, 1536
3072, 6144, 12288, 24576, 49152, 98304, 196608
393216, 786432, 1572864
(20th step)
1572864 DOTS

all I did was follow the pattern

Facilitator's guide for the Marcy's Dots activity

Marcy's Dots

1. To get participants involved in thinking about content and learning, have them solve Marcy's Dots, a problem in the content area of algebra and function from the 1992 National Assessment of Educational Progress (NAEP) Grade 8 Test. About 20% of the test for grade 8 assessed algebra and function, and this is typical of an extended constructed-response question.

The following information might be shared after or at an appropriate time during the discussion. Do not start off with this but use it after people have become engaged and come to some conclusions about the problem and about the ways students found their solutions. Only 6% of the students provided a satisfactory or better response; 6% provided a generalization; 10% made some attempt at a pattern; 63% provided inaccurate or irrelevant information; and 16% did not respond. (Remember that this test is a no stakes test for students.)

2. Investigate Student responses. Points that might be made in the discussion:

Wrong answers usually occurred because they had the wrong notion of the pattern.

- Student 1 alternated between adding 4 and adding 6.
- Student 5 multiplied by 3 then by 2 as the pattern.
- Student 7 multiplied by 3 then by 2.
- Student 12 increased by multiplying by 2.

No recognition of pattern:
- Student 9 added the numbers in the problems.
- Student 3 added 6, the last set of dots.

Right Answers:
- Student 2 used the pattern within the pattern and the picture; wrote out all steps (recursion).
- Student 4 used relation between rows and columns and was able to generalize to a rule.
- Student 6 used relation between rows and columns from picture and was able to generalize to a rule.
- Student 8 used the pattern within the pattern: recursively adding two more each time (4, 6, 8, ...)
- Student 10 focused on relationship between rows and columns, wrote out all steps (recursion).
- Student 11 used relationship numbers and was able to generalize to a rule.

3. Discuss the problem from the perspective of its role in the middle grades mathematics curriculum. How does the plenary session on content and learning relate to the problem? How does the problem fit into the larger picture of algebra and algebraic reasoning? Why is it important for students to recognize and be able to work with patterns?

4. Hand out the excerpts from the draft section of the middle grades algebra section from *"Principles and Standards for School Mathematics*: Discussion Draft," the Standards 2000 draft being prepared for dissemination, comment and input this fall. Provide a few minutes for people to read the excerpts. How does the mathematics in this task relate to the discussion of algebra in the document?

Resources for Marcy's Dots

Dossey, J.A., Mullis, I.V.S., & Jones, C.O. (1993). *Can students do mathematical problem solving? results from constructed-response questions in NAEP's 1992 Mathematics Assessment.* Washington, DC: National Center for Education Statistics.

Kenny, P.A., Zawojewski, J.S., & Silver, E.A. (1998). Marcy's Dot Problem. *Mathematics Teaching in the Middle School, 3(7),* 474-477.

TABLE 2.11 National Results for Demographic Subgroups for the Extended-Response Task, Marcy's Dot Pattern, Grade 8

	No Response	Incorrect	Minimal	Partial	Satisfactory	Extended	Satisfactory or Better
Nation	16 (1.0)	63 (1.3)	10 (0.7)	6 (0.7)	1 (0.2)	5 (0.6)	6 (0.7)
Northeast	18 (3.2)	61 (3.2)	10 (1.9)	4 (0.7)	2 (0.5)	6 (1.8)	8 (1.6)
Southeast	20 (2.0)	64 (2.2)	9 (1.5)	3 (0.7)	1 (0.4)	4 (1.1)	4 (1.3)
Central	10 (1.5)	65 (2.1)	10 (1.4)	8 (1.4)	1 (0.4)	6 (1.1)	7 (1.4)
West	16 (2.0)	62 (2.8)	10 (1.1)	7 (1.8)	0 (0.2)	4 (1.1)	4 (1.1)
White	12 (1.1)	63 (1.5)	11 (0.8)	7 (0.8)	1 (0.2)	6 (0.8)	8 (0.9)
Black	24 (2.9)	67 (2.9)	6 (1.6)	2 (0.9)	0 (0.0)	1 (0.5)	1 (0.5)
Hispanic	28 (2.8)	61 (3.1)	7 (2.0)	3 (1.2)	0 (0.0)	1 (0.5)	1 (0.5)
Male	19 (1.5)	63 (2.2)	8 (1.0)	5 (0.9)	1 (0.2)	5 (0.9)	5 (0.9)
Female	13 (1.2)	63 (1.6)	12 (1.1)	6 (1.0)	1 (0.3)	5 (0.8)	6 (0.9)
Advantaged Urban	8 (2.9)	62 (5.1)	10 (1.9)	6 (1.6)	1 (0.6)	11 (2.5)	13 (2.6)
Disadvantaged Urban	32 (3.9)	59 (4.7)	4 (1.3)	4 (1.9)	1 (0.6)	1 (0.5)	1 (0.7)
Extreme Rural	16 (2.9)	69 (3.6)	8 (2.3)	2 (1.1)	1 (0.7)	4 (2.0)	5 (2.3)
Other	15 (1.3)	62 (1.5)	11 (0.9)	6 (0.9)	1 (0.2)	4 (0.7)	5 (0.7)
Public	16 (1.2)	64 (1.4)	9 (0.8)	6 (0.7)	1 (0.2)	4 (0.6)	5 (0.6)
Catholic and Other Private	11 (1.7)	56 (2.7)	12 (1.6)	7 (1.2)	2 (0.9)	10 (2.2)	13 (2.0)

The standard errors of the estimated percentages appear in parentheses. It can be said with about 95 percent certainty that for each population of interest, the value for the whole population is within plus or minus two standard errors of the estimate for the sample. In comparing two estimates, one must use the standard error of the difference (see Appendix for details). When the proportion of students is either 0 percent or 100 percent, the standard error is inestimable. However, percentages 99.5 percent and greater were rounded to 100 percent and percentages 0.5 percent or less were rounded to 0 percent. Percentages may not total 100 percent due to rounding error.

SOURCE: National Assessment of Educational Progress (NAEP), 1992 Mathematics Assessment

DISCUSSION SESSION WORKSHEETS

DISCUSSION SESSION 1

Saturday, 11:00 a.m. - 12:30 pm

Content and Learning Issues

1. Read Marcy's Dots and find a solution. How do you think students might solve the problem? What errors do you think they would make?

2. Examine the student solutions. What observations can you make?

3. Does the problem address an important mathematical concept? What mathematical areas are involved? Should these areas be in the middle grades curriculum and where? What mathematical knowledge would students need to solve the problem? How might that knowledge be built in grades K-6? What follow-up activities might be used to help students be successful on such a problem? How does this problem connect to mathematics after grade 8?

4. Read the draft section on algebra for the middle grades from "Principles and Standards for School Mathematics: Discussion Draft." What does Marcy's Dots have to do with algebra as content?

DISCUSSION SESSION 2

Saturday, 4:00 p.m. – 5:30 p.m.

Participant Sheet

Reflect on the videos you saw in the plenary session and the panel discussions that followed. Think about your reactions, particularly in light of the focus points for the session.

What are the important characteristics of effective teaching in the middle grades? Of effective teaching of mathematics in the middle grades?

How can instruction in middle grades classrooms be organized to maximize learning? How can we tell when learning is happening?

What tools and strategies will make a difference in how middle grades students learn mathematics?

Observations:

DISCUSSION SESSION 3

Sunday, 10:30 a.m. – 11:30 a.m.

Participant Sheet

Certain issues are associated with teaching and learning mathematics in the middle grades. These issues range from how teachers are prepared to what students do in the classroom to what the system and community expects mathematics to look like in those grades.

As a group, what statements can you make about each of the following issues? You might think in terms of:

- 3 areas of agreement
- 3 challenges/issues needing more work.

Content and learning mathematics in the middle grades

In particular, as you think about the issues surrounding content and learning, some of the points that might frame your discussion are:

1. the role of number, specifically rational numbers

2. algebra and linearity as a major element in the middle grades

3. integration of mathematics content with other discipline areas

4. focusing the mathematics content without eliminating important mathematics for middle grades students

Teaching in middle grades

In particular, what can you say about successful teaching in the middle grades and about successful teaching of mathematics. Some of the points you might think about are teaching

5. for thoughtful engagement and learning with understanding

6. competence without acceleration and specialization

7. mathematics to young adolescents

8. preparation and certification for middle grades mathematics teachers

BACKGROUND PAPER FOR THE CONVOCATION

What Is 8th Grade Mathematics: A Look from NAEP

John Dossey
Mathematics Department, Illinois State University

One of the few sources that mathematics educators, or policy makers, have upon which to base judgments about 8th grade is the data from the National Assessment of Educational Progress in Mathematics (NAEP). This federal large-scale assessment has been collecting data about the mathematical experiences of the eight graders (or 13-year olds), as well as data on fourth graders (or 9-year-olds) and twelfth-graders (or 17-year olds), since 1973. These random samples of the nation's students at these grade/age levels are taken to provide a picture of the status of mathematics education at critical junctures in their schooling.

The national NAEP assessment, has been given in 1973, 1978, 1983, 1986, 1990, 1992, and 1996. There is a NAEP Trend assessment that employs forms of the 1973 examination to provide a trend knowledge relative to basic skills and knowledge in school mathematics over time since 1973. This test was given in the same years as NAEP, as well as in 1994.

ACHIEVEMENT RESULTS

National NAEP Achievement Results

What kind of picture do the results of these assessments paint? First, they show that our eighth grade students have made consistent progress over time in mathematics. The achievement trend on national NAEP is split into two sections, as the nature of the NAEP assessment was changed in 1990 by the National Assessment Governing Board to reflect more open-ended problem solving and to narrow the number of different content areas in mathematics that were to be assessed. Since that time, the assessment has focused on student work in Number and Operations, Measurement, Geometry, Algebra, and Data Analysis/Statistics/

Probability. The mean student scores on the NAEP assessment from 1978 through 1986 were developed on random samples of the nation's 9-, 13-, and 17-year olds. The results for 13-year-olds showed a consistent picture, with improvement for students in the last two assessments given under the framework (Dossey, Mullis, Lindquist, & Chambers, 1988). The scores for these assessments are shown in Table 1.

Table 2 shows the scores for the new NAEP scale for 8th graders initiated in 1990 with the first assessment to be given under the new NAEP framework. Note that the scores shown in Table 1 should not be compared with those

shown in Table 2 as they are from two different scales, representing different content and different formats of examinations. These results show a steady and consistent improvement from 1990 through 1996.

An analysis of the scores in Table 2 indicate a strong and significant increase in scores over the six year period of time. Comparing the increases to the benchmark of 10 NAEP score scale points equals one grade-placement level of progress, the data suggest that the nation's eighth graders' achievement has increased essentially one grade placement since 1990! This is an indication of good things happening in the school classroom (Reese, Miller, Mazzeo, & Dossey, 1997).

Table 1. NAEP Trend Scores for 13-year-olds for National NAEP: 1973-1986

Assessment Year	1973	1978	1983	1986
National Mean	266	264	269*†	269*†

*† indicates that the score is significantly greater than the score in 1978 at the 0.05 level.

Table 2. NAEP Trend Scores for 13-year-olds for National NAEP: 1990-1996

Assessment Year	1990	1992	1996
National Mean	263	268*	272*†

* indicates that the score is significantly greater than the score in 1990.

*† indicates that the score is significantly greater than the score in 1992.

NAEP TREND ASSESSMENT RESULTS

One might look at the above results and have a feeling that the improvement in achievement is really only since 1990, as there was a dip in 1978 in the data and that we essentially made up in 1983 and 1986. Besides this, critics of school reform and change in mathematics education might also indicate concern over the changed nature of the test and feel that the "basics" have been left out of the new NAEP assessment starting in 1990

Table 3. NAEP Trend Assessment Scores for 13-year-olds for Trend NAEP: 1973-1996

Assessment Year	1973	1978	1983	1986	1990	1992	1994	1996
National Mean	266	264	269	269	270*†	273*†	274*†	274*†

*† indicates that the score is significantly greater than the score in 1973 at the 0.05 level.

since it has been somewhat loosely based on the NCTM Standards.

It was just this concern that the Department of Education and NAGB had in deciding at the inception of NAEP to continually give the 1973 examination to random samples of 13-year-olds over time as a measure of change from a baseline examination. This examination was, and is, heavily grounded in paper-and-pencil skills and knowledge that was considered basic in 1973, a period marked by "back-to-the-basics" following the New Mathematics of the 1960s. Table 3 shows student performance on this examination over time. Again note, one should not compare the scale numbers for this assessment with the previous two, as it is a third different assessment.

However, the data here, together with the two previous sets of assessment data, suggest that the mathematics achievement, be it on new content, or on traditional content, is improving over time (Campbell, Voelkl, & Donahue, 1997). None of the assessment results suggests that the "baby has been thrown out with the bathwater" in the move to reform school mathematics.

OTHER NAEP RESULTS

In addition to the achievement information, the National NAEP program collects information from the students relative to their beliefs and demographic backgrounds, from their teachers relative to their instruction and their education, and from their schools about the organization and curriculum of the school program. These data permit the description of the context in which these students encounter mathematics and the resources that they have as they approach the study of mathematics.

Course Taking

Data from the 1996 NAEP assessment indicated that 81 percent of the nation's eighth graders attended a school that offered the study of Algebra I as an option in the eighth grade curriculum. Further, the data indicated that 25 percent of the nation's eighth graders actually enrolled in Algebra I as their eighth grade mathematics course. The remaining students either participated in a classroom where mathematics was taught from an eighth grade text from a basal K-8 curriculum series (43%), participated in a prealgebra class (26%), or were in some other form of mathematics instruction (6%) (Hawkins, Stancavage, & Dossey, 1998).

Calculator Usage

Data from the 1996 assessment indicated that 80 percent of the nation's eighth graders have access to school-owned calculators. This percentage was the same whether students were in Algebra 1, prealgebra, or eighth-grade mathematics. No significant difference was noted between the performance of the students having and not having access to school-owned calculators (Hawkins, Stancavage, & Dossey, 1998).

Teacher Backgrounds

The teaching of eighth-grade mathematics falls between elementary and secondary preparation in many states, as few states have a special middle school/ junior high school certification level. Data from the teachers of the students in the 1996 NAEP sample indicated that 62% of these teachers either had degrees in mathematics (49%) or mathematics education (13%). The remaining teachers either had degrees in education but not mathematics or mathematics education (32%), or had degrees in some other discipline (7%). Analysis of the student achievement of the students of these four groups of teachers by collegiate major indicated that the students whose teachers had degrees in mathematics outper-

formed the students of teachers whose degrees were either in education (but not mathematics education) or in another discipline. The students whose teachers had degrees in mathematics education had achievement scores that were not significantly different from the achievement of students whose teachers had degrees in either mathematics or education/other discipline (Hawkins, Stancavage, & Dossey, 1998).

Professional Development and Knowledge of the NCTM Standards

Eighth-grade teachers reported that on average 26% of them had had less than 6 hours of professional development in mathematics during the past year, 29% had from 6 to 15 hours of professional development in mathematics during the past year, and 45% had over 15 hours of professional development in mathematics during the past year. When one considers that 15 hours of professional development is less than two working days' time, one recognizes that over half of the nation's eighth-grade students are being taught by teachers who are receiving precious little opportunity for growth in their major teaching field.

Teachers were also asked about the level of knowledge they felt they had of the *NCTM Curriculum and Evaluation Standards for School Mathematics*

(NCTM, 1989). The teachers of 16% of the students said that they felt they were very knowledgeable, 32% were knowledgeable, 33% somewhat knowledgeable, and 19% reported having little or no knowledge of the Standards. Analysis of the mean achievement scores of students related to these four groups of teachers indicated that students of teachers who reported being knowledgeable or very knowledgeable of the Standards performed significantly higher than those of teachers reporting little or no knowledge of the Standards. However, one is unable to determine the cause for this difference. It may be in hiring practices of districts, or that some districts have more resources, give more professional development, or pay higher salaries (Hawkins, Stancavage, & Dossey, 1998).

Performance in Content Sub-Areas

When students' achievement work is examined by content sub-areas, their performance in each area showed a significant increase from 1992 to 1996. The sub-areas and 1996 achievement scores for each are as follows: Number Sense, Properties, and Operations (274), Measurement (270), Geometry and Spatial Sense (269), Data Analysis/ Statistics/Probability (272), and Algebra and Functions (273). Like the results from TIMSS, the lowest performance areas were Geometry and Measurement

(Mitchell, Hawkins, Jakwerth, Stancavage, & Dossey, 1999).

Item Types and Special Studies

The items in the 1996 NAEP were approximately distributed as follows: 55% multiple choice, 38% short student constructed answer, and 7% extended student constructed answer format. Overall it was expected that students would have spent about 40% of their response time working on items that called for student constructed responses of one type or another. Results of the testing showed improvement on students' abilities to construct answers to questions in 1996 over prior years. This was an indication that communication and reasoning are playing greater roles in classroom assessment programs across the nation. However, when one looks at the results of student performance on extended student constructed response items, graded by a 5 point rubric, one sees that there is still considerable room for improvement, as few students achieved the highest levels of score on these items.

As part of the 1996 assessment, eighth-grade students were also given a block of items where the context for the block was common, although the actual items were locally independent—that is, no item's answer depended on the answer to another item. Student performance on these items, including the extended constructed response items tended to be slightly higher than that on similar format items in the regular NAEP. This may indicate that the changing of contexts within regular NAEP from item to item may slightly suppress student performance levels, or alternatively, maintaining a context helps students develop a positive focus (Hawkins, Mitchell, Stancavage, & Dossey, in press).

Summary

While this is but a brief overview of teh eighth-grade results from 1996 NAEP, these data and results provide a gestalt for the context and nature of eighth-grade students' achievement patterns at present. A thorough reading of the NAEP reports will provide an even more complete picture of eighth-grade mathematics in the United States today.

References

Campbell, J.R., Voelkl, K.E., & Donahue, P.L. (1997). *NAEP 1996 Trends in Academic Progress*. Washington, DC: National Center for Education Statistics.

Dossey, J.A., Mullis, I.V.S., Lindquist, M.M., & Chambers, D.L. (1988)). *The Mathematics Report Card: Are We Measuring Up?* Princeton, NJ: Educational Testing Service.

Hawkins, E.F., Mitchell, J.H., Stancavage, F.B., & Dossey, J.A. (in press). *Focused Studies in the NAEP 1996 Mathematics Assessment: Findings from the National Assessment of Educational Progress*. Washington, DC: National Center for Education Statistics.

Hawkins, E.F., Stancavage, F.B., & Dossey, J.A. (1998). *School Policies and Practices Affecting Instruction in Mathematics: Findings from the National Assessment of Educational Progress*. Washington, DC: National Center for Education Statistics.

Mitchell, J.H., Hawkins, E.F., Jakwerth, P.M., Stancavage, F.B., & Dossey, J.A. (1999). *Student Work and Teacher Practices in Mathematics*. Washington, DC: National Center for Education Statistics.

Nationa Council of Teachers of Mathematics. (1989). *Curriculum and Evaluation Standards for School Mathematics*. Reston, VA: Author.

Reese, C.M., Miller, K.E., Mazzeo, J., & Dossey, J.A. (1997). *NAEP 1996 Mathematics Report Card for the Nation and the States*. Washington, DC: National Center for Education Statistics.

Appendix 7

RESOURCES

Curriculum integration: proceeding with cautious optimism. (1996). *Middle School Journal, September 1996*, pp. 3-26.

Alexander, W.M. (1965). The junior high: A changing view. In G. Hass & K. Wiles (Eds.), *Readings in curriculum*. Boston: Allyn and Bacon.

Arnold, J. (1993). A responsive curriculum for emerging adolescents. In T. Dickinson (Ed.), *Readings in middle school curriculum: A continuing conversation*. Columbus, OH: National Middle School Association.

Beane, J.A. (1993). *A middle school curriculum: From rhetoric to reality* (2nd ed.). Columbus, OH: National Middle School Association.

Bitter, G.G., & Hatfield, M.M. (1998). The role of technology in the middle grades. In L. Leutzinger (Ed.), *Mathematics in the Middle* (pp. 36-41). Reston, VA: National Council of Teachers of Mathematics.

Carnegie Council on Adolescent Development. (1990). *Turning points: Preparing American youth for the 21st century* (abridged version). Washington, DC: Carnegie Council on Adolescent Development.

Chiu, M.M. (1996). Exploring the origins, uses, and interactions of student intuitions: Comparing the lengths of paths. *Journal for Research in Mathematics Education, 27*(4), 478-504.

Clark, T.A., Bickel, W.E., & Lacey, R.A. (1993). *Transforming education for young adolescents: insights for practitioners from the Lilly Endowment's middle grades impovement program, 1987-1990*. New York: Education Resources Group.

Council of Chief State School Officers, & Carnegie Corporation of New York. (1995). *The middle school: Professional development for high student achievement*. Washington, DC: Council of Chief State School Officers.

Davis, B. (1997). Listening for differences: An evolving conception of mathematics teaching. *Journal for Research in Mathematics Education, 28*(3), 355-376.

English, L., Cudmore, D., & Tilley, D. (1998). Problem posing and critiquing: How it can happen in your classroom. *Mathematics Teaching in the Middle School, 4*(2), 124-129.

Felner, R.D., et al. (1995). The process and impact of school reform and restructuring for the middle years: A longitudinal study of Turning Points-based comprehensive school change. In R. Takanishi & D. Hamburg (Eds.), *Frontiers in the education of young adolescents*. New York: Carnegie Corporation.

Felner, R.D., et al. (1993). Restructuring the ecology of the school as an approach to prevention during school transitions: Longitudinal follow-ups and extensions of the School Transitional Environment Project (STEP). *Prevention in Human Services, 10*, 103-136.

Felner, R.D., Jackson, A.W., Kasak, D., Mulhall, P., Brand, S., & Flowers, N. (1997). The impact of school reform for the middle years: Longitudinal study of a network engaged in *Turning-Points*-based comprehensive school transformation. *Phi Delta Kappan*.

Friel, S.N., Bright, G.W., & Curcio, F.R. (1997). Understanding students' understanding of graphs. *Mathematics Teaching in the Middle School, 3* (3), 224-227.

George, P.S., & Alexander, W.M. (1993). *The exemplary middle school* (2nd ed.). New York: Harcourt Brace Jovanovich.

Jackson, A.W. et al. (1993). Adolescent development and educational policy: Strengths and weaknesses of the knowledge base. *Journal of Adolescent Medicine, 14*, 172-189.

Lamon, S.J. (1993). Ratio and proportion: Connecting content and children's thinking. *Journal for Research in Mathematics Education, 24*(1), 41-61.

Lara, J. (1995). *Second-language learners and middle school reform: A case study of a school in transition*. Washington, DC: Council of Chief State School Officers.

Leinwand, S.J. (1998). Classroom realities we do not often talk about. *Mathematics Teaching in the Middle School, 3*(5), 330-331.

Lewis, A.C. (1995). *Believing in ourselves, progress and struggle in urban middle school reform, 1989-1995.* New York: Edna McConnell Clark Foundation.

Lipsitz, J., Jackson, A.W., & Austin, L.M. (1997). What works in middle-grades school reform. *Phi Delta Kappan 78*(7), 517-519.

Lipsitz, J., Mizzell, M.H., Jackson, A.W., & Austin, L.M. (1997). Speaking with one voice: A manifesto for middle-grades reform. *Phi Delta Kappan, 78*(7), 533-540.

Manauchureri, A., Enderson, M.C., & Pugnucco, L.A. (1998). Exploring geometry with technology. *Mathematics Teaching in the Middle School, 3*(6), 436-443.

McEwin, C.K., & Dickinson, T.S. (1995). *The professional preparation of middle level teachers: Profiles of successful programs.* Columbus, OH: National Middle School Association.

McEwin, C.K., Dickinson, T.S., & Jenkins, D.M. (1996). *America's middle schools: Practices and progress: A 25 year perspective.* Columbus, OH: National Middle School Association.

National Board for Professional Teaching Standards. (1993). *The early adolescence/ generalist standards.* San Antonio, TX: National Board for Professional Teaching Standards.

National Middle School Association. (1995). *This we believe: Developmentally responsive middle level schools.* Columbus, OH: National Middle School Association.

National Center for Educational Statistics. (1996). *Pursuing excellence: A study of U.S. eighth-grade mathematics and science achievement in international context.* Washington, DC: Author.

National Center for Educational Statistics. (1997). *Pursuing excellence: A study of U.S. fourth-grade mathematics and science achievement in international context.* Washington, DC: Author.

Oldfather, P., & McCaughlin, H.J. (1993). Gaining and losing voice: A longitudinal study of students' continuing impulse to learn across elementary and middle level contexts. *Research in Middle Level Education*, Fall 1993, 1-25.

Phillips, E., & Lappan, G. (1998). Algebra: The first gate. In L. Leutziner (Ed.), *Mathematics in the Middle* (pp. 10-19). Reston, VA: National Council of Teachers of Mathematics.

Reese, C.M., Miller, K.E., Mazzeo, J., & Dossey, J. (1997) *NAEP 1996 mathematics report card for the national and the states: Findings from the National Assessment of Educational Progress.* Washington, DC: National Center for Education Statistics.

Reys, B.J. (1994). Promoting number sense in the middle grades. *Mathematics Teaching in the Middle School, 1*(2), 114-120.

Reys, R. E. (1998). Computation versus number sense. *Mathematics Teaching in the Middle School, 4*(2), 110-119.

Reys, R. E., Reys, B. J., Barnes, D. E., Beem, J. K., Lapan, R. T., & Papick, I. J. (1998). Standards-based middle school mathematics: What do students think? In L. Leutzinger (Ed.), *Mathematics in the Middle* (pp. 153-157). Reston, VA: National Council of Teachers of Mathematics.

Romberg, T. A. (1998). Designing middle school mathematics materials using problems created to help students progress from informal reasoning to formal mathematical reasoning. In L. Leutzinger (Ed.), *Mathematics in the Middle* (pp. 107-119). Reston, VA: National Council of Teachers of Mathematics.

Rosenzweig, S. (1997). The five foot bookshelf: Readings on middle-level education and reform. *Phi Delta Kappan 78*(7), 551-556.

Silver, E.A., & Cai, J. (1996). An analysis of arithmetic problem posing by middle school students. *Journal for Research in Mathematics Education, 27*(5), 521-539.

Silver, E.A., & Kenney, P. (1993). An examination of relationships between 1990 NAEP mathematics items for grade 8 and selected themes from the NCTM standards. *Journal for Research in Mathematics Education, 24*(2), 159-167.

Silver, E.A., Mamona-Downs, J., Leung, S.S., & Kenney, P. A. (1996). Posing mathematics problems: An exploratory study. *Journal for Research in Mathematics Education, 27*(3), 293-309.

Silver, E. A., Shapiro, L. J., & Deutsch, A. (1993). Sense making and the solution of division problems involving remainders: An examination of middle school students' solution processes and their interpretations of solutions. *Journal for Research in Mathematics Education, 24*(2), 117-135.

Silver, E.A. (1998). *Improving mathematics in middle school: Lessons from TIMSS and related research*. Washington, DC: U.S. Department of Education.

Swafford, J.O., Jones, G.A., & Thornton, C.A. (1997). Increased knowledge in geometry and instructional practice. *Journal for Research in Mathematics Education, 28*(4), 467-483.

Swaim, J.H., & Stefanich, G.P. (1996). *Meeting the standards: Improving middle level teacher education*. Columbus, OH: National Middle School Association.

Task Force on Education of Young Adolescents. (1989). *Turning points: Preparing American youth for the 21st century*. New York: Carnegie Council on Adolescent Development.

Warrington, M. (1997). How children think about division with fractions. *Mathematics Teaching in the Middle School, 2*(6), 390-397.

Wheelock, A. (1992). *Crossing the tracks: How "untracking" can save America's schools*. New York: New Press.

Wheelock, A. (1995). *Standards-based reform: What does it mean for the middle grades?* New York: Edna McConnell Clark Foundation Program for Student Achievement.

Yershalmy, M. (1997). Designing representations: Reasoning about functions of two variables. *Journal for Research in Mathematics Education, 28*(4), 431-466.

Zucker, A.A. (1998). *Middle grades mathematics education: Questions and answers*. Arlington, VA: SRI International.